# Metapop

*Studies in Popular Culture*
*M. Thomas Inge, General Editor*

# Metapop

*Self-referentiality
in Contemporary American
Popular Culture*

MICHAEL DUNNE

UNIVERSITY PRESS OF MISSISSIPPI
*Jackson & London*

Paperback Edition 2010

The paper in this book meets the guidelines for permanence and durability of the Committee on Production Guidelines for Book Longevity of the Council on Library Resources.

Library of Congress Cataloging-in-Publication Data

Dunne, Michael, 1941–
    METAPOP : self-referentiality in contemporary American popular culture / Michael Dunne.
        p.  cm. — (Studies in popular culture)
    Includes index.
    ISBN 1-60473-513-9
    1. United States—Popular culture.  2. Arts, American.  3. Arts, Modern—20th century—United States.  I. Title.  II. Series: Studies in popular culture (Jackson, Miss.)
    E169.12.D86  1992
    306.4'8'097309049—dc20                                    91-35995
                                                                  CIP

British Library Cataloging-in-Publication data available

# CONTENTS

# INTRODUCTION

When I began writing about country music in 1983, I set out to show that the amazingly popular songs written and performed by country music "outlaws," such as Willie Nelson, Waylon Jennings, and Jerry Jeff Walker, were actually about their professional lives in the music business and not about the rugged lives of cowboys or bandits on the lone prairie. While listening to this music, I realized that pop and rock musicians—Leo Sayer, Paul Simon, and Bob Seger—were equally likely to produce songs that were thinly disguised references to themselves and their musical careers. I decided to probe further, hoping to detect some sort of pattern in this self-referentiality.

As usually happens following such a decision, examples began to appear everywhere. Soon, not only the songs I was hearing, but also the films I saw, the comic strips I faithfully followed, and the commercials I watched on television seemed to scream out their self-referentiality. I felt like the character in a sci-fi movie who detects an alien presence that no one else seems able to see. When I voiced my discoveries to others, however, I found that I was not alone. Students, colleagues, relatives, and casual acquaintances might not immediately recognize the term *self-referentiality*, but everyone seemed familiar with the songs and shows I mentioned, and most were eager to draw other examples to my attention. In a variant on the sci-fi plot, I then began to suspect that everyone knew about self-referentiality in popular culture but for some unspoken reason was keeping mum about it.

Subsequent research demonstrated that this conspiracy of silence was by no means unbroken. Literary critics, including John Barth, Robert Scholes, and Linda Hutcheon, had written very provocatively about the self-referentiality of postmodern metafiction and fabulation. Film critics interested in Federico Fellini and Jean-Luc Godard had commented on their self-referential techniques. Media scholars Lawrence Mintz and Joann Gardner had connected self-referential devices with the nature of film and television comedy. That all these practices might fit together, however, was not a common assumption. Thus, further scrutiny was required.

Soon, the signals grew stronger. In 1987, *It's Garry Shandling's Show* debuted on television, and the animated *The Completely Mental Misadventures of Ed Grimley* followed the next year. Both shows openly advertised, through their subject matter and technique, that they were TV shows and that they assumed their audiences knew this perfectly well. Why pretend that they were simulations of reality, when everyone knew that they were not? Perhaps more significantly, 1988 first saw network news reporters interviewing "spin doctors" about how they intended to manage the news media's treatment of the ongoing presidential election. As in the case of the Shandling and Grimley shows, both sides in this mediated political transaction seemed confident that viewers and voters would understand what was going on and would accept their intervention in the process. Clearly, self-referentiality was attaining greater and greater degrees of sophistication and visibility.

I therefore decided to write about the entire phenomenon. Along the way, I made a number of decisions. First of all, I decided that there was nothing wrong with self-referentiality, that it was a technique naturalized by the omnipresence of television in our culture, and that it was not a sign of cultural illiteracy or postcapitalist decay. Then I reluctantly decided that I could not treat as many manifestations as I would like. I could not write about animation, despite the temptations offered by the Grimley show, *Who Shot Roger Rabbit?*, and the fascinating precedents set by the wonderful old Warner Brothers cartoons featuring Bugs Bunny, Daffy Duck, and Porky Pig. Putting aside the rhetorical issue of the completely different vocabulary required to analyze them, animated cartoons are cartoons, just as comic strips like "Bloom County" are cartoons; furthermore, animated cartoons are either films, as *Spaceballs* is a film, or TV programs, as *SCTV* (*Second City Television*) is a TV show. Neither could I treat in detail the bizarre self-referentiality of the 1988 presidential election, since this might also be plausibly considered just another TV show, advertisement, or media event. In the end, and because everything must have an end, the chief examples would have to be restricted to television, film, rock and country music, music videos, and comic strips.

Even within these reasonable limitations, there remained problems of selection, which I approached pragmatically. Since the omnipresence of television seems to have been the precipitating factor in promoting self-referentiality from the margins to the center of American culture, the most useful television shows would be those that most ostentatiously proclaimed their status: *Second City Television*, *Saturday Night Live*, *Moonlighting*, and *It's Garry Shandling's Show*. From a practical standpoint, these choices naturally ruled out others: *Pee Wee's Playhouse*, for example, or *Twin Peaks*. Similar factors governed my choice of film-makers. Because they all started out in television, Woody Allen, Mel Brooks, Rob Reiner, and Jim Henson seemed likely to shed light on the case. At the same time, other promising television-bred directors—Carl Reiner, Richard Benjamin, and James Brooks, for example—were excluded.

Selection was even more problematic regarding songs and music videos. For every one chosen, dozens of others had to be rejected for simple reasons of available space. Furthermore, I arbitrarily picked a cut-off point after which I would add no new songs or videos, no matter how appropriate, lest the project reach even more elephantine dimensions. This arbitrariness also governed my choice of comic strips. Long after I tied up that chapter, wonderful examples kept appearing in the morning and Sunday papers and, except for one "Ziggy," I had to let them all go by. Eventually, enough is enough. Even Samuel Johnson wisely observed about *Paradise Lost*, "No one ever wished it longer."

Either there are enough illustrations in this book to prove that self-referentiality exists throughout our hypermediated culture or there are not. I am willing to submit the evidence at this point to the judgment of others, hopeful that their responses will be similar to those I have been encountering for the last several years: "I know what you mean! How about . . . ? Have you ever seen, read, heard, it? It's very self-referential too."

The many people who have been saying this to me have materially advanced my work, and I would like to thank as many of them as my notes and memory will permit. The friends who have made suggestions include: Jim Card, Virginia Crank, Don Cusic, Dennis Hall, Rebecca King, Lloyd Michaels, Claudia Spivey, Jerome Stern, Richard M. Turner, Tom Tyner, and James M. Welsh. Linda and Bill Badley, Steve Dale, Cindy Duke, Larry Gentry, Tom Inge, Jerry McGeorge, J. D. Scarbrough, Elizabeth Turpin, Paul Wells, and Charles Wolfe all contributed by lending me books, records, tapes, videos, and comic strips. Betty McFall, who handles interlibrary loans at the Andrew M. Todd Library, secured a variety of print sources for me without once implying that she found anything inappropriate in an English professor's doing such reading. The same must be said of Ellen Garrison and Sarah Long of the MTSU Center for Popular Music, who shared with me their research skills and excellent memories.

The research and writing of this book was made possible by released time funded by several sources at Middle Tennessee State University: The Center for Popular Music, The Research Committee, and the Non-Instructional Assignment Committee. The university's generous support is hereby most gratefully acknowledged.

Portions of this work have appeared in somewhat different form in scholarly journals. I here express my gratitude to the editors of these journals for permission to reprint material that earlier appeared under the titles: "Stardust Memories, The Purple Rose of Cairo, and the Tradition of Metafiction," Film Criticism 12, no. 1 (1987): 19–27; "'I Fall Upon the Cacti of Life! I Bleed!': Romantic Narcissism in 'Outlaw' Cowboy Music," Studies in Popular Culture 11, no. 2 (1988): 22–39; "Metaleptical Hijinx in Woody Allen's Stardust Memories," Literature/Film Quarterly 19, no. 2 (1991).

M. Thomas Inge not only shared with me his unparalleled collection and knowledge of comic strips, but he also provided encouragement and valuable advice on the project overall, including the title Metapop. Rebecca King contributed substantially to the preparation of the manuscript. Gwen Duffey's meticulous editing helped me say what I wanted to say.

My sons Paul and Matthew listened to music with me, watched movies, TV shows, and videos, made funny and helpful suggestions, and provided emotional support. My wife Sara did all of these things too, and because she has been doing so for twenty-five years, this book is for her.

# Metapop

CHAPTER I **Contemporary American**

**Popular Culture**

You're So Vain, You Probably

Think This Chapter

Is About You

Acts of human communication are usually understood and discussed primarily in terms of their content. This is true whether the
act occurs toward the more expressive and aesthetic end of the communication spectrum designated in Aristotle's *Poetics* or the more
instrumental end discussed in his *Rhetoric.* Of course, Aristotle and
his responsible descendants have always acknowledged the significance of the formal or stylistic elements of art and rhetoric. Any
theory of aesthetic organicism or rhetorical effectiveness must origi-
nate in the assumption that content and means of communication
should interact so as to be indistinguishable from each other. Even
so, content has been so privileged by critics that stylistic elements
drawing the audience's attention away from content and toward the
communicative act have historically been condemned as inappropriate.

The problem with such stylistic techniques, it has often been
argued, is that they signify the artist's presence at the expense of the
artist's content. Throughout Western cultural history, however,
some artists have very deliberately signaled their own presences by
emphasizing the process of communication as well as the content.
Such signals can also be visualized on a spectrum, in this case running from subtle stylistic winks at the audience to ostentatious
flaunting of the communication process. In the most extreme cases,
in fact, content can become merely the occasion for an artist's self-

advertisements—what Susan Sontag called "stylization" in her essay "On Style" (19). Whether in subtle or extreme form, such advertisements of a communicator's presence may be designated by the term self-referentiality.

Contemporary American popular culture resounds with self-referentiality of many kinds. For example, an actor wearing a white lab coat appears on television and says, "I am not a doctor, but I play a doctor on TV." Having admitted that—like most of the actors playing doctors in commercials—he possesses no particular medical knowledge, he then proceeds to pitch a cough medicine that he promises will bring us improved health. That is to say, this commercial italicizes the convention by which actors pretend to be doctors so that an actor may do something that viewers have probably grown tired of seeing. Shortly afterwards, a commercial for a collection of rock oldies appears, mostly familiar shots of lovers grooving happily to the music of their youth. Suddenly, this idyll is interrupted by a mechanical bunny who crosses the screen beating on a drum. The voice-over switches from hawking oldies to proclaiming the endurance of Eveready Energizer batteries. Apparently this is not the annoying repeat that it seemed at first to be, but it is a commercial nevertheless. Instead of pretending that they are not selling us anything, these advertisers brazenly admit it, and then go on to try to sell us anyway. These commercials openly admit that they are commercials, because their creators realize that viewers already know this. Such television advertising uses self-references to conduct business as usual with an audience grown jaded through long exposure to advertising that tried to conceal its designs.

Print advertisers today are often equally ostentatious in announcing their rhetorical intentions. The cover of an October 1990 "Extra" catalog from Land's End Direct Merchants, for example, features a cartoon of a man shoveling through waist-high snowdrifts to get to a mailbox jammed with catalogs. Facing upward in the mailbox is the same Land's End catalog with the cover cartoon of the man shoveling through waist-high drifts. A more traditional approach to the cover would have produced a staged photograph of models in front of a cheery fireplace, pretending to be satisfied customers who were glowing with the happiness created by their Land's End clothing. The unstated implication would be that buying similar clothing would bring the customer similar joy. This 1990 cover cancels the intermediate step by admitting that the purpose of catalogs is to sell products, not joy—except perhaps the joy of shopping. Through the bulging cartoon mailbox, moreover, the cover makes the flattering acknowledgement that desirable customers, such as the reader, probably receive many catalogs. Then Land's End pretends, even in the face of such knowledge, that customers will find this catalog somehow better, or more useful, or more worth digging through the snow for.

Another striking example appears in the glossy pages of *The New Yorker* for 22 October 1990. This full-color, full-page print advertisement consists of a photograph of Cutty Sark whiskey on the rocks, centered on a gray-toned page. Near the bottom of the page is the Cutty Sark logo with its striking flash of yellow. Between, slightly below the photograph, appears the following text: "This is a glass of Cutty Sark. If you need to see a picture of a guy in an Armani suit sitting between two fashion models drinking it before you know it's right for you, it probably isn't." Predictably, this whiskey ad appeals to the snobbery long attributed to the magazine's upscale target audience. Here, however, the snobbery takes on a peculiarly contemporary coloration. The advertisement flatters readers not merely for the material sophistication that makes them familiar with Armani suits and fine whiskey but also for the mediated sophistication that would keep them from being fooled by glitzy photographs of elegantly dressed models. As the careful use of the casual term *guy* connotes, experienced readers understand that fashion models—perhaps like the ones appearing elsewhere in the magazine—probably possess no more special knowledge about whiskey than TV actors wearing white lab coats do about medicine. However, these readers also know that advertising is just as much a staple of *The New Yorker*, as it is of television. Perhaps the slick advertisements are among the reasons many readers subscribe. Thus, they can be expected not to feign Marxist horror when a product is hawked in their direction. As a matter of fact, one is being hawked right now: Cutty Sark.

In these examples, and in dozens of television and print ads like them, advertisers use rhetorical appeals that are surely subtle, but they are hardly subliminal. Along the way, the ads successfully complete the familiar rhetorical transaction in which viewers and readers are encouraged to buy. Perhaps the potential customers actually will buy the products. Whether anyone buys anything, however, the advertisers have succeeded in exposing their products to carefully targeted audiences made leery of advertising through long and continuing exposure. Self-referentiality has made possible a rhetorical communication that overfamiliarity might seem to have forbidden.

Of course, advertising is not the only—or even the principal—manifestation of self-referentiality in contemporary American culture. Something similar has been happening in electoral politics. Especially during the 1988 presidential election, both print and non-print media analysts paid far less attention to the substance of the campaign than to what Joan Didion called "Insider Baseball," intricate details of the process of campaigning (*The New York Review of Books*, 27 October 1988). Before the televised debates between Michael Dukakis and George Bush, for example, William Safire wrote a *New York Times* column entitled "Debate Advice" (8 September 1988, A29) in which he counseled Dukakis: "Appeal to the media by exposing the heavy-handed spin-doctoring; we hate to be seen being manipulated." Among many significant factors in the statement are Safire's assumptions that operatives of the Bush campaign had been effectively managing the news; that Safire could call the process "spin doctoring" with some likelihood of being understood; and that political insiders were not the only ones who know about this, that his general readers were also familiar with the process.

Safire was correct in all of these assumptions. Following the debates, network reporters interviewed Lee Atwater and other campaign functionaries who, first of all, agreed to be called "spin doctors" and then explained to the national television audience how they intended to manipulate media sources in favor of their candidates. Around the same time, ABC television news conducted on-the-street polls to find out how previous ABC news polls on the candidates' relative standings were affecting the general perception of the candidates' chances for election. As with the advertisements cited previously, the people who were sending the signals admitted that they were doing so, in large part, because they knew that their audience already understood that such signals were being sent. The primary and presidential election campaigns still took place, and a president was elected, even though the number of actual voters continued to decline, as *The New York Times* pointed out in their morning-after coverage of the election on 9 November 1988.

Although it appears everywhere in contemporary American popular culture, self-referentiality is neither new nor solely a property of popular culture. Many of William Shakespeare's love lyrics, for example, refer directly to themselves and their author. Sonnet 63 typically claims that the speaker's lover will outlast his mortal days because "His beauty shall in these black lines be seen." In a more famous variant of the theme, Sonnet 65 develops a paradoxical "miracle" in which "my love may still shine bright" in time to come through the poem's "black ink." In both cases, the poet subtly advertises that his speaker and the speaker's lover have their most significant existence in poems, rather than in the "real" world. In fact, Sonnet 55 makes the point emphatically in terms highly prejudicial to physical reality: "Not marble nor the gilded monuments / Of princes shall outlive this pow'rful rime." Shakespeare leaves little opportunity for anyone to assume that these are spontaneous outpourings of a lover's heart. They are poems, he insists, poems written by someone with ink on paper; and because they are poems, they will be more enduring than even the most sublime human beauty. As the speaker concludes in the famous "Shall I Compare Thee to a Summer's Day," Sonnet 18: "So long as men can breathe or eyes can see, / So long lives this, and this gives life to thee." It is obvious from these poems that self-referentiality in literature is at least five hundred years old.

Lyric poetry is not the only genre that has afforded authors opportunities to engage in self-references. Henry Fielding's neoclassical "rehearsal" plays, such as *The Author's Farce* (1730) and *Eurydice Hissed* (1737), were comic dramas about staging dramas. Fielding's best-known work, *Tom Jones* (1749), presents a highly diverting tale of comedy, adventure, and romance, but the novel also presents extensive commentary on literature in general and on the current story in particular. Thus, for example, Fielding feels free to open Book XV with a short chapter in which he first ponders the relations of virtue to happiness overall and then ironically contrasts "the most virtuous part imaginable" being enacted by Tom Jones to "the ruin of his Sophia" (644). Fielding's readers probably derive some deepened understanding of the story as a result of this chapter, but they surely get a deepened sense of Fielding's wit and sophistication. Through such self-referential passages, readers enter into a community of understanding with the author which allows him to make comments of this sort: "It would be unpleasant and tedious to paint this scene in full length. Let it suffice to say, that the behavior of Jones was kind to excess" (811). Readers thereby acquire the knowledge they need to follow the fictional proceedings, but they also learn a good deal about reading and writing fiction.

Self-referential devices also appear often in American fiction during the next century. In "The Big Bear of Arkansas" (1841) by Thomas Bangs Thorpe, a genteel, totally fictional narrator introduces Jim Doggett, the rough backwoodsman who will narrate the tale that gives the story its title, by emphasizing Doggett's "happy manner . . . of emphasizing the prominent parts of his conversation." Then the narrator says, "As near as I can recollect, I have italicized the words, and given the story in his own way" (83). Nathaniel Hawthorne begins his story "Rappaccini's Daughter" (1844) with a mock critical essay on the fiction of M. "Aubépine," the French word for *hawthorn*. Adopting a fictionalized editorial voice, Hawthorne speaks with mild irony about the literary efforts of this Aubepine and refers to several of Hawthorne's own tales by invented French titles. "The Balloon Hoax" (1844) by Edgar Allan Poe begins with a fictional frame in which Poe, posing as an editor of the *New York Sun*, introduces a stunning, but fictitious, trans-Atlantic balloon crossing by vouching for its authenticity: "The particulars furnished below may be relied on as authentic and accurate in every respect, as, with a slight exception, they are copied *verbatim* from the joint diaries of Mr. Monck Mason and Mr. Harrison Ainsworth. . . . The only alteration in the MS. received, has been made for the purpose of throwing the hurried account of our agent, Mr. Forsyth, in a connected and intelligible form" (225). As in the case of Fielding's *Tom Jones*, these stories by Thorpe, Hawthorne, and Poe succeeded in being told to their readers, and the readers probably derived appropriate aesthetic satisfaction from them. By expending so much energy in explaining *how* the stories were told, however, the authors were clearly reminding readers of the creators' controlling presence behind the scenes. They were being self-referential.

In the early twentieth century, self-referentiality continued to appear, usually in conjunction with literary works exploring the outer limits of what many call High Modernism. No one could believe for a moment, for example, that Wallace Stevens's poem "Thirteen Ways of Looking at a Blackbird" (1923) or James Joyce's novel *Finnegans Wake* (1939) were direct transcriptions of reality, because the authors' styles ostentatiously advertised their artificiality. Luigi Pirandello's *Six Characters in Search of an Author* (1921) is even more self-referential since it exacerbates this stylistic eccentricity by direct commentary on the theatrical process. Somewhat in the manner of Fielding's plays two centuries before, Pirandello's characters both act and comment on acting. Thus, in Act I, the character called The Son tells the character called The Manager, "I am an 'unrealized' character, dramatically speaking," and, in Act III, The Father admits, "We have no other reality beyond the illusion" (233, 264). We must, of course, recognize that the very different artistic intentions among High Modernists such as Pirandello, Stevens, and Joyce resulted in significantly different reader responses to their texts and created widely various thematic impressions. It is equally significant, however, that a foregrounding of technique is apparent in all these cases and that this foregrounding attracts the attention of the audience to the creator as well as to the creation. Readers and viewers who are consistently reminded in these ways that their experience is being artistically shaped must inevitably grow more sophisticated in their understanding of artistic mediation.

Even when many writers deliberately tried to break with High Modernism later in this century, they often enacted their rebellion in terms of an acute self-referentiality. Postmodern literary texts such as John Barth's *Lost in the Funhouse* (1968), Robert Coover's *Pricksongs and Descants* (1969), and William Goldman's *The Princess Bride* (1973) rely heavily on devices that should seem familiar from even this very schematic exercise in literary history. The title story of Barth's collection presents a narrative about a young boy named Ambrose who goes to Ocean City, Maryland, with his family. It also presents commentary on the art of fiction—including a diagram of Freitag's Triangle (95)—and on the current story, as in the following: "At this rate our hero, at this rate our protagonist [sic] will remain in the funhouse forever. Narrative ordinarily consists of alternating dramatization and summarization" (78). Coover's "The Babysitter" consists of 104 discretely marked narrative units that recount the experience of Mr. and Mrs. Tucker, an ordinary suburban couple who go to an ordinary suburban party while an unnamed babysitter takes care of their children, Jimmy and Bitsy. In the course of the story, the babysitter may get raped by her boyfriend or Mr. Tucker. Perhaps she is murdered. Perhaps the children are murdered too, or perhaps Bitsy drowns. Perhaps the suburban party turns out to be an orgy. Perhaps none of this happens. Because Coover's story is so obviously a story both typographically and stylistically, it encourages readers to accept any or all of these possibilities.

Goldman's novel also offers multiple possibilities. At one point, Westley, the hero, definitely dies, but then he returns to life. At one point, Buttercup, the heroine, marries the evil prince, but then she turns out to have been dreaming. All of these plot shifts are subject to commentary, moreover, by a narrator who calls himself Goldman and by S. Morgenstern, the supposed author of the original story. In a strategy that would probably please Poe and Thorpe, this commentary is presented in red type rather than the "black ink" used in the rest of the novel. All such self-referential texts remind readers that they are reading words on a page written at an earlier time by an author; they are not eavesdropping on life.

Silvio Gaggi makes some highly illuminating comments on these issues in his *Modern/Postmodern: A Study in Twentieth-Century Arts and Ideas* (1989). He also demonstrates, in a stimulating analysis of *Las Meninas* by Diego Velázquez (1656), that self-referentiality has had a long tradition in painting. Gaggi and others have remarked that recent artists—Andy Warhol, Roy Lichtenstein, M. C. Escher, and Shirley Levine—have productively interacted with this tradition. When associated with comparable examples in architecture and literary criticism, these postmodern literary texts and works of fine art may be understood to exhibit forms of self-referentiality similar to those we have seen operating in contemporary advertising and political campaigning.

Historically, American popular culture has often been highly self-referential. In his essay "Broadcast Humor," Lawrence E. Mintz insists that during its "golden age . . . radio comedy evinces a humor that is conscious of the medium" (95) in self-referential ways. Throughout the Marx Brothers films of the 1930s, Groucho addressed the audience directly. In *Horse Feathers* (1932), for example, while Baravelli (Chico) plays the piano for Connie Bailey, "the college widow," Groucho walks toward the camera and says, "I've got to stay here, but there's no reason why you folks shouldn't go out into the lobby till this thing blows over." Bob Hope and Bing Crosby were similarly self-referential during the 1940s in their "road" pictures with Dorothy Lamour. According to Wes D. Gehring's essay "Film Comedy," the apex of the latter occurred early in *The Road to Morocco* (1942), when Hope said to Crosby, "I'll lay you eight to five that we'll meet Dorothy Lamour" (78). In the 1950s, guest stars such as Lucille Ball played themselves in episodes of the *Jack Benny Program* in which Benny played himself as host of a show built around these same guest stars. Typically, the guest star would walk on stage during Benny's monologue, supposedly startling him into a surprised exclamation: "Lucy! Lucille Ball!" During the same years, George Burns explained the plots of his sitcom to the viewers as each episode developed and often watched this same episode developing on a TV set in his den.

Even while acknowledging these precedents in both hieratic (high) and demotic (popular) art, we must recognize that self-referentiality has become much more common and more elaborate in today's popular culture. Because of the increasing immersion of contemporary Americans in all forms of mediation, moreover, the rhetorical intention of the self-references has shifted considerably, shifting away from the artist's self-expression and toward an affirmation of the mediated community that is embracing both creator and audience.

This shift is apparent in all segments of the American entertainment industry. At the end of the film *Ferris Bueller's Day Off*, Matthew Broderick comes on screen and tells the viewers that the movie is over and they should go home. At the end of *Pee Wee's Big Adventure*, the cast watches the film, as is also true of the casts in Woody Allen's *Stardust Memories* and Jim Henson's *The Muppet Movie*. In Allen's *The Purple Rose of Cairo*, characters freely move between a fictional, full-color New Jersey and the black-and-white Manhattan on a movie screen. At the end of Mel Brooks's parodic western *Blazing Saddles*, the film's two stars ride off into the sunset in a studio limo. While long experience has taught viewers unconsciously to expect certain conventions to govern film narrative, in all of these cases the conventions are violated right in front of the viewers. These violations then become part of a different narrative based on another rhetorical compact, one postulated on the audience's heightened awareness of how film conventions operate. Once again, a much exploited popular medium can be seen to draw sustaining energy from the audience's understanding of what is "really" going on.

Brooks, Allen, Henson, and other motion picture directors such as Rob Reiner got started in show business by working in television, and it is in television that the contemporary trend toward self-referentiality is most clearly displayed. During the late 1970s, *Saturday Night Live* and *SCTV* took television as their subject matter as well as their medium of communication. Thus, their satiric sketches often ridiculed game shows, talk shows, and TV news, as well as the business practices and aesthetic standards of their industry. In addition, they often comically emphasized the devices of their medium—dream focus, theme music, laugh tracks,—instead of trying to use them to create illusions of verisimilitude.

This was also the rhetorical strategy of Jim Henson's brilliant syndicated TV program from the same period, *The Muppet Show*. Since, with the exception of a guest star, all the actors on the show were puppets, this open acknowledgement of artifice was probably a very good idea. In any case, the show's rhetorical approach may be typified by an episode of the recurring soap opera parody called *Veterinarians' Hospital*, from the show starring Lou Rawls which was broadcast during the second season (1977–78). As usual, the sketch was constructed of a series of corny medical jokes, mostly delivered by Miss Piggy. Eventually, as usual, an unseen announcer broke in. Then, as usual, all the Muppets in the sketch looked at the ceiling in surprise, trying to figure out where the voice was coming from. In this case, Dr. Bob asked the ceiling, "Who are you?" The voice replied, "I'm the one who says, 'And now for another episode of Veterinarians' Hospital.'" Then the Muppets began the sketch over again at manic speed, racing though the jokes in acknowledgement of their staleness. Since the viewers can hardly have laughed at these tired jokes the first time around, no loss of comic immediacy occurred. Rather, the real joke became the shared recognition by Henson's writers and viewers of what had been going on in this sketch—and in all the ones preceding it. On such TV programs, the creators' obvious rhetorical assumption was that viewers already knew they were watching "television" and not reality, or even a simulacrum of reality, and so why not admit this?

In the 1980s, TV programs such as *It's Garry Shandling's Show* and *Moonlighting* built on these foundations, confident that their viewers had been fully enrolled in a rhetorical community based on a common experience of television and its conventions. Even when self-referentiality was not basic to a TV show's premises in the 1980s, however, it was assumed to be a valid and easily recognizable technique. Rick Ducommun's HBO comedy special during the summer of 1989, for example, opened with Ducommun watching his closing credits on a TV set. He rewound this tape, and the viewing audience then saw Ducommun's performance, composed of segments filmed at earlier times. When all the jokes had been told, Ducommun went home, turned on his TV set, and watched himself go home and turn on his TV set. In a *Twilight Zone* allusion, a voice-over said that Ducommun was caught in a "nightmare," but the experienced viewer understood that this was merely an advanced degree of self-referentiality. Similarly, on an episode of Candice Bergen's *Murphy Brown* sitcom during the fall 1989 season, the executives at Murphy Brown's network decided to produce a sitcom about a TV newswoman and so sent Morgan Fairchild, the actress slated to play Murphy Brown, to the studio to observe the "real thing." When the sitcom's filming actually got underway, Murphy was given a walk-on part. After the filming, when Murphy was back in her own "real" studio, Connie Chung did a walk-on. Both the framing device of the Ducommun special and the play within a play of the *Murphy Brown* episode depended, for their comic references, on the audience's close familiarity with the medium of television, with guest stars, with videotaping, with cutting for continuity, and—above all—with the understanding that television is television and not life.

It is probably unsurprising that self-referentiality is itself almost a convention in music videos, a form of popular culture largely developed in the 1980s, after the practices already cited had grown entrenched in film and television. The typical music video today has as its plot the making of a music video. Thus, production techniques are frequently translated from signifiers to signifieds, and back again, in the space of three minutes. This exploitation of convention was probably necessitated by a combination of creative exhaustion and escalating production costs. Whatever the causes, however, this kind of self-referentiality has authorized the continuing production of music videos. In this respect, Phil Collins, the singer, is often cast, as an actor in one of his music videos, in the same sort of role played by the actor in the television commercial who says he plays a doctor on television. A new rhetorical community based on a mutual recognition of conventional devices thus allows the genre to continue even though some supposedly necessary illusions have been deconstructed.

Even without the videos, contemporary popular music is often highly self-referential. The rigors of life on the road, the disappointments of the music business, the hollowness of success, the burdens of stardom—all provide subject matter for hit songs. Significantly, the popularity of these topics even crosses the rigid boundaries observed elsewhere in the pop music industry. Country musicians are as likely as rockers to demand sympathy for the supposed agonies of superstardom. Bob Seger and Larry Gatlin could hardly be more unlike musically, and yet they both assume that their listeners know enough about how the music business operates to empathize with their self-referential performances. This seems, moreover, a perfectly legitimate assumption. Who can be totally ignorant about today's pop singers? Even if the listener does not read *Rolling Stone* and *Spin* or one of the country music fan magazines, the news will get out through *Entertainment Tonight*, the MTV *Music News*, or *Time* magazine. And then, there are always the supermarket tabloids. Who in America can claim to know nothing about Madonna's private life? The fans of popular music naturally wish to make no such claim. They eagerly consume information about their favorite musicians, especially if the fact or gossip is advertised as "inside" information. Here we see another way in which a new rhetorical community emerges. The consumers of popular music willingly enter into a compact in which they agree to absorb and retain information about their favorite stars' lives as well as their art. This information thus becomes legitimate subject matter for self-referential performances by the stars.

Even many comic strips have accepted these rhetorical assumptions. Ziggy tells his therapist about a nightmare of being naked because "he" forgot to draw Ziggy's clothes. Adam collides with the right-hand panel of the strip while chasing a fly ball. Boner sails his ark through the line dividing two cartoon panels. Readers have probably always known, in some sense, that cartoon conventions like these lines existed, but only the more creative strips—"Pogo" and "Li'l Abner," for example—openly acknowledged them. In the self-referential rhetorical community of today, even strips like "Frank & Ernest" and "Marvin" make such jokes, comfortably assuming that their readers will comprehend.

The more intellectual strips are even more self-referential. Even though some comic artists believe, as Charles Schulz told James O. Clifford, that strips should not make "self-conscious statements," the majority opinion increasingly seems to hold otherwise. "Doonesbury" took no parting shot on Ronald Reagan's last day as president and made this decision the joke of the day. "Doonesbury" also ran a series of strips about "sweeps week" on the comic pages. Characters in "Bloom County" often refer to where they live as "this strip." Bill the Cat is repeatedly compared to Garfield. As in the case of pop singers, it is unsurprising that cartoonists assume their readers' familiarity with their lives and business. No matter what he says about self-referential strips, Charles Schulz has been a public figure for years, and a very wealthy one at that. Garry Trudeau has been on the cover of *Newsweek*. His sabbatical in 1983 was not only a major news story but a subject for other comic strips, including "Frank & Ernest" and "Bloom County." Berke Breathed's decision to close down the latter strip and replace it with *Outland* was also treated as a major entertainment industry event. It is probably as hard not to know about the major cartoonists as about the major rock stars and TV personalities.

The key to understanding the rhetorical community now supporting American popular culture surely lies somewhere around here. How can we not know about Roseanne Barr's version of the national anthem? about Michael Jackson's plastic surgery? about Barbara Hershey's lips and Paul Newman's eyes? about Pete Rose's gambling and Kitty Dukakis's drinking? We don't have to go out in pursuit of this information. We don't even have to watch television all the time. Think how many TV shows we know about that we have never seen, how many movies, how many best sellers! We don't need to hear an actual recording by Two Live Crew to know—or to think we know—about their lyrics. We don't have to taste blue tortilla chips or see Andrew Dice Clay or read Stephen King. We exist in a culture that is brokered for us primarily by the mass media.

Evidence began to appear many years ago that this mediated sensibility was emerging. In December 1965, Pauline Kael commented in *The Atlantic* on what she took to be a peculiar phenomenon: "Now advertising kids advertising, TV commercials kid TV commercials, movies kid movies." Kael did not specifically call these tendencies self-referential in her article and, furthermore, did not approve of them: "It's as embarrassed and half-hearted a strategy as that of a fatman who makes himself a buffoon so that you can't make more fun of him than he has already" (85). She did, however, cite a plausible explanation of the movement's etiology that a marketing expert had provided earlier in *The New York Times:* "They're coming. The new generation of young adults, wise, hip, skeptical. . . . A new breed of sophisticates who have been deluged by advertising since they were 3. Bred to a new wisdom at television's knee" (84). Perhaps the forced enthusiasm of his rhetoric distracted Kael from the perceptiveness of the ad man's observation. Perhaps in 1965 the signs were not yet clear enough to interpret. By 1983, however, an equally unsympathetic observer, the Marxist critic Fredric Jameson, was fully convinced that American popular culture had been infused by "an ever more rapid rhythm of fashion and styling changes; the penetration of advertising, television and the media generally to a hitherto unparalleled degree throughout society" (124). If we can put aside the alarmist tone of such commentary, we may profit from its insights.

The thoroughness of the penetration, for one thing, may be seen in highly varied situations. Writing in the *New Republic* about Roger Ailes, the conservative "media consultant," Fred Barnes recounts several anecdotes to show the effectiveness of rehearsed ad libs in politics. He recalls first how Ronald Reagan mooted any question about his advanced age by saying in his debate with Walter Mondale, "I am not going to exploit for political purposes my opponent's youth and inexperience." Barnes credits the line originally to Reagan but explains that, if he had "not had time to recall and practice the line, he probably wouldn't have come up with it in time to give a quick riposte on national television" (12). Another success was the following quip by George Bush during another debate: "To hear the Democrats wringing their hands about all that's wrong . . . I'm depressed. I want to switch over and see 'Jake and the Fatman' on CBS." Barnes reports that Roger Ailes actually invented the zinger and adds, "Bush had never seen the show, but the line worked. Again he dominated the sound bites" (12). Even if George Bush had never seen this show, Ailes had, or at least he knew about it, and he could assume the same about most of the audience tuning in to the debates or watching a few seconds of film on the evening news. Probably, like most other Americans, Bush had at least heard of the show.

Like most other Americans, including my son Paul, George Bush probably also knew at one time that Oprah Winfrey had lost sixty-seven pounds, even if—like Paul—Bush had never watched Oprah's show. This highly mediated dieting by Oprah Winfrey might be taken synecdochally to represent the whole rhetorical environment in which contemporary self-referentiality occurs. On 9 November 1990, two years after the famous weight loss, Richard Prince wrote an entire column on Oprah's decision not to attempt another diet to shed the seventeen pounds she had regained. In the process, he referred to the size ten Calvin Klein jeans she wore on the 15 November 1988 show and to the scandal in which *TV Guide* superimposed Oprah's face on Ann-Margret's body. Surely it is symptomatic of a larger climate of understanding that Prince would devote this space usually focused on significant political, social, and racial issues to the diet plans of a media celebrity and that he would do so with the confidence that his readers could understand his references. Probably we may all testify that Prince's confidence was well placed.

Further evidence is refracted through a piece written by Andrew Sarris for the *Village Voice* (19 July 1983) on Woody Allen's film *Zelig*, starring Allen and Mia Farrow. Like several other reviewers, Sarris associates Allen's use of fictional interviews in this mock documentary with Warren Beatty's earlier use of the technique in *Reds*, starring Beatty and Diane Keaton. Sarris then goes the other critics one better by writing, "Allen's 'joke' about witnesses is of course double-edged in the sense that those of us who read page six of the *Post* slavishly are aware that both Woody Allen and Warren Beatty have been involved with Diane Keaton in the muse-is-a-jealous-mistress department" (39). In this observation, Sarris assumes that his readers either know about these celebrities' romantic entanglements already or can reconstruct them easily from some minimal references. Despite the self-defensive irony suggested through the word *slavishly*, Sarris also assumes that it is acceptable for him to know and recount this gossip because it has already been reported in the *Post* and other places. We may wonder whether George Bush and Roger Ailes also know about Keaton and Allen. Oprah almost certainly does.

We know about Woody and Oprah because they are among the elements constituting contemporary American culture, as are Jesse Helms, Madonna, and Beaver Cleaver. We must recognize, first of all, that our familiarity with these people has primarily come to us not through immediate personal experience but through the mass media, from mass-circulation magazines, films, radio, advertising, the covers of supermarket tabloids, and—chiefly—television. We should realize further that these media are also the sources through which we have learned about Ollie North, Manuel Noriega, Mikhail Baryshnikov, and Mother Teresa. This is how information of all sorts reaches us in America today.

Furthermore, most Americans are conscious of this process, at least to some degree. They know that the medium, especially television, is inseparable from the message it conveys. The naive masses who allegedly cannot distinguish between Joan Collins and the fictional character she played on *Dynasty* are surely a fiction themselves. Although some gullible dolts certainly exist, there are probably no more of them than there are people who sincerely believe that professional wrestling is on the up-and-up or that they will end up looking like Christie Brinkley if they use the same makeup she uses. Views to the contrary are largely the creation of media critics eager to stigmatize the choices of free agents with tastes different from their own.

The more likely case is cogently presented by Jeff Greenfield in his book, *Television: The First Fifty Years* (1981). Greenfield writes: "Many of television's critics worry that it is creating a generation of 'zombies,' staring slack-jawed at the screen, obeying the advertisements as so many automatons. But every generation grows up to learn that its elders distort, avoid, and lie; in the case of this generation, that insight has come from the same source as its dominant diversion: television" (234). By extending Greenfield's observation, we may say that, through prolonged exposure, this generation has become accustomed to assuming that the media mediate experience, that representations are not reality. A corollary of this assumption might be a definition of culture for this generation as: what we are really all in together. In this light, our highly mediated culture is not some pale platonic reflection of the culture we need or should desire but the only living culture we have. This conclusion certainly accords more closely with the evidence provided by the self-referential forms with which we are all—creators and consumers of popular culture alike—surrounded today.

WORKS CITED

Alter, Jonathan. "Real Life with Garry Trudeau." *Newsweek*, 15 Oct. 1990, 60–66.
Aristotle. *Rhetoric*. Translated by W. Rhys Roberts. *Poetics*. Translated by Ingram Bywater. New York: Modern Library, 1954.
Barnes, Fred. "Pulling the Strings." *New Republic*, 22 Feb. 1988, 11–14.
Barth, John. "Lost in the Funhouse." In *Lost in the Funhouse: Fiction for Print, Tape, Live Voice*, 72–97. 1968. Reprint. New York: Grosset, 1969.
Clifford, James O. "Charlie Brown Turns 40." *The (Nashville) Tennessean*, 5 Oct. 1989: 1E+.
Coover, Robert. "The Babysitter." In *Pricksongs and Descants*, 206–39. 1969. Reprint. New York: New American Library, 1970.

Didion, Joan. "Insider Baseball." *The New York Review of Books*, 27 Oct. 1988, 19–30.

Dionne, E. J., Jr. "Bush is Elected by a 6-5 Margin." *The New York Times*, 9 Nov. 1988: A1+.

Fielding, Henry. *The History of Tom Jones, A Foundling.* 1749. Reprint. New York: Washington Square, 1963.

Finch, Christopher. *Of Muppets and Men: The Making of the Muppet Show.* New York: Knopf, 1981.

Gaggi, Silvio. *Modern/Postmodern: A Study in Twentieth-Century Arts and Ideas.* Philadelphia: University of Pennsylvania Press, 1989.

Gehring, Wes D. "Film Comedy." In *Humor in America: A Research Guide to Genres and Topics*, edited by Lawrence E. Mintz, 91–108. Westport, Conn.: Greenwood, 1988.

Goldman, William. *The Princess Bride: S. Morgenstern's Classic Tale of True Love and High Adventure, The "Good Parts" Version.* New York: Harcourt, 1973.

Greenfield, Jeff. *Television: The First Fifty Years.* New York: Crescent, 1981.

Hawthorne, Nathaniel. "Rappaccini's Daughter." In *Mosses from an Old Manse*, edited by J. Donald Crowley, 91–128. Columbus: Ohio State University Press, 1974.

Jameson, Fredric. "Postmodernism and Consumer Culture." In *The Anti-Aesthetic: Essays on Postmodern Culture*, edited by Hal Foster, 111–25. Port Townsend, Wash.: Bay, 1983.

Joyce, James. *Finnegans Wake.* New York: Viking, 1939.

Kael, Pauline. "Spoofing and Schtik." *The Atlantic*, Dec. 1965, 84–85.

Mintz, Lawrence E. "Broadcast Humor." In *Humor in America: A Research Guide to Genres and Topics*, 91–108. Westport, Conn.: Greenwood, 1988.

Pirandello, Luigi. *Six Characters in Search of an Author.* 1922. In *Naked Masks*, edited by Eric Bentley. New York: Dutton, 1952. 211–76.

Poe, Edgar Allan. "The Balloon-Hoax." In *Prose Tales*, edited by James A. Harrison, 224–40. New York: Crowell, 1902. New York: AMS, 1965.

Prince, Richard. "Backsliding Back into Size 16." *The (Nashville) Tennessean*, 9 Nov. 1990, 13A.

Safire, William. "Debate Advice." *New York Times*, 8 Sept. 1988, A29.

Sarris, Andrew. Review of *Zelig, Village Voice*, 19 July 1983, 39.

Shakespeare, William. *Sonnets.* Edited by Douglas Bush and Alfred Harbage. The Pelican Shakespeare. Baltimore: Penguin, 1961.

Sontag, Susan. "On Style." In *Against Interpretation and Other Essays*, 15–36. New York: Farrar, Straus & Giroux, 1966.

Stevens, Wallace. "Thirteen Ways of Looking at a Blackbird." In *Collected Poems*, 92–95. New York: Knopf, 1978.

Thorpe, Thomas Bangs. "The Big Bear of Arkansas." In *The Hive of "The Bee-Hunter": A Repository of Sketches*, 72–93. New York: D. Appleton, 1854.

CHAPTER 2 **Saturday Night Live**

**and *SCTV***

Live from New York!

It's Television Like

You've Never Seen It Before

Self-referentiality is perhaps inseparable from television because of the audience's relation to the medium. Unlike a drama or film, which we encounter by deliberately going through time and space to a legitimate theater or motion picture house, television programs actually come to us, to our living rooms, dens, bedrooms, kitchens, and motel rooms. With the use of portable TV's such as the Sony Watchman, television programs can even follow us to a ball park, a boat, or a stretch limo. As Gerald Mast wittily observes in his *Film/Cinema/Movie: A Theory of Experience* (1977), because TV "is something we can so easily grasp (literally and, hence, figuratively)" (102), situational distinctions crucially affect our differing rhetorical relations to theater, film, and television.

It is probably true, as Samuel Johnson pointed out in his "Preface to Shakespeare" (1765), that spectators at a play "are always in their senses, and know, from the first act to the last, that the stage is only a stage, and that the players are only players" (214). Even so, their individual decisions to attend the play and their physical separation from the stage seem to create some sort of neutral zone of imagination. Thus, although the members of the audience know, as Johnson argues, that the stage is not really Egypt and the actor not Cleopatra, in another sense, simply by sitting in a darkened theater and facing toward a stage, the members of the audience agree to what Samuel Taylor Coleridge calls in chapter 14 of his *Biographia Literaria* a "willing suspension of disbelief" (376). Once again in Johnson's words, the play "is credited with all the credit due to drama" (215). In Mast's more recent formulation one might say that "the successful work of mimetic representation makes us *know* we are undergoing an experience at the same time that we know we are sitting in a theater" (46).

The same may be said in a slightly different way about the experience of watching a motion picture in a downtown theater, a multi-screened mall film emporium, or even a darkened gymnasium. Again, the circumstances of deliberately going to the film site, of (usually) sitting in the dark, and of facing a remote screen operate on the audience to create some sort of "suspension of disbelief." Consider the episode in which Holden Caulfield attends the Christmas show at Radio City Music Hall in J. D. Salinger's novel *The Catcher in the Rye* (1951). Holden says about the live stage show, "It's supposed to be religious as hell, I know, and very pretty and all, but I can't see anything religious or pretty, for God's sake, about a bunch of actors carrying crucifixes all over the stage" (178). Perhaps fortunately, Holden has focused on the presentational dimensions of the show to such an extent that he cannot accept its content. He pretends to be equally unaffected by the sentimental film and says, "Don't see it if you don't want to puke all over yourself" (180). Significantly, however, Holden can recount the plot of the film almost frame by frame, testifying to his original attention to its content. Holden's differing reactions, though fictional, illustrate the different demands made on an audience by film and live performance, even when presented side by side. (These distinctions were probably sealed forever by the disappearance of the Music Hall's live shows in 1983.) It is evident that the rhetorical community between the creators of a film and their viewers resembles the one that Johnson and Coleridge posit between the audience and the dramatic stage. Both of these relations differ substantially, however, from that existing between Holden and the Rockettes and between the viewer and television.

Another ground of distinction should be noted. Until motion picture theaters recently adopted the television practice of showing filmed commercials before the feature, audiences at either a legitimate play or a movie could reasonably anticipate a discrete experience. A legitimate theater might pair a farce with a tragedy, or a Saturday matinee at the Bijou might consist of a western, a comedy, several cartoons, and a newsreel. Even so, in the first case, the theater provided only plays and in the second, only films. Surely an audience habituated to such generic consistency would share different rhetorical expectations than those developed by a television audience habituated to continual content shifts.

A dramatic chase on television, for example, may be suspended, to be followed by a series of commercials for soft drinks, imported cars, insurance, and soap, interspersed with station identification, promotional material for upcoming shows, and perhaps a summary of news headlines or weather conditions. A credit establishing the return to the dramatic show would probably conclude the interruptions and reintroduce the chase. Since this whole series of viewing experiences would very likely be preceded and followed by other commercials, promotions, and public service presentations—as well as by generically different programing such as sitcoms, newsmagazine shows, sports and talk shows—the constant shifting of content and appeal becomes more rhetorically significant. Hovering over all such transactions, moreover, both in the realm of broadcast possibility and in the viewer's previous experience of the medium, is a potential interruption by some sort of presentational programing: a news flash, a weather alert, an election report. Experienced TV watchers are constantly aware, even if not consciously, of such possibilities. This constitutes, in fact, the very nature of watching television.

This varied and constantly changing content has a leveling effect on all of its components. Dramas, live news events, commercials, and music videos are all in an important sense merely parts of "television." As many observers have remarked, the correlative developments of cable television and the remote control unit have only served to intensify this effect. In Salman Rushdie's novel *The Satanic Verses*, for example, Saladin survives a period of existential alienation by watching "a good deal of television with half an eye; channel hopping compulsively." The experience leads him to observe, "[W]hat a leveller this remote-control gizmo was, a Procrustean bed for the twentieth century; it chopped down the heavyweight and stretched out the slight until all the set's emissions, commercials, murders, game-shows, the thousand and one varying joys and terrors of the real and imagined, acquired an equal weight" (405).

Interestingly, David Marc draws similar conclusions in his study

*Comic Visions: Television Comedy and American Culture,* and he presents them in a more lively style than the novelist:

> PBS penguins roosting on the ice floes. Boxcar Willie is a guest on *Nashville Now.* Lucy smuggles a giant provolone cheese onto an airplane by disguising it as a baby. The House is holding hearings. A rerun of a college basketball game; I think I know the score. Kill cockroaches with sonic waves. Could that really be Deputy Dawg? A new show— does the star cue psychosexual responses? A different Lucy episode arrives from a neighboring market. It's the one where Lucy goes to the eye doctor and gets a glaucoma test that impairs her vision just before she's supposed to do a dance number down at the club with a professional jitterbug. Whole minutes of duelling Lucies; a woman with a real baby sits down next to Lucy; the jitterbug, wearing a zoot suit, calls Lucy a "chick"; Fred and Ethel reluctantly agree to help; Ricky's anger sends him into Spanish. I pray to the god of HBO; oh no, not *The Black Stallion* again! This guy is either the Herbalife guy or the guy who tells you how to become a millionaire by taking over bad mortgages. *The PTL Club* without Tammy or Jim? No thanks. Sally Jessy Raphael—the poor woman's Phil Donahue. Didactic *Starsky and Hutch:* a Soviet ballerina falls in love with Hutch and defects to the West Coast. Julia Child is adding butter. Mark Goodman is announcing concert dates for incomprehensible pop bands. Fred Flintstone is yelling for Wilma. (204)

Amid such proliferation, the claim of any single TV entity on viewers' disbelief must obviously be slight. When so much is being incessantly communicated, viewers can only grow more aware of the means of communication. As receivers of signals, viewers must therefore enter into a community of reference with the people sending the signals. It is this TV community that authorizes such advanced degrees of self-referentiality.

Furthermore, something similar seems to have been true of television from its earliest days. In a very helpful study entitled "Self-referentiality in Art: A Look at Three Television Situation Comedies of the 1950s," Joann Gardner analyzes the interplay between television itself and the sitcom content on *The George Burns and Gracie Allen* show, the *Jack Benny Show,* and *I Love Lucy.* As Gardner shows, all three programs attempted to exploit the new medium of television as a source of comic possibility. Among others, Lawrence E. Mintz has emphasized how, during this same period, Ernie Kovacs turned the focus of his comedy away from predictable sketch material toward the medium he was using. In his essay

"Broadcast Humor," Mintz says that Kovacs "was always aware of the potential of the camera, and his metacomedic, satiric references to other aspects of his own medium such as commercials and variety entertainment were unparalleled" in that era (97).

Later, *Rowan & Martin's Laugh-In* (1968–73) built on two decades of audience exposure to television to authorize a much more obvious interplay among subject matter, technique, and field of comic allusion, thus attaining an advanced degree of self-referentiality. Contemporaneously (1969–74), the British import *Monty Python's Flying Circus* confirmed this direction, not only in the creators' exploitation of the medium for comic effect, but also—and more significantly—in their assumption that their viewers were equally aware of the medium's involvement in the message even if, again, this awareness was unconscious and unexamined. Roger Wilmut supports such conclusions in his informative book *From Fringe to Flying Circus* when he quotes John Cleese's recollection of the show's original motivation: "The whole idea of breaking a convention was right in the front of our minds; but very rapidly, once you've destroyed a convention then the fact that the convention no longer exists itself becomes a convention" (218). The audience's complicity in this rhetorical communion authorized all sorts of self-referentiality on the Python show, and these tendencies were developed even more explicitly on *Saturday Night Live* and *SCTV* during the late 1970s.

Although, as Joann Gardner has persuasively argued, this consciousness has long been a part of television, there has unquestionably been an increase in the frequency and intensity of the sort of self-referentiality that makes this consciousness manifest. As the audience has grown more steeped in the medium with the passage of four decades, the basic rhetoric of TV communication has subtly changed. In 1981 Jeff Greenfield observed presciently in *Television: The First Fifty Years* that "it was to be expected that [TV] should find itself changing shape under its own impact" (23). Events have vindicated Greenfield's perception.

This shape-shifting was apparent in *Monty Python's Flying Circus*. The rhetorical assumptions of the Python show were clear first of all in the group's deliberately mixed content of costumed sketches, live-action role-playing, animation, and supposed public reactions such as the recurring shots of the same, elderly, female audience applauding, letters of complaint from offended viewers, and

Graham Chapman's humorless Colonel who canceled sketches for being "too silly." This last element especially underlined the rhetorical convention that, in any given situation, the Python troupe was a group of comic actors playing written parts on a television program that consisted of many such parts. Since Chapman's Colonel was so obviously fictional, his role doubly demonstrated all these assumptions.

One example must suffice to illustrate the series' self-referential exploitation of television as a medium as well as an object for satire. In one sketch, Michael Palin plays a working-class British citizen who is eating dinner in the kitchen with his wife, played by Terry Jones. A letter arrives from the head of the BBC asking Palin's character to play a walk-on role in a comedy sketch. Since the viewers have already seen Eric Idle and John Cleese unaccountably standing about nervously in a lingerie shop set, it is easy to guess which sketch is in need of a bit player. Although Palin's character is reluctant, he is persuaded by his wife to do his civic duty and play the one-second part. Palin thus enters the shop-sketch set and walks immediately off. Idle and Cleese then enact a silly robbery sketch. Jones, at home, flips on the telly just in time to see Palin's back disappearing through the lingerie shop door, too late to alert the neighbors who are coming to watch her husband's TV debut.

The content of the unfunny robbery sketch cannot be considered the focus of this extended comic performance. Rather, the humor is created by acknowledging that the sketch is a piece of comic drama, that the participants are actors who, like Palin's character, have lives elsewhere, and that anyone might someday be "on television"—if not in a BBC comedy sketch, then in an on-the-street interview, a studio audience, or perhaps just in the security monitor of a convenience store. In these respects, the audience's expectations concerning television differ vastly from those concerning films or theater. The contrast is especially clear when we recall that the very possibility of appearing on stage or in the movies has long been a staple of popular fantasy projection, whereas the possibility of appearing on television can function as an element of rhetorical commonality. Presidential aspirant Richard Nixon appeared on *Rowan & Martin's Laugh-In* in 1968, and presidential handler Lee Atwater played very unfunky blues guitar on the David Letterman show in 1989. In a column written in April 1990, Ellen Goodman predicted with alarm that anyone with sufficient perseverance might appear on *America's*

*Funniest Home Videos* next year, or the year after that. Thus, a whole mediated realm of possibilities supports, and perhaps demands, self-referentiality.

Since the Python show was British and was long unavailable to American viewers except for a small-scale syndication on a few PBS affiliates after its first-run demise, it cannot be considered central to a discussion of how such self-referentiality has flourished in American television. Even so, as Richard A. Blake recognized early on, the show did epitomize an evolving form of TV programing. During 1975, the show's syndication market vastly increased and the film *Monty Python and the Holy Grail* was released, thus creating considerable media interest in the troupe. Writing at that time in *America*, Blake observed about the TV show:

> Cleese and his collaborators have . . . captured a sense of the television medium itself. To revert to a mildly quaint McLuhanism, they have exploited the medium so completely that the Albion-bound message is really reduced to an insignificant position of importance. . . .
>
> Like its linear ancestor on American television, *Laugh-In*, the *Flying Circus* has mastered the principle of television timing. It uses the commercial as the measure of the longest possible attention span of its audience. Television pace, if it is authentic, disregards the content of the program, which is merely a derivative of literature and literary-conditioned continuity. . . . A viewer can tune in at any point in the program and not miss any background; an editor can jumble the parts and rearrange them in any sequence and nothing would be lost. The generic model is the cascade of commercials that floods the living room during a two-minute station break. (348)

In spite of some condescending archness, Blake's comments are highly instructive since they touch on so many of the elements that constitute self-referentiality on television: a shared sense of the medium's presence, of its artificial arrangement of highly discrete segments, of its possible discontinuity, and of its inextricable involvement in commerciality. All of these assumptions can be seen at work in the now readily available videotapes and reruns of the Python show, and they can be seen (probably daily) in reruns of the show's much more familiar American cousin, *Saturday Night Live*.

In their very interesting history, *Saturday Night*, Doug Hill and Jeff Weingrad discuss the powerful influence of *Monty Python's Flying Circus* on Lorne Michaels, the creator of *Saturday Night Live* (*SNL*). As Hill and Weingrad explain, from *SNL*'s beginnings in 1975,

Michaels hoped to produce an American television comedy equivalent in sophistication to the Python show, both in video technique and in breadth of comedic reference. Michaels even favored the Python troupe's practice of breaking through the "fourth wall" and truncating sketches at their peak of comic effectiveness, rather than trying to develop some sort of traditional closure (133–35). On *SNL* the practice was called "dropping the cow," and it can be illustrated by a "Killer Bee" sketch featuring—appropriately enough—Eric Idle.

In this sketch, the male cast members and Idle, dressed in preposterous bee costumes complete with wildly springy antennae, attempt to rob a swine flu vaccine center staffed by two nurses, played by Jane Curtin and Gilda Radner. During the robbery, Idle forgets to use the *Treasure-of-Sierra-Madre* Mexican accent used by the other bees and lets slip the term *bloke*, leading Curtin and Radner to claim that the Idle bee is not truly Mexican. The John Belushi bee admits that the Idle bee may have had "two semesters at Cambridge" but insists that he still is not British. When Idle's use of further British slang makes the Mexican imposture insupportable, the other actors break character and claim that Idle has "ruined the sketch." Garrett Morris says, "*Monty Python's Flying Circus!* They must be willing to laugh at anything in England!" The cast members then walk off, leaving an embarrassed Idle on stage. Laraine Newman, who was not in the sketch, enters and tells Idle that she thinks he is "wonderful." He asks her to go back to his dressing room, and they exit romantically, hand in hand.

In this sketch, the "cow" is not "dropped" to cut off the humor at its peak. In fact, the swine flu sketch contains no intrinsic humor. Whatever laughter the sketch produces comes as a result of its obviousness as a performance: the absurd premise of machine-gun-toting giant bees, the ridiculous costuming, the bogus accents with their allusions to John Huston's classic film. The sketch also depends heavily on the audience's familiarity with earlier, equally silly, "Killer Bee" sketches, such as the one recounted by Hill and Weingrad (133) in which the bee played by Elliott Gould cannot stay in camera focus because the director is supposedly drunk, and another sketch in which Rob Reiner berates the killer bees for ruining a romantic sketch, only to be berated in turn by the bees and his wife, Penny Marshall, for his display of superstar egotism. In all three bee sketches, then, the separate elements of comic silliness provide incidental laughs, but the overall humor results, as Richard A. Blake might observe, from the medium of television not from the content of the sketch.

Surely this is even truer of the fake debacle with which the Eric Idle sketch ends. The viewers know that this is only a brief comic segment in a larger program. They know further that Idle is not a bee, that he is not even a regular performer on the show, that—like Gould and Reiner—he is merely a guest host, a changing element of the show's structure. Morris's identification of Idle as a member of the Python troupe is another joke based on the same sort of audience awareness. The point is not that the Python show is not as funny as *SNL*, but that viewers of *SNL* may be assumed to know about the Python show—and probably to be fans. That is to say, the humor is self-referential.

All of these remarks may be applied equally to one of *SNL*'s most famous sketches, "The Last Voyage of the Starship *Enterprise*." This sketch opens with John Belushi playing the role of Captain James Kirk in a set representing the flight deck of the Starship *Enterprise*. For the first few minutes, the sketch consists of typical *Star Trek* business about the mission and the ship's course, with Chevy Chase playing Mr. Spock and Dan Ackroyd, Dr. Bones. As always on *Star Trek*, trouble arises, this time in the form of two earth creatures from the mid-twentieth century: an NBC program executive named Herb Goodman (Elliott Gould) and his flunky Curtis (Garrett Morris). These two have come to announce that low Nielsens have led to the cancelation of the show, the firing of the actors, and the striking of the set. At first, the members of the *Enterprise* crew attempt to resist in character, but soon Bones/Ackroyd reverts to DeForrest Kelley and goes off to get a drink, inviting "Leonard" to join him. Spock/Chase stays in character until Goodman repossesses his Vulcan ears. Then, as Leonard Nimoy, Chase goes off crying. Kirk/Belushi stays in character during the dismantling of the set, even when Goodman calls him "Shatner" and mentions the offer of a margarine commercial.

The sketch ends with Belushi alone on the struck set, still in character, dictating the final entry into his Captain's log: "We have tried to explore strange new worlds, to seek out new civilizations, to boldly go where no man has gone before. And except for one television network, we have found intelligent life everywhere in the galaxy" (Hill and Weingrad, 138). Hill and Weingrad are probably correct in their judgment that this piece of comedy "is unanimously considered by those on *Saturday Night* to be one of the best sketches ever on the show" (136). We should add that the sketch's effectiveness derives as much from the viewer's mediated experience as from the excellent writing and acting. The sketch assumes the audience's familiarity with *Star Trek*, with the personalities of its characters and the names of its stars, with the significance of Nielsen ratings, with the way television programing decisions are made, with the functioning of TV props and sets. Most likely, another sort of self-referentiality is also involved in *SNL*'s apparently daring ridicule of its own network, NBC, which actually canceled *Star Trek* in 1969. If the viewer is aware of this last fact, a further form of self-reference can be discovered in the implied parallels between space exploration and innovative television comedy such as that practiced on *SNL*.

Although some of the humor on *SNL* would probably have been accessible, at the time of its original broadcasting, to a viewer who had never seen television before and who thus had little idea of the conventions and modes of operation involved, such a viewer would surely have missed the point of most of the show's humor. Clearly, such was not the audience for whom *SNL* was designed and on whom the show's rhetorical community of reference was postulated, as David Marc explains in *Demographic Vistas* (151-55). These assumptions are even more significant when considering a program that many regard as superior in every way to *SNL* as quintessential TV humor: *Second City Television* or, as it soon came to be known, *SCTV*.

*SCTV* began in 1977 as an outgrowth of the Toronto branch of Chicago's Second City improvisational comedy troupe. In those days, the membership of the Toronto cast consisted variously of Brian Doyle Murray, Joe Flaherty, Rick Moranis, Dave Thomas, John Candy, Eugene Levy, Andrea Martin, Martin Short, Dan Ackroyd, and Gilda Radner. As Tony Hendra reports in *Going Too Far*, this roster was raided by the Canadian, Lorne Michaels, for the original cast of *Saturday Night Live*, and Hill and Weingrad add that Michaels's successor, Dick Ebersol, followed suit in signing up Catherine O'Hara, Robin Duke, Mary Gross, Tim Kazurinsky, Tony Rosato, and Martin Short from the Chicago and Toronto Second City companies as *SNL* replacements when members of the original cast graduated to motion pictures or just burned out. Not all Second City performers defected immediately to NBC and *SNL*, however, and those who stayed behind—Flaherty, Candy, Levy, Moranis, Thomas, Martin, O'Hara, Rosato, Duke, and Short—constituted the cast of the original half-hour programs produced by *SCTV*. Ironically enough, *SCTV* moved to NBC in 1981 for two years, in a ninety-minute format called *SCTV Network 90*, broadcast at 12:30 A.M. on Friday nights. When the show grew too expensive—$400,000 per program, according to Sally Bedell's 1983 report in *The New York Times*—NBC replaced it with *Friday Night Videos*, a brainchild of Dick Ebersol. Later moving to the Cinemax cable network, as *SCTV Network*, the remaining cast members briefly tried two forty-five minute shows per month before finally calling it quits in 1984.

The original half-hour format was probably ideal for the show because it eliminated the intimidating challenge of filling vast stretches of TV time with a few extended pieces in the manner of *SNL*, while affording opportunities for great versatility in six or more pieces of varying lengths. The show could thus accommodate nearly any topic despite several commercial breaks and a two-minute segment consisting of 100 percent Canadian content, mandated by Canadian labor laws. As Christopher Connelly discovered for his *Rolling Stone* article "Two Nerds from Canada," these two-minute pieces featuring Bob (Moranis) and Doug (Thomas) McKenzie, the beer-drinking, back-bacon-eating, "hoser" hosts of *The Great White North* TV show, were almost entirely improvised. A supposedly regular feature of the SCTV network, the McKenzie segments typified *SCTV* both in their satiric bite and in their brevity.

In his highly appreciative essay, "Satire Comes to Video," Richard T. Jameson wrote that *SCTV* threw away more comic ideas in mini-sketches and supposed promotions for upcoming, but never developed, programs than most shows used during their entire first-run lives. Although *SCTV*'s thirty-minute programs were not as frenetic in production style as *Rowan & Martin's Laugh-In* or the Python show, the creators obviously assumed that rapid shifts in content were perfectly legitimate, perhaps—as Richard A. Blake might observe—even necessary on television. It is apparent, in other words, that *SCTV* was a truly self-referential enterprise: TV made for viewers familiar with TV by writers equally familiar with TV.

Even the show's basic premises emphasize self-referentiality. SCTV was supposedly an independent television network headed by Guy Caballero, "owner and president of SCTV." As played by Flaherty, Caballero neatly echoed Ricardo Montalban and other TV performers of his ilk through a three-piece white suit. Caballero's unnecessary wheelchair surely echoed Raymond Burr's Chief Robert Ironside, and Caballero's name and general sliminess probably alluded to Caballero Films, the famed producers of pornographic movies and videotapes. This congeries of sleaze, humor, entertainment, and commercialism, epitomized by Caballero, usually characterized the perspective on television animating all of *SCTV*'s activities.

A typical *SCTV* program would probably begin with a brief sketch involving one of the network's regular performers in a simulated broadcast or promotion: John Candy's hard-drinking, scheming, womanizing Johnny LaRue, for example; or Andrea Martin's Edith Prickley, the acerbic, crazed, oversexed station manager. Other recurrent network characters included: Dave Thomas's pointlessly abrasive critic, Bill Needle; Flaherty's revoltingly insincere Vegas-style talk-show host, Sammy Maudlin; Eugene Levy's cigarette-wielding, gold-chain-wearing, chest-hair-baring ratpack entertainer, Bobby Bittman; Martin Short's manic nerd, Ed Grimley; Catherine O'Hara's blonde bombshell, Lola Heatherton; or the network's news anchor team, Earl Camembert (Levy) and Floyd Robertson (Flaherty). This opening piece, developed to whatever length the writers deemed appropriate, would be followed by the credits and theme song, terminating in the promise: "Television like you've never seen it before! This is the SCTV television network!" Following might be another sketch, a parody commercial, or a real commercial—the uncertainty operating as another element of the show's innovative creativity.

Central to whatever might follow, however, would be the audience's previous immersion in other television experiences. In one sketch, for example, the retired Walter Cronkite, played by Thomas, visits the newsroom and replaces Earl Camembert. Because the trivial local news that Camembert has uncovered compares so unfavorably with Robertson's world-shaking scoops, Cronkite finds himself inventing bogus disasters to compete. Clearly the viewer's amusement depends entirely on what he knows already about Cronkite and about TV news broadcasts. A similar exposure, to game shows, would be required to appreciate Edith Prickley's *The Mating Game*, with its bachelor lineup of Scotsman Angus Crock (Thomas), Chef Marcello Sebastiano (Rosato), and Rabbi Itzak Karloff of the Benihana Synagogue (Moranis). Many hours of TV exposure to entertainment "personalities" must prepare the way for an appreciative viewing of *Jackie We Hardly Knew Ye*, a testimonial by the albino celebrity, Jackie Rogers, Jr. (Short), to his equally celebrated performer father, Jackie Rogers, Sr. (also played by Short), whose comeback special was tragically cut short when he was killed by a cougar during his rendition of "If I Could Talk to the Animals."

The appropriate viewer response to all of these highly allusive sketches involves not only a sense of having spent countless hours watching television programs like these but also some questioning of whether the time was well spent. *SCTV* was not only highly allusive and self-referential, but—as Richard T. Jameson perceptively discovered—satiric. The SCTV network series *The Adventures of Shake 'n' Bake*, for example, was supposedly based on the literary lives of William Shakespeare and Sir Francis Bacon, but the only episode filmed consisted almost entirely of low-comedy homosexual mincing, duels, and views of buxom serving wenches. Some localized humor undoubtedly resulted from such burlesquery, but the principal source of humor was, just as undoubtedly, the television industry's abject slavering over high culture and its equally fundamental practice of reducing all programing to the same insultingly low level.

These basic constituents of television programing were also satirized in the *SCTV* shows devoted to Sweeps Week, during which the network planned to air *The Dallas Cowgirls Salute to (Aaron) Copeland* and *Night of the Prime Time Stars*, featuring Linda Lavin (Martin), Gavin McLeod (Flaherty), Merlin Olson (Candy), Lorne Greene (Levy), and Jamie Farr (Short). Interspersed with segments of these blockbusters and with aggressively sincere appeals from Guy Caballero, was a fantasy plot in which SCTV employees were sucked into a time warp with figures from early TV such as Ralph Kramden and Arlene Francis. It is significant, first of all, that the fictional Kramden and the actual Francis were given historical equivalence. It is further significant that an atmosphere of commercialism and mediocrity is assumed to have characterized the medium from the beginning.

Another form of satire practiced on *SCTV* was parodic, as when Andrea Martin's Linda Lavin plays and sings "I Loves You Porgy" dreadfully, but with exaggerated sincerity, on *The Night of the Network Stars*. Martin's body language brilliantly parodies Lavin's, and her request to the director not to film her hands during the portion of the song that she cannot play acutely skewers show-biz posing and insincerity. The recurrent *SCTV* sketch *The Days of the Week* also used uncanny parody to echo the production techniques of TV soap operas while satirizing the shallow values that motivate the characters on soaps. If some criticism attaches to the viewer, the effect is not altogether unintentional. As the Linda Lavin number attests, *SCTV*'s parodies were often multimediated. A good example was the remake of *Midnight Cowboy* with John Candy's lisping ghoul character, Dr. Tongue, in Jon Voight's role and Eugene Levy's horribly deformed Woody Tobias, Jr., in Dustin Hoffman's. That both characters regularly appeared on SCTV programs, moreover, resulted in the film's being reabsorbed into the medium of television.

The same may be said of the more extended, two-part film parody, *Maudlin's Eleven*. Since all the gang members—with the lunatic exception of Johnny Puleo and the Harmonica Gang—were regular *SCTV* characters, the parodic film somehow became part of the network, a bizarre sort of made-for-television movie. In this black-and-white film, supposedly directed by the early TV figure Hy Averback, Sammy Maudlin organizes a mob consisting of Puleo and his harmonica band, the Ed McMahon clone from Maudlin's talk show, William B. Williams (Candy), Bill Needle, Bobby Bittman, and Bittman's younger brother, Skip (Moranis), who is employed at the time as a warm-up comic on *Make Room for Daddy*. As is consistent with the parodic authenticity of the film, Skip's jokes concern Mr. and Mrs. Kruschev. Bobby Bittman's coffee-house musical number cultivates an accurate historical note also, as does the mob's objective: to rob Danny Thomas, "the richest man in television," in his dressing room at Desilu Productions. The continual shocks of recognition elicited from the viewer by the parody result in a laughing acknowledgement that *Ocean's Eleven* and other ratpack enterprises were incontestably awful. The artful recreation of an early stage of black-and-white television also calls forth negative recognitions concerning Danny Thomas and TV sitcoms, Ed Sullivan and TV vaudeville, and the "golden age of television" in general.

Multiple recognitions of this sort also attend the final example in which we may indulge: *The Lone Ranger Show*. Here again several levels of entertainment experience were layered into a hypermediated form of television presentation. The basic premise is that the Lone Ranger as played by Clayton Moore (Moranis) has a talk show much like Johnny Carson's, with Tonto (Flaherty) filling Ed McMahon's sidekick role and Doc Watson (Rosato) replacing Doc Severnsen as the band leader. As the sketch opens over the "William Tell Overture," the Lone Ranger comes through the curtains to great applause. He greets Tonto with rim-shotted cracks about drinking firewater and Doc with cracks about his outfit. When the gags in the subsequent monologue bomb, the audience begins shooting. Tonto and the Lone Ranger duck behind the papier-mâché boulders familiar from the old series and return fire. Since the parody is filmed in black and white, this scene—and the whole sketch—draws heavily on the audience's familiarity with the look and tone of the old Lone Ranger TV series, the sort of experience that David Marc calls "television shadow memory" in *Demographic Vistas* (135). A complex perspective is maintained, however, through devices such as Tonto's comment during the resumed monologue, "Plenty good segue, Kemosabe!"

In front of a *Tonight Show* set in which western scenes have replaced the urban skyline, the Lone Ranger dons a turban to answer Karnac-like questions about cattle rustlers. Then the first guest, comedian Kip Adatta (also Moranis), performs an unfunny series of jokes about cows, even though he is dressed in a tuxedo. The Lone Ranger soon shoots the microphone out of Adatta/Moranis's hand, and assistants come out to hog-tie and brand the comedian. When Tonto expresses sympathy for Adatta, the Lone Ranger responds: "Tonto, in a way he deserved it. No one can insult the intelligence of this or any audience and expect to get away with it. That material was substandard and below network quality. Let that be a lesson to all young comedians—make sure your material is damn funny, and you'll be loved by good people everywhere!" A drum roll and tumultuous applause follow.

Although this sketch continues for a while with other incidental references that layer the Johnny Carson show on the old western—such as having Wishbone come on to plug his new cookbook, *Grub*—the climax must surely be the Lone Ranger's lecture about comedy. This ironic sermon is also the quintessence of self-referentiality. The particular references of the Lone Ranger and the *Tonight Show* vividly awaken the viewer's memory of earlier TV watching, but this heightened awareness is then converted into an occasion for considering the medium of television itself. The tone of the sketch is assuredly arch, ironic to the point of encouraging the viewer to discount most of what the Lone Ranger says. In this sense, it is both parodic of the high-minded "commitment" of TV talk-show hosts and satiric of their basic insincerity. Even so, considerable truth is communicated by—or despite—this speech. Most television does "insult the intelligence" of the audience. Most viewers are conscious of this to some, probably unexamined, degree. Most viewers are also conscious that the violators are seldom shot or branded, and this sketch might lead them to think, "More's the pity!" Whatever conclusion the viewers might reach, this sketch was obviously designed to remind them that they are not watching the Lone Ranger or Johnny Carson; they are watching *television*.

WORKS CITED

Bedell, Sally. "SCTV Moves to Cable." *New York Times*, 18 May 1983, C27.

Blake, Richard A. "Python, Python, Burning Bright." *America*, 3 May 1975, 348–49.

Brooks, Tim, and Earle Marsh. *The Complete Directory of Prime Time Network TV Shows, 1946-Present*. 4th ed. New York: Ballantine, 1988.

Coleridge, Samuel Taylor. *Biographia Literaria*. In *Criticism: The Major Texts*, edited by Walter Jackson Bate, 376–87. Enlarged ed. New York: Harcourt, 1970.

Connelly, Christopher. "Two Nerds from Canada." *Rolling Stone*, 4 Feb. 1982, 76–79.

Gardner, Joann. "Self-Referentiality in Art: A Look at Three Television Situation-Comedies of the 1950s." *Studies in Popular Culture* 11, no. 1 (1988): 35–50.

Goodman, Ellen. "Americans Racing to the TV for Chance to See Themselves." *The (Nashville) Tennessean*, 13 Apr. 1990, 11A.

Greenfield, Jeff. *Television: The First Fifty Years*. New York: Crescent, 1981.

Hendra, Tony. *Going Too Far: The Rise and Demise of Sick, Gross, Black, Sophomoric, Weirdo, Pinko, Anarchist, Underground, Anti-Establishment Humor*. New York: Dolphin/Doubleday, 1987.

Hill, Doug, and Jeff Weingrad. *Saturday Night: A Backstage History of Saturday Night Live*. New York: Beech Tree/Morrow, 1986.

Jameson, Richard T. "Satire Comes to Video." *Film Comment*, May–June 1981, 76–77.

Johnson, Samuel. "Preface to Shakespeare." In *Criticism: The Major Texts*, edited by Walter Jackson Bate, 207–17. New York: Harcourt, 1970.

Marc, David. *Comic Visions: Television Comedy and American Culture*. Boston: Unwin Hyman, 1989.

———. *Demographic Vistas: Television in American Culture*. Philadelphia: University of Pennsylvania Press, 1984.

Mast, Gerald. *Film/Cinema/Movie: A Theory of Experience.* New York: Harper, 1977.

Mintz, Lawrence E. "Broadcast Humor." In *Humor in America: A Research Guide to Genres and Topics,* edited by Lawrence E. Mintz, 91–108. Westport, Conn.: Greenwood, 1988.

Rushdie, Salman. *The Satanic Verses.* New York: Viking, 1989.

Salinger, J. D. *The Catcher in the Rye.* Boston: Little, Brown, 1951.

Wilmut, Roger. *From Fringe to Flying Circus: Celebrating a Unique Generation of Comedy, 1968–1980.* London: Methuen, 1980.

## CHAPTER 3

**TV in the 1980s**

This Is the Theme

to Garry's Show

(and David and Maddie's Too)

In a book published in 1976, John G. Cawelti identified the perennial subjects of popular literature as *Adventure, Mystery, and Romance.* It is evident that Cawelti's formula applies beyond these genres of print since, with the addition of comedy, these categories could also function as a taxonomy of prime-time television programing from its earliest days to the present. Such continuity provides some security for viewers but inevitably occasions problems for artists attempting to develop novelty within the familiar forms. In this respect, television writers in the 1980s might often be seen to share the historical dilemma of Renaissance artists confronting a conventionalized literary tradition. Ben Jonson, for example, lamented in *Timber* (1641) that "a man cannot invent new things after so many" (113). Significantly, Jonson continued to write anyway, acknowledging conventions in his work but escaping their paralyzing influences. When faced with comparable circumstances, Glenn Gordon Caron, the creator of *Moonlighting* (1984–89), followed a similar strategy by adopting the route of self-referentiality.

As our examination of *SCTV* reveals, both producers and consumers of network television might be expected by the late 1980s to be thoroughly conversant with TV conventions. After all, how many times does a viewer have to hear a real or canned audience laugh at what a wife says to a husband in the kitchen to realize that the couple exist "on television" rather than in real life? By 1989, even some TV commercials were conceding this awareness, as in a Ragu commercial showing a grandmother and granddaughter sampling spaghetti sauce from a pot on the stove. When the girl says that the sauce tastes "like grandma's," the older woman says, "I'll get them," and an unseen audience laughs. The television audience can only conclude that the two females are actresses appearing in a commercial rather than actual people recorded by a hidden camera. This advertiser clearly acknowledges the audience's familiarity with TV conventions, but the sauce still is advertised. In this way, self-referential television can accommodate the pressures generated by an ever-increasing audience awareness.

*Moonlighting* did for adventure, mystery, and romance what this Ragu spot tried to do for commercials. By referring directly and ironically to generic conventions, the series exploited the audience's familiarity rather than being restricted by it. The producers thus had access to all the devices of conventional production techniques without seeming conventional, and the viewers could relish familiar forms of escapist entertainment without seeming to watch the same old kind of TV show. As is so often the case with self-referentiality, then, the parties involved could both have their cake and eat it.

The basic premises of *Moonlighting* obviously follow the conventions familiar to viewers of TV adventure series. Maddie Hayes (Cybill Shepherd) and David Addison (Bruce Willis) operate Blue Moon Investigations, a detective agency. They are assisted in the enterprise by an annually increasing staff of associates, including one named—in a probable allusion to *Lucy*—MacGilicuddy. Especially useful members of this supporting cast are Agnes DiPesto (Allyce Beasley) and Herbert Viola (Carlin Armstrong) since they can supply comic relief to lighten the tensions of the mysteries and serve as a parallel romantic couple to Maddie and David. The day-to-day operations of the agency and the interactions among the staff at the beginning and end of each episode serve the conventional function of supplying continuity to the series. Within this continuity, the adventure plots permit the stars to have romantic involvements with different characters who can conveniently disappear at the end of one or two episodes, a series variation that the experience of Richard Diamond, James Rockford, and even Chief Robert Ironside earlier showed to be desirable. Another predictable element of the show's basic premises is the romantic battle of the sexes between the two stars—here updated for contemporaneity through references to women's liberation and sexual equality. Little in these basic ingredients would seem to suggest any radical departure from the conventions of this sort of programing, but the series revealed considerable ingenuity even so.

On the simplest level, the scripts of *Moonlighting* reinvigorate familiar devices through various forms of self-reference. When a sexual harassment case in a 1989 episode pits Maddie against David in a sleuthing competition, Maddie sneaks into David's office late at night to discover his evidence. This break-in takes place over the Henry Mancini theme music from the Pink Panther movies, thus offering the audience the first set of self-referential italics. When David catches her, as the suspense genre demands, the conventionality of his apt arrival is not concealed but self-referentially emphasized. Thus, David says to Maddie, "Do you think the writers would let you break into my office without me catching you?" On one level, the ironic italics in this scene provide an insider's joke for the hip viewer. Structurally, and more significantly, the device allows the suspense plot to continue.

References to "the writers" are common features of the scripts, but they are not the only form of ingenuity turned on generic conventions. In some cases, classic comic devices such as pies in the face and pratfalls exercise the two-fold function of comic relief and displacement of the romantic or mystery plot. The final episode of the series, for example, romantically builds toward the wedding of Agnes and Herbert. In a displacement of this sentimental resolution, Herbert's broken jaw prevents his reading of the mawkish wedding vows that he has composed. Eventually, however, Agnes reads them for him. A burlesque conclusion in which everyone falls or is pushed into a swimming pool further disguises the sentimentality of this romantic resolution. Significantly, even though everyone ends up dripping wet, the two characters are still happily married. In other words, the scripts of *Moonlighting* usually follow traditional patterns, both in overall plotting and in the devices used to advance these plots, but the self-referential writing cleverly disguises this conventionality through appeals to the reader's previous experience of similar, less self-conscious programs.

Although the basic premises of *Moonlighting* were derived from the traditions of adventure, mystery, and romance, the need to adapt these premises for the hypermediated audience of the 1980s also demanded some acknowledgement of television formalism throughout the series. Thus, the adventure show adopted many devices familiar from the comedy on *SCTV* and *Saturday Night Live,* most especially an ostentatious self-referentiality. This dimension of *Moonlighting* was apparent to TV critics and viewers almost from the beginning. In a 1986 article in *The New York Times Magazine,* for example, Joy Horowitz writes of the Hayes and Addison characters, "Like Burns and Allen or Hope and Crosby, they often break the 'fourth wall' with a wink at the audience, admitting they exist within a 19-inch frame" (26). The comment is significant not only in its testimony to the series' self-referentiality but also in its easy shift from the dramatic to the comedic plane in order to find an apt analogy. Such blurring of generic distinctions led, in fact, to the peculiar development in which some episodes of *Moonlighting* were nominated for Emmy awards in 1986 in the comedy category and others as serious dramas.

The confusion is understandable in light of the show's frequent exploitation of *SCTV*'s most reliable form of comedy, parody. An excellent illustration is "The Dream Sequence Always Rings Twice," a black-and-white film-noir parody broadcast on *Moonlighting* in 1985. This program could easily have appeared on *SCTV* with the substitution of Catherine O'Hara for Cybill Shepherd and Dave Thomas for Bruce Willis. An important difference lies in the fact that the *Moonlighting* parody also served to further the ongoing development of the Hayes and Addison characters since each was supposedly responsible for fantasizing half of the echoic plot.

This episode advertises its self-referentiality even before it actually opens since Orson Welles, acting as the host, assures the viewers that, when their screens later shift from color to black and white, the effect is intentional and "special." In fact, Welles continues as announcer through the episode, intoning at each commercial break, "This special black-and-white episode of *Moonlighting* will continue in a minute." A viewer can hardly believe that a "screen" that can change generic conventions is actually "life," although the clever script permits as much suspension of disbelief as the viewer is willing to supply.

Many of the script's best effects are purely technical. After Maddie and David argue in the present and in full color about who was the guilty party in the Flamingo Cove Murder of the late 1940s, Maddie falls asleep, listening to a swing record on her stereo. Having faded out on the spinning LP, the next shot shows a 78 RPM record turning on a black-and-white turntable; thus, the scene has shifted to Maddie's dream. When Maddie awakens about fifteen minutes later, the needle on her stereo has stuck in a groove, and she lifts her phone to scream at David whom she holds guilty as a representative of the male species. After a brief scene on the phone, David falls asleep to dream his version of the same story, also in black and white. Just as his dream is ending in the electric chair, he is awakened by the buzzing of the telephone that he has left off the hook. By beginning and ending the episode in the world of Blue Moon Investigations, the script gave the viewers what they tuned in to see. By presenting the murder plot as a film-noir parody, the script opened the series to new possibilities. By using Welles as host, moreover, the script allowed the audience to take some mild aesthetic chances without serious disruptions to their usual televiewing experience.

In Maddie's version of the mystery, Rita Adams, the nightclub singer, is manipulated by Zack McCoy, a cornet player, into complicity in the murder of her husband Jerry, who plays clarinet in the same swing band. She is then betrayed to the police by McCoy. Maddie's version of the murder plot allows Shepherd to dress in 1940s high chic and to sing "Blue Moon," the song after which her agency is named. She may also parody female acting styles perfected by the likes of Ann Sheridan and Ginger Rogers but rendered obsolete by the hypermediation of the television audience. Since the whole experience is doubly italicized by the plot device of Maddie's dream and by the technical device of the black-and-white photography, both the producers and the viewers can relish their indulgence in outmoded styles without sacrificing their knowingness.

Willis's portrayal of Zack McCoy in David's dream superimposes Alan Ladd on John Garfield on Humphrey Bogart in a parody of stunning accuracy. In this version, Zack is a foolish innocent in love, and Rita is a cold-blooded temptress. Thus, Shepherd's Rita must become more sensual and brazen; her theme song changes from "Blue Moon" to "I Told You I Love You, Now Get Out!" And yet, Shepherd layers many of Maddie's looks and gestures over Rita's so that the romantic tangle of the overall series is never lost. Another difference in the two dreams is the greater attention in David's to the cinematic qualities of the story. He is not so much dreaming about a murder as dreaming about a movie about a murder. Thus, when Zack sits in an open window, dressed in an undershirt, playing his cornet against the backdrop of a flashing neon sign, his voice-over says that this is his favorite way to practice. When, after Jerry's murder, Zack walks the streets against a backdrop of flashing neon signs, he acknowledges his familiarity with convention by asking, "How long was I supposed to walk the streets? . . . How long would these signs float over my head?"

This dream sequence parodies many other film-noir conventions. One is the use of absurd front-page headlines to advance the plot. When the condemned McCoy asks the prison guard, "Didn't the Governor call?" the headline announces, "Governor Doesn't Call." Another is the exaggeration of hard-boiled prose style. Zack says about Rita, "She was like peanuts: the more I had, the more I wanted." Echoes of the Carl Reiner/Steve Martin parody *Dead Men Don't Wear Plaid* surely resonate in such writing, probably on purpose. To push the device a step further toward absurdity, Zack recalls, "Then we began to plan the murder, what to wear, what to bring." Speeches of this sort serve partly to enhance the development of David's wise-guy personality in the series; after all, this is his dream. They also jar the viewer into noticing the conventions of this film genre and to recognizing the intervention of an artistic medium between the steamy murder and a secure living room.

This line of thinking receives its strongest push from self-referential remarks such as Zack's summary of his first romantic interlude with Rita: "That night was the beginning. We would see more of each other. Then, all of each other. But this is television, so we won't get into that." To involve David and Maddie in a fictional murder for which either might be executed would fall outside the possibilities of the series. To involve them in a highly sexual romance would move the series along faster than seemed appropriate in 1985. To involve them in a self-referential parody was probably the best of all possible solutions. Possibly there is a veiled admission of this when David wakes from his dream and questions the ceiling, "Auntie Em? Uncle Henry?" In an allusive joke, David is back from Oz, but there are signs—chiefly the smirk on Willis's face by which he advertises how clever the whole process has been—that he may return there sometime if the experiment proves popular.

The evidence that it did prove so can be seen in the series' most widely acknowledged—and, at $3 million, most expensive—single episode, the *Taming of the Shrew* program (1986). In this show, on-going character development was maintained by replacing the Maddie-David romance with the more famous one between Katherina and Petruchio and by the updated 1980s resolution in which successful marriage is defined in terms of sexual equality. Both the tension between the principal characters and the series' endorsement of raised gender consciousness were maintained, while variety was introduced into the continuing story line. As in the "Dream Sequence" parody, audience disruption was kept to a minimum by means of a framing device, in this case not Orson Welles but a family in which a young boy is supposed to read his Shakespeare assignment rather than watch *Moonlighting*.

The more comic dimensions of this parody, on the other hand, have little relation to the series overall. For example, when Carlin Armstrong opens the parody in the role of Lucentio, he is rejected by all the characters on the streets of Padua, thus leading him to lament, "It's my fault I get stuck with all the exposition?" The comic referent here is dramatic construction far more than the viewer's sense of Herbert Viola's usual plot function on the series. The same is true when Petruchio declaims at his first entrance, "To be or not to be!" and then essays familiar tag lines from *Richard II* and *Julius Caesar* before taking out his script and finding the correct speech. The joke is independent of Willis's David Addison character, and even of *Moonlighting*. Its antecedents lie in a long line of demotic cultural burlesques extending back at least as far as the Duke's soliloquy in *The Adventures of Huckleberry Finn*. Lawrence W. Levine traces the practice back even further in his study *Highbrow/ Lowbrow: The Emergence of Cultural Hierarchy in America* (1988), but for our purposes it is enough to see that the energy derives from sources other than this single TV series. The script's contrived passages of verse surely derive from these same anti-aesthetic sources, as is evident in the final line that Katherina and Petruchio speak in unison: "We hate iambic pentameter."

Nondramatic cultural comedy is also evident as Baptista examines the wedding contract that Petruchio has drawn up. When Baptista reads, "Your own Winnebago, a chance to direct, a piece of the syndicated," the source of the humor is the star system in general— or perhaps the entertainment persona of Bruce Willis—but it is not David Addison, the fictional detective. David is not developed on the series as a rock-and-roll performer either, and so Petruchio's rendition of "Good Lovin'" during the wedding scene, complete with dancing and harmonica playing, can only refer to Willis's alternate career as Bruno, the singer, not to any aspect of the *Moonlight-*

*ing* scripts. As on *SCTV*, every element of the hypermediated culture is available for comic reference in this parody.

Just as the script takes for granted the audience's familiarity with Bruno, it assumes a thoroughly mediated knowledge of other cultural icons. In one scene, Petruchio echoes Jackie Gleason's Ralph Kramden by threatening to send Kate "to the Moon" during their argument about a husband's authority. In another scene, Petruchio breaks through Katherina's door with an axe and echoes Jack Nicholson in *The Shining* by announcing, "Here's Petruchio!" Since the earlier line was an allusion to the *Johnny Carson Show*, the levels of reference here are fairly complicated. This door to Katherina's room is used to initiate another set of references when Petruchio's attempts to woo Kate are repulsed with cartoon-like violence, including a firecracker dropped into his suit of armor, while *Loony Tunes* music plays. Motion pictures are the referent for another device by which Katherina's acceptance of Petruchio's proposal of marriage is presented through black-and-white film of a ticker-tape parade and a revolving front page with the headline, "Kate to Wed Today."

Popular music also figures prominently as a source of reference. In one scene, Petruchio sings an abbreviated version of Shirley Ellis's 1965 hit, "The Name Game." Later he parodies Helen Reddy's feminist hit by declaiming, "I am man. Hear me roar, in numbers too great to ignore!" When the lute and hautboy orchestra at Lucentio and Bianca's wedding plays "Close to You," the joke primarily turns on an anachronism (as it does in the earlier scene in which Petruchio and his horse wear sun glasses), but this wedding-reception joke also relies on the audience's sense of musical hipness. Watchers of *Moonlighting*, it is implied, would never be caught listening to "Close to You" as performed by the Carpenters or by a live-musak, wedding-reception combo. References of this sort ultimately must be understood as self-references, signs that, even though a media transaction is taking place, it is not naive or without ironic self-recognition. In fact, to establish this recognition is often the main point.

When operating outside the indirect self-referentiality of parody, *Moonlighting* was sometimes just plain outrageous. The first show of the final season, for example, "A Womb With a View," has as its premise that the growing child in Maddie's womb (played by Bruce Willis in a diaper) should learn from a supernatural visitor named Jerome about the life he is about to be born into. Since most viewers of this much-delayed premiere episode would know about Cybill

Shepherd's pregnancy, the plot's ingenious accommodation of the star's condition probably served as a kind of self-reference. Since the baby's instruction about his parents' ancestry comes in the form of film clips from the "Dream Sequence" and *Taming* episodes, another layer of self-reference develops. When the baby grows alarmed at film depicting Nazis, atomic bombs, and the Ku Klux Klan, Jerome acknowledges the process of mediation by saying soothingly, "That's all right. We'll go to commercial now." When "the creator" finally decides that the baby will not be the child of David and Maddie after all, Jerome offers the consolation that he will become "either Kirk Cameron's little brother or Bill Cosby's grandchild." That the baby will live on a TV show rather than in anyone's real home directly advertises the presence of the medium, but the ambiguity concerning the identity of "the creator" does so as well. Is the antecedent God or Glenn Gordon Caron? No matter what Jerome says, the audience probably assumes the latter.

Caron and his production team are forcefully present in this episode in several more obvious ways. The show opens with Agnes DiPesto answering the office telephone in verse: "We can't solve your case 'cause we don't have a show. / We went off the air at the end of last season / 'Cause management wouldn't listen to reason." When Agnes looks up and notices the camera, she says excitedly, "It's you! You came back!" Shortly afterwards, she and David look directly into the camera and identify members of the viewing audience: "Cathy! . . . and Arnold! . . . and Dawn!" When Herbert Viola seems unexcited by the audience's return, Agnes tells him to forget his obscure roles in the past and look forward to "a new season, a great season, your season." Since Carlin Armstrong has become a featured player on the series, the point of the reference should be clear. To leave even less doubt, the members of the Blue Moon office staff soon begin to dance and sing to a familiar melody from Cole Porter's *Kiss Me Kate*: "Another season, another try, to make twenty-two shows before we die." Amid references to critics, reruns, production delays, and the likelihood that they will probably make no more than sixteen shows, the actors dance though the fourth wall, out into the production area filled with cameras, ladders, director's chairs, technicians, and grips. The ensuing musical number is not particularly well done, but that is surely part of the self-reference. *Moonlighting* is not a Busby Berkeley musical, nor is it a Bugs Bunny cartoon, as another allusion testifies. However, it *is* a highly mediated experience, as the audience is clearly expected to recognize.

Such—usually unstated—assumptions about the viewers' awareness resonate throughout the series, but nowhere more emphatically than in the final episode. Following the wedding of Herbert and Agnes, the burlesque debacle, and everyone's arrest, David returns to Blue Moon Investigations the next morning to find workmen dismantling the office and removing the furniture. In a scene echoing the *Saturday Night Live* sketch about the cancellation of *Star Trek*, David encounters Walter Wiperad, an ABC functionary who is overseeing the striking of the *Moonlighting* set. The premise here is that David, unlike the viewer, is unaware that this is the last show of the series. Wiperad says that he used to be a fan of the series and so is sorry to report that David has only eight minutes and thirty-six seconds to live. MacGilicuddy is already dead, not because of his bad heart, as Herbert guiltily assumes, but because he has no more scenes. When Maddie arrives seconds later, she is also unaware of the cancellation and is shocked to see "Red" carrying off their view of the skyline. Wiperad's astonishment that the two stars have not been notified is expressed in an acutely self-referential manner: "You don't know, do you? Somebody from current programs was supposed to call you. Well, I guess that's why NBC is number one!" This line brings the scene perilously close to presentational rather than representational television, but the script quickly returns to the business at hand.

As has been his role throughout the series, David proposes a plan of action: that they go to see their producer, Si, in an attempt to avert extinction. Along the way, they meet a grief-stricken Agnes who says—plausibly, in the light of TV history—"If there's a God in heaven, He'll spin Herbert and me off in our own series." Having created another ambiguity in connection with the identity of the creator, the script then carries David and Maddie to a projection room in which earlier scenes from the final episode are running for Si. Si confesses that he is also a fan of the series but says, "Even I can't get people to tune in to watch what they don't want to watch anymore." Again, the self-referentiality becomes almost presentational, but Si's explanation returns attention to the dramatic. He says that David and Maddie have become victims of low ratings, not because of the production delays and reruns to which the first show of the season referred and of which viewers surely were well aware, but for a reason more consistent with the show's basic premises: the viewers' supposed dissatisfaction with the progress of David and Maddie's romance. When the two characters attempt to get married in a last-ditch effort to save the show, a kindly Irish priest rejects their request as hasty and irresponsible.

It is significant that in these scenes they are still David and Maddie, not Willis and Shepherd, even though they are operating outside the romantic plot of Herbert and Agnes's wedding and the mystery plot of "the Anselmo case" in which Blue Moon Investigations was supposedly engaged. As in the episode during the first season on which David and Maddie answered viewer mail, the show's self-referentiality is directed to a play outside the play, rather than to the professional careers of the stars. Thus, Maddie and David are supposedly the ones filled with nostalgia as they sit on the altar steps, not Cybill and Bruce. When Maddie says, "If we could just have these five years to do over again," the sound track plays Ray Charles and Betty Carter's rendition of "We'll be Together Again," and the two characters seem to consider life without each other.

The clips that then fill the screen, and supposedly the characters' memories, show Willis and Shepherd at all stages of the show's run, looking younger and older, and wearing all sorts of costumes. The principal effect for the faithful viewer was surely to recall favorite episodes in the series rather than significant moments in the lives of fictional characters, but the self-referential angle of presentation successfully obscured any clear-cut distinctions.

Such doubled references clearly resemble the way in which *SCTV* surrounded the parodic film *Polynesiantown* with the SCTV network career of Johnny Larue and another parody, *Maudlin's Eleven*, with the SCTV careers of Sammy Maudlin, Bobby Bittman, and Bill Needle. This sort of self-referentiality is not confined to any particular genre of TV program, then, not to comedy, adventure, mystery, or romance. It requires only that a television program acknowledge that it is a television show and not a record of experience, whether real or fictional. Such an acknowledgement has the paradoxical effect of enhancing rather than confining the production since it only cooperates with what a hypermediated audience knows to be the truth in any case.

The contemporary trend toward self-referentiality exemplified by *Moonlighting* was epitomized by *It's Garry Shandling's Show.* With the possible exception of *SCTV,* no other television show relied so consistently on the fact of its being a TV show to provide substance as well as technique. In this respect, the Shandling show was—as John J. O'Connor recognized—quintessentially postmodern, a reflection of the hypermediated age in which we live.

The Shandling show, first of all, fulfilled the requirements of a conventional sitcom as they are set forth by David Grote in *The End of Comedy: The Sit-Com and the Comedic Tradition* (1983). Throughout the series, Shandling played a young man named Garry Shandling, unmarried until the final season, who coped inefficiently with society at large, his career, his friends, and women. This Garry was, predictably, surrounded by an "artificial family," other tenants of the Sherman Oaks, California, condo community in which he lived. These supporting characters consisted of his platonic girlfriend Nancy, Nancy's lover Ian, the condo president Leonard Smith, and the Shumaker family: Pete, Jackie, adolescent Grant, and baby Blue Suede Shumaker. In the final season, the cast was expanded to include Phoebe Bass, played by Jessica Harper, Garry's nonplatonic girlfriend and eventual wife. Often, Garry's mother, who lived elsewhere, also appeared.

The plots of the Shandling show also follow conventional patterns identified by Lawrence E. Mintz in his essay "Situation Comedy," in *TV Genres: A Handbook and Reference Guide* (1985). Each episode begins with the situations of normalcy that provides continuity to the series. This equilibrium is disturbed by forces unleashed by one of the supporting players or by some external agency. A friend of Nancy's, Richard Kimble, is being pursued by a Lieutenant Girard. Leonard Smith has a Vietnam flashback. Grant Shumaker is jealous of the attention his parents are bestowing on the baby. Garry's old college professor, Paul Bozgang, visits, bringing back memories of late-sixties student activism. Confusion predictably ensues, but by the end of the thirty-minute time slot, the status quo has been reestablished, perhaps enriched by some important lesson learned.

This adherence to sitcom conventionality is perfectly understandable in light of the previous experience of the program's two creators. Stephen Farber reports that before starring in his own series, and even before becoming a stand-up comedian, Garry Shandling wrote for *Sandford and Son* and *Welcome Back, Kotter.* Doug Hill and Jeff Weingrad report that Shandling's partner, Alan Zweibel, won an Emmy award in 1976 as a writer on *Saturday Night Live.* Moreover, Zweibel told Hill and Weingrad that he conceived his ambition to become a TV comedy writer by watching the *Dick Van Dyke Show* as a child (484). Clearly these two should know how to create a typical sitcom. In this respect, they might seem to illustrate a negative model proposed by Harry F. Waters in *Newsweek:* "By and large the young comedy writers who have begun setting the tone of the tube have never written for—nor studied—any other show biz form. That, combined with TV's intrinsically imitative nature, gives Ben Stein justification for charging: 'Television has become so derivative of other television that it is cut off from any vitality. We're now at the fourth remove from reality'" (71). Ben Stein is the author of the highly critical study of television *The View from Sunset Boulevard* (1979). Layering Waters on Stein thus produces a purely negative view of hypermediation that would seem to foreclose any sort of creativity or originality from Shandling and Zweibel, or—by extension—the potential audience of *It's Garry Shandling's Show.*

Fortunately, such shortsighted projections are erroneous. One explanation lies in Zweibel's earlier association with *Saturday Night Live,* a self-referential program that often satirized other TV shows, particularly conventional sitcoms. Most long-term fans of *SNL* can easily recall John Belushi's playing the Beaver, for example, or—in the parody happily recreated in David Marc's *Demographic Vistas* (153–54)—Ricky Nelson's coming home from school to a *Twilight-Zone* sequence of wrong 1950s TV households: the Cleavers, the Andersons, the Williamses, the Ricardos. Such creative precedents on *SNL* suggest that protracted exposure to conventional television programing can produce something other than the replicating vision of imitation—namely, the double vision of irony.

This was certainly the perspective operating in the Shandling show. To begin with Shandling's character, the Garry he played was also named Shandling, and he was also a successful stand-up comedian. This fictional Garry even told jokes about his hair and his inept relations with women, which the viewers would most likely have heard the real Garry tell on the *Johnny Carson Show* or an HBO comedy special. This self-reflexiveness would probably strike critics such as Waters and Stein merely as an imitation of the premise underlying the old Jack Benny and Danny Thomas shows—that the sitcom's plot complications all involve the star's putting on a TV show. And yet, the premise of the Shandling show was not quite that. Although Shandling's character was a professional comedian, his involvement with the sitcom plot was that of a participant not a producer. This was the case even when the plot involved putting on a show, as when Garry does part of his stand-up act at Mr. Peck's comedy club as a replacement for Grant Shumaker, who has been caught plagiarizing the jokes of comedian David Wood in a bid to win his parents' affection back from the new baby. Significantly, Garry's performance is neither very funny nor very well received. That is to say, Shandling was truly acting in the series even though the part he played carried his own name. A moment's reflection should reveal, though, that Jack Benny and George Burns were only acting on their series too. The split focus of Shandling's show made this dramatic dimension evident, however, by simultaneously presenting and ironically italicizing the action through self-referentiality.

This sort of irony is especially clear in the Shandling show's approach to guest stars. As on earlier TV comedy shows, guest stars often appear in roles that supposedly reveal their real offscreen lives. Just as Lucy Ricardo interacted with William Holden and Tallulah Bankhead in stories that required the actors to play scripted versions of themselves, so Garry complies with Martin Mull's invitation on one show to play in a celebrity golf tournament, and in another show he goes to Jeff Goldblum's house to play *Win, Lose, or Draw* with a group including Burt Convy. It is probably significant in a larger context that these plots turn on some aspect of mediated celebrity, but it is certainly significant as a reflection of this show's use of devices familiar to viewers of its predecessors.

The episode in which Garry and Phoebe finally get married depends almost entirely on recognizable guest stars for its self-referential comedy. After having spent several episodes working out the details of the wedding, the couple have agreed on a tasteful marriage at the Edgewood Manor resort. The plot complication arises when this place burns down and Philip H. Stravely, the head of Garry's network, decides to hold the wedding on television. Stravely says, "We want to recreate in the studio the interior of the Edgewood Manor," perhaps a subtle reminder that this discussion is taking place in an apartment that is also "in the studio." In any event, Stravely promises that everything will go exactly as Garry and Phoebe have planned.

Predictably, nothing goes as planned, and a TV "spectacular" complete with songs, dances, and guest stars is mounted to simulate the quiet ceremony the lovebirds wanted. This self-referential joke surely focuses on the vapid artificiality of much television, especially of TV variety shows. This joke is authorized, however, primarily by the audience's familiarity with such shows and with the entertainers who appear on them. The quintessential TV "personality" Charles Nelson Reilly, for example, has been chosen to direct the marriage ceremony. According to the wedding's opening credits, guests will include: "June Lockhart, Scott Baio . . . the honorable Tip O'Neill, Roy Rogers, Dale Evans, and Billy Dee Williams." Randy Gardner and Tai Babilonia are scheduled to perform some role as yet unspecified because of the absence of ice in the studio. Connie Stevens, on the other hand, has been confirmed to sing the prenuptial production number. Ned Beatty, who has been cast as the best man, is slated to do "a bit with the ring" when the solemn moment arises. Everything is SHOWBIZ. Nothing is "real." Garry and Phoebe refuse to participate in the farce, but they get married anyway. Perhaps the viewer has an indistinct sense of having seen all this some time before—perhaps on a show starring Perry Como or Andy Williams or Bob Hope. If so, that is probably part of the joke too. Garry's wedding episode is a television program about television, in large part about how television has traditionally used guest stars.

In some scripts, guest stars play roles that approach their actual characters even more closely. In one episode, for example, Carl Reiner comes to console Garry after one of his jokes has caused Norman Wax, a member of the studio audience, to die from laughter. After encouraging Garry to work through his guilt by attending Wax's funeral, Reiner asks, "Am I in the funeral scene?" When Garry says no, Reiner replies, "Your mother called me for this one lousy scene? . . . Gar, I've got a suit and my toupee in the car." Surely the levels of reference here are multiple. On one level, the fictional Garry's mother calls an older man to console her son; on another, an actor refers to scenes and camera exposure; on a third, a television personality recalls the audience's memory of him as sometimes bald, sometimes with hair; on a fourth, a conversation between two supposedly actual persons is admitted to be a prelude to an already written "funeral scene." That is to say, the Shandling show used guest stars, as *I Love Lucy* did, but presented them italicized with a reminder that they were only acting, a reminder likely to strike a responsive chord in a hypermediated audience.

The Shandling show would probably have been intelligible to a viewer only minimally familiar with television history, since each episode tied up the loose plot ends within the allotted time. Such a viewer then or now would probably find the show trite and unamusing, however. To appreciate the program's humor required considerable experience with TV watching. In addition to the presumably familiar guest stars, the show frequently alluded to other television personalities and shows as reference points for plotting or as specific imagery for humorous asides. Pat Harrington and Bonnie Franklin from *One Day at a Time* are used in one episode to exemplify a form of sexuality peculiar to sitcoms, while in another, Wink Martindale and Bill Cullen stand synecdochally for the whole game-show industry. Garry belongs to the "television Biography Book of the Month Club" from which he has received books about Vanna White, Merv Griffin, Gavin McLeod, and Desi Arnaz. When Garry visits the cemetery to discuss a problem with his dead father, the quick and the dead get into an argument about the avatars of Lucille Ball's sitcom persona. When Pete Shumaker's occupation is suddenly changed from shoe salesman to lawyer, Garry explains the transformation by saying, "Pete was on *Paper Chase* for three years and those credits will transfer." These references operate, as allusions always do, to establish a community of understanding between speaker and hearer—in this case, a community of mediated hipness.

This allusiveness reaches its utmost sophistication and depends most strongly on the audience's experience in the show's sustained parodies. As was the case on *SCTV* and *Moonlighting*, these parodies echo their originals technically and stylistically as well as thematically. The Shandling show's parody of the Robert Redford film *The Natural* parodies baseball in Ping-Pong and Glen Close's Iris character in Charlene, the goddess of Ping-Pong. More strikingly, though, the parody recalls the texture of the film by simulating its romantic camera focus, echoing its film score in some brilliantly Elmer-Bernsteinesque instrumental music, and reproducing the film's more dramatic technical effects. Especially in the climactic scene in which Garry's Ping-Pong ball shatters all the overhead spotlights in the studio, an experienced viewer would laughingly recognize the allusions to *The Natural*, while the inexperienced viewer could see only foolishness.

Accuracy of technique is crucial in TV parody, as David Marc makes clear in *Demographic Vistas* when writing about the parodies on *Saturday Night Live:* "Performance telerealism of appearance, voice, gesture, and camera address constitutes one of [the] essential elements of this comedy" (152). Although *The Natural* parody accurately illustrates Marc's point, the series' most uncanny parodic effects were achieved in *The Fugitive* episode. On this show, Nancy's old friend Richard Kimble is being pursued by police Lieutenant Girard for the murder of Kimble's wife. Kimble claims that the actual murderer was a one-armed man and that he needs to escape to Mexico to follow the killer. These plot allusions are reenforced by the theme song from *The Fugitive* and some black-and-white film from the final episode of the original series. The episode transcends simple parody at a crucial point, however. When Lieutenant Girard shouts that the police have surrounded the apartment, Garry says to Nancy and Richard, "He's waiting at the door when there's not even a wall on this whole side of the apartment." The three then escape through the tabooed "fourth wall" of the set and flee through the studio, asking directions from the announcer, Dick Tufeld, along the way. In the end, Kimble is exposed as the murderer and arrested. Nancy and Garry patch up the squabble that Kimble's presence caused, and the episode ends on some heartwarming, syrupy music. Many sitcom conventions have been observed in this parody, but they certainly have not been observed conventionally.

Ironic italicizing of conventions is a major source of humor throughout the series. When Garry and Jeff Goldblum carry party food into Goldblum's walk-in freezer, Garry bumps into the door, locking them in, as Lucy, Laverne, or Shirley would have done. Just before doing so, however, Garry turns to the camera and asks, "Can you see this coming?" Of course the viewers can, since they have seen it happen so many times before. And yet, by breaking through the convention by means of an implied allusion, Garry suborns the viewer into seeing it just one more time.

The same may be said concerning the episode in which Garry meets a sexy girl named Sylvia in the laundry room. The meeting is surprising since Garry earlier predicted that nothing unusual would take place on that show. Significantly, his prediction occurs as part of another allusion to sitcom conventionality: "Did you ever notice on a lot of other television shows all the exciting stuff just *happens* to happen on the day they do the show?" Despite the prediction, Garry does meet Sylvia, a woman so erotic that her every movement is accompanied by theatrical steam and a wailing saxophone. Since these are conventional production techniques, they are naturally available as comic referents. Later in the episode, Sylvia's jealous boyfriend tracks her to Garry's apartment. When she asks how he found her, the boyfriend replies, "Oh, like I couldn't see the steam or hear the saxophone music?" This is a revealing exchange since it follows the conventional sitcom dialogue pattern of setup and one-liner but does so in an unconventional manner, by turning the joke toward the technical device itself rather than toward the situation it presumably enhances.

All such jokes depend heavily on audience participation. First of all, the writers must rely on what David Marc calls "electronic shadow memory" (165), on the viewer's past experience of other TV programs on which devices such as theatrical steam and sultry music were used univocally, without ironic implications. Secondly, the humor depends on the audience's unexamined acceptance of conventionality as the defining context of the sitcom. When Garry helps Richard Kimble escape through the fourth wall of the set, the humor results from a challenge to the audience's sense of what is conventionally possible in that situation. Since, as David Barker demonstrates in his essay "Television Production Techniques as Communication," so much sitcom humor has been authorized by the kind of performer blocking possible in a familiar TV sitcom set, simply walking out of the set is equivalent to walking out of the restrictions of conventionality. The shock produces laughter.

A similar challenge to convention occurs during the episode in which Pete Shumaker makes his career change. In one scene, Garry has supposedly been sitting in a cafe for an hour, munching on rolls and waiting to have lunch with Pete. Because of the long wait, Garry has asked the waiter to give complimentary rolls to the members of the studio audience. When Pete finally arrives, surly and insulting, the audience throw rolls at him. Garry says to the audience, "You're gonna get us thrown out of here." By authenticating the cafe, this line brings the action back within the conventional sitcom plot in which the hero deals with a friend's problem. Before this line, however, Garry and the audience have been briefly operating in unconventional sitcom territory, free of the confining possibilities of the set. Merely recognizing the presence of the audience, moreover, challenges the viewers' acceptance of the laugh tracks that have punctuated their previous sitcom watching, whether these tracks were generated entirely by machine or partly by a "live studio audience."

By recognizing conventions in this way, the Shandling show was able to exploit the entire sitcom repertoire while avoiding imitation and stale conventionality. When Garry wants to know why Pete is so unhappy, he makes use of a "dream hat" to visualize Pete's dreams. Everyone in the cast knows that Garry owns this dream hat and knows further that he has been "forbidden by a judge" to use it. The dream hat looks at best like a cheap prop from a 1950s science fiction program and at worst like a kitchen colander. The audience thus laughs at the obviousness of the device, but the viewers still learn of Pete's secret desire to become a lawyer, and the plot is consequently advanced. In the same way, Garry comprehends his unwillingness to fight with Sylvia's boyfriend through the use of the "flashback booth" that he had built as a child. In a similar fashion, whenever the plot calls for a fantasy, dream, or memory, the dissolving camera focus causes Garry to feel woozy. He usually asks Nancy to stay with him during this techno-psychic experience. Again the audience laughs at a reference to a tired old convention, but the scene of alternative experience is still communicated.

In several scripts, Garry even comments on camera location, as when he says to another customer at the post office, "Excuse me! I'm just trying to talk to the camera." On another occasion, Garry is counseling Grant Shumaker backstage at Mr. Peck's comedy club when he turns to the camera and says, "Could we use the camera angle into the mirror? I think the scene will play more dramatic." When the camera angle shifts, Garry says, "Thank you," and resumes his sincere talk with Grant. In both of these scenes, the plot is advanced, and in both cases the advance is postulated on the viewer's awareness of production techniques.

Other elements of the Shandling show also relied heavily on the audience's familiarity with the operations of the entertainment industry. The Shumaker baby got the name "Blue Suede" from Donna Taylor of Wilmington, Ohio, winner of the "Name the Shumaker Baby Contest," who appeared on the episode in which the baby finally receives his name. When Garry introduces the proprietor of the local newsstand on another episode, he seems surprised that the audience does not respond with the expected enthusiasm. Then he observes, "You don't know Eddie, and that's why you're not applauding." On another episode, Garry tells the audience that they are applauding too much for Martin Mull. When a set recreating the jungles of Vietnam, complete with Viet Cong, appears in the corner of Gilda Radner's apartment, Gilda orders the set raised and chases the Cong out the door by shouting in Vietnamese. As the set ascends, Gilda is conked on the head by a prop coconut and gets to do some knockout shtick reminiscent of her performances on *Saturday Night Live.* In many episodes, Garry refers to the presence of commercials on his show, as when he says during the Shumaker baby episode, "If those seem like a lot of commercials, it's because five days have passed."

The series' theme song provided another opportunity to emphasize that it was not only a sitcom but also a TV show. Scripts frequently have characters commenting on the length of the theme song: exactly forty-one seconds. On the 1960s activism episode, the theme is sung by Flo and Eddie of the Turtles, whom Garry introduces by means of a historically appropriate Ed Sullivan impersonation. On another episode, the deceased Norman Wax plays the closing theme on a harp as he hovers angelically over "the funeral scene" that Carl Reiner finally gets to participate in. As a rule, however, the theme song was performed by Bill Lynch, who even appears with Shandling at the end of the neighborhood-walk episode, ostensibly to fill two minutes of unscripted air time. In any form, the song's lyrics are blatantly self-referential, from the first line, "This is the theme to Garry's show," through the explanation: "This is the music that you hear /while you watch the credits." Surely this musical explanation was unneeded by the audience for whom the show was intended, hypermediated viewers long habituated to theme songs, opening and closing credits, and the concept of TV programing built around a star's personality. Such viewers could easily recognize the likelihood that "Garry called me up and asked if /I would write his theme song." When sung by the unknown Lynch, if not by Flo and Eddie, such testimony probably seemed plausible, even though the lyric was actually written by Shandling and Zweibel.

This kind of ironic self-reference is admittedly contrary to the received wisdom of the television industry, as the show's creators were well aware. Shandling's agent, Bernie Brillstein, told Stephen Farber of *The New York Times* that such conflicting perceptions of how sitcoms may operate were responsible for the Shandling show's appearance on cable rather than network TV. According to Brillstein, when he approached the network executives on behalf of Shandling and Zweibel, "They said you can never break the fourth wall. . . . I said George Burns had done that in his television series and Hope and Crosby had done it in their movies, and their answer was that those were done a long time ago, and no one would accept it now." The fact that the show prospered on Showtime and went into syndication on the Fox network would seem to argue that the network executives were mistaken in their understanding of what viewers would accept. On the other hand, the show went out of production with Garry's wedding in the spring of 1990, thus demonstrating the demographic enormity of network programing considerations.

The reference to George Burns is significant, however, since it suggests another set of sitcom conventions that echoed through the Shandling show. On the *George Burns and Gracie Allen Show* (1950–57), Burns addressed comments on each episode's plot directly to the camera. Joann Gardner's study, "Self-Referentiality in Art," shows how Burns also exploited self-referentiality as a comic device by watching the progress of the plot on a TV set in his study. Some antecedents of Shandling's techniques surely lie here, as was suggested by several critics, including John O'Connor. In the same review in which he called *It's Garry Shandling's Show* "postmodern," O'Connor also drew parallels hieratically to Luigi Pirandello and demotically to the Burns and Allen show. Naturally, such parallels must include the function of the framing monologues in which Burns and Shandling introduced and concluded each episode. Not only did these monologues provide opportunities for additional jokes and character development, but they underscored the fact that the intervening situation comedy was not a transcription of actual experience but a performance, a form of mediated experience with which the TV viewers of the 1980s were even more familiar than their parents in the 1950s.

WORKS CITED

Barker, David. "Television Production Techniques as Communication." In *Television: The Critical View,* edited by Horace Newcomb, 179–96. 4th ed. New York: Oxford University Press, 1987.

Cawelti, John G. *Adventure, Mystery, and Romance: Formula Stories as Art and Popular Culture.* Chicago: University of Chicago Press, 1976.

Farber, Stephen. "54 Shandling Episodes Ordered for Showtime." *New York Times,* 7 Apr. 1987, C18.

Gardner, Joann. "Self-Referentiality in Art: A Look at Three Television Situation-Comedies of the 1950s." *Studies in Popular Culture* 11, no. 1 (1988): 35–50.

Grote, David. *The End of Comedy: The Sit-Com and the Comedic Tradition.* Hamden, Conn.: Archon, 1983.

Hill, Doug, and Jeff Weingrad. *Saturday Night: A Backstage History of Saturday Night Live.* New York: Beech Tree/Morrow, 1986.

Horowitz, Joy. "The Madcap Behind 'Moonlighting.'" *The New York Times Magazine,* 30 Mar. 1986, 24+.

Jonson, Ben. *Timber: or Discoveries.* In *Criticism: The Major Texts,* edited by Walter Jackson Bate, 112–16. Enlarged ed. New York: Harcourt, 1970.

Levine, Lawrence W. *Highbrow/Lowbrow: The Emergence of Cultural Hierarchy in America.* Cambridge, Mass.: Harvard University Press, 1988.

Marc, David. *Demographic Vistas: Television in American Culture.* Philadelphia: University of Pennsylvania Press, 1984.

Mintz, Lawrence E. "Situation Comedy." In *TV Genres: A Handbook and Reference Guide,* edited by Brian Rose, 107–29. Westport, Conn.: Greenwood, 1985.

O'Connor, John J. "Following His Whimsy, Shandling Finds Success." *New York Times,* 14 April 1987, C18.

Stein, Ben. *The View from Sunset Boulevard: America as Brought to You by the People Who Make Television.* New York: Basic Books, 1979.

Waters, Harry F. "TV Comedy: What It's Teaching Kids." *Newsweek,* 7 May 1979, 64–72.

CHAPTER 4 **Mel Brooks and Woody Allen**

Purple Memories

of Blazing Spaceballs

In his essay "Film Comedy" in Lawrence E. Mintz's *Humor in America: A Research Guide to Genres and Topics,* Wes D. Gehring persuasively argues in favor of a connection between television and the kind of cinematic self-referentiality epitomized by the parody or "spoof" film. Although motion pictures have served as sketch material for TV comedians as varied as Bob Hope, Carol Burnett, and the casts of *SCTV* and *Saturday Night Live,* the nurturing matrix for this sort of comedy, according to Gehring, was the epoch-making TV variety program *Your Show of Shows,* broadcast weekly on NBC from 1950 to 1954. The show starred Sid Caesar, Imogene Coca, Carl Reiner, Howard Morris, and—of course—guest stars in a wide assortment of comedy formats, as Ted Sennett has lovingly demonstrated in his study, *Your Show of Shows* (1977). One form of sketch comedy examined by Sennett (120–52) is crucial to Gehring's thesis, namely the TV program's elaborate parodies of popular films, for example, *From Here to Obscurity* and *Trolley Car Named Desire.* The consequences of this early TV exposure on Carl Reiner's career in films might be conjectured from his 1982 parody of the film-noir private eye genre, *Dead Men Don't Wear Plaid,* starring Steve Martin. Of even greater significance, however, was the influence of *Your Show of Shows* on two of the staff writers, Mel Brooks and Woody Allen.

As Gehring argues more extensively in his essay "Parody," in his

*Handbook of American Film Genres*, the effects of writing the film parodies for *Your Show of Shows* can be seen in the film work of Woody Allen as early as *What's Up, Tiger Lily?* and in Mel Brook's *The Producers* in 1967. Following these suggestions, we may testify to the effects' continuing through Brooks's *Spaceballs* (1987) and Allen's *The Purple Rose of Cairo* (1985). Central to the vision of these film-makers, it can therefore be argues (and to the aesthetic dispositions of their audiences), is the assumption that movies are deliberately created art forms, not simple reflections of life. A film audience is always aware, to some degree, of watching a film, just as a TV audience is always aware, to some degree, of watching television.

The implications of such assumptions are significant, as can be seen through an examination of Mel Brooks's highly successful early film *Blazing Saddles* (1974). Brooks's consciousness that *Blazing Saddles* is a film surfaces even in the opening credits, which are shot against a background of conventional western scenery in the over-lush technicolor familiar to viewers of the formula westerns of the 1950s. The voice of Frankie Laine singing the title song—"He rode a blazing saddle . . . "—should focus the audience's memories even more vividly on the milieu and plot of *High Noon*, for which Laine also sang the theme song. One message to the viewer is that this will be another movie about a sheriff, the townspeople, and an outside threat.

Other, similar allusions deliver similar messages throughout the film. When the townspeople assemble in a white clapboard church to discuss finding an accomplished gunslinger to defend them against attack, dozens of similar scenes from earlier westerns re-echo, especially the church scene from Glenn Ford's *The Fastest Gun Alive* (1956), the likely source for this parody. Gene Wilder's role as the drunken, debased Waco Kid should also call up many other echoes. The same might be said of the striking impression of Gabby Hayes performed by Claude Ennis Starrett, Jr., in the church scene and elsewhere in the picture, since Hayes was an actor who might almost stand by himself as a synecdoche of the formula western film. Brooks's minutely accurate imitations of costuming and set design from earlier western films confirm the viewer's understanding that *Blazing Saddles* is not a window on reality but another rendition of a familiar theme.

Because much of the viewer's pleasure in the film depends on such an understanding, Brooks does not trust solely to the viewer's acuity to establish his references. The script written by Brooks (in collaboration with Norman Steinberg, Andrew Bergman, Richard Pryor, and Alan Uger) often refers directly to the story's generic character. For example, when Cleavon Little, as Sheriff Bart, asks the townspeople to give him twenty-four hours to figure out a plan, they refuse, prompting him to complain, "You'd do it for Randolph Scott!" The townsfolk doff their hats in reverence, and a background choir sings Scott's name as if it were a hymn. The self-referential point of the scene seems inescapable. Less obvious, perhaps, is the fact that Little's heroic character is literally a black Bart, the name of the villain in many formula westerns. Somewhere between these two examples on the scale of subtlety is the Waco Kid's boast, "I must have killed more men than Cecil B. DeMille." For one thing, DeMille's name has become almost synonymous with studio film-making, and, for another, this pairing of the gunfighter and the movie mogul guarantees that the violence sure to follow in this film should be accepted by the viewer as theatrical, comic, cinematic—not as real.

Another aspect of the Waco Kid's joke is its anachronicity. There were, of course, no films in the days of the Wild West and so no Cecil B. DeMille. Nor was there a track star named Jessie Owens or an ice-cream-maker named Howard Johnson, and yet both are mentioned in the script, as in the TV series, *The Wide, Wide World of Sports*. Such anachronisms are not defects in the script, however, but strengths. As Gehring points out in his "Parody," films like *Blazing Saddles* constitute "a genre of indeterminate time and space *but with a difference*" (154). The difference is—as Gehring explains and as Brooks's work confirms—intentionality. These films violate historical probability, not because their creators inadvertently shatter an illusion of historical verisimilitude, but because they choose to do so as a coded sign of artistry.

Especially in the film's overt sense of "Jewishness," Brooks is signaling the audience that this film is not really "about" the Wild West so much as it is "about movies." When playing the Indian Chief who spares the young Bart's family, Brooks speaks Yiddish. The villainous Hedley Lamarr (Harvey Korman) rejects a plan to kill the firstborn of each family in Rock Ridge as "too Jewish." The bimbo secretary of Governor William J. LePetomane (also Brooks) is his "beloved Miss Stein." In a story supposedly set in 1884, Lamarr uses the Yiddish terms *putz* and *shmuck,* confident that they will be understood by his cowboy thugs as well as by the audience. A similar assumption governs the coarse name of Lili Von Shtupp, the seductress played by Madeline Kahn, in a parody of Marlene Dietrich's role as Frenchy in *Destry Rides Again* (1939). In semiological terms, the "signified" for all these ethnic "signifiers" is SHOWBIZ, the cultural agency that has made the American viewing audience— irrespective of family background—familiar with these Yiddish terms, and others such as *chutzpah* and *shtick.*

Many other elements of the script also signal the popular entertainment industry of which this film is part. Hedley Lamarr's name conjures up Heddy Lamarr, not only as an actress, and thus an ancestor of the actors in this film, but also as a celebrity notorious for her nudity in the film *EXTASE* (1933) and her scandalous autobiography *Ecstasy and Me* (1966). Another form of mediated celebrity is signified through Sheriff Bart's flamboyant style of dress, particularly by his Gucci saddle, surely suggesting the artificial aura of the TV talk-show "personality" so brilliantly satirized by *The Sammy Maudlin Show* on *SCTV.* Very likely, the scene in which Sheriff Bart and the Waco Kid share marijuana in the jailhouse signifies the same sort of celebrity hipness. While listing these other anachronistic references, we should also comment on the Ku Klux Klan members enlisted in Lamarr's gang. The backs of their robes display two signifiers of mediated commercialism, a yellow smiley face in a circle and the ubiquitous slogan, "Have a Nice Day." All of these references come from within SHOWBIZ and assume the audience's unquestioned familiarity with the originals. Perhaps they also imply an invitation to the audience for a secondary kind of participation in some form of mild satire.

These attitudes are also conveyed through the film's musical allusions. Surely a significant part of the joke surrounding Frankie Laine's singing of the theme song arises from the relative obscurity into which Laine had fallen by 1974. The members of Brooks's audience are expected to know this, as they are expected to recognize the Las Vegas lounge sleaze in Little's rendition of Cole Porter's "I Get a Kick Out of You," offered in response to a bigot's request for a worksong. Porter is probably the American composer least likely to be a favorite of the former slaves comprising a Wild West railroad gang. Porter is very likely to be recognized by Brooks's audience, however, and so the script alludes to his work again when Lamarr encourages his criminal gang to attack Rock Ridge with the order, "Do, do that voodoo that you do so well!" Once again, part of the anachronistic joke is that the criminals are supposed to catch the allusion. Another two-fold musical joke is made when Bart rides his palomino through the Wild West in time with a soundtrack featuring the Count Basie orchestra. When the sheriff then encounters the actual orchestra playing in the desert, Gehring notes the probable influence of Jean-Luc Godard's 1967 film *Weekend* ("Parody" 155). Gehring does not note, however, the "swinging" arrangement that the band is playing, the trademark yachting cap that Basie is wearing, and the tune itself, "April in Paris." Here is a total musical experience as inappropriate to the Wild West as Cole Porter would be.

More appropriate—at least thematically—is "The Ballad of Rock Ridge," which recounts the coming of violence to a peaceful western community. Since the music and lyrics both come from Brooks himself, the song might be understood to be thematically appropriate, and it is—perhaps too appropriate. In fact, "The Ballad of Rock Ridge" is not a piece of film music in any real sense. It more nearly resembles the expository theme songs associated with TV shows such as *The Beverly Hillbillies* and *Gilligan's Island*. Such songs articulate a set of comic premises available to situational variations. The theme thus signals "sitcom" to the audience. By concluding the introductory sequence within the formulaic church scene, moreover, with the congregation singing the last lines of the "Ballad," Brooks directly signals the audience that he is setting up a comic situation, not recounting a purportedly historical event.

Much more blatant forms of self-referentiality appear elsewhere in the film. Sheriff Bart often addresses the camera directly, as does an old woman who is being beaten by two of Lamarr's men. When she says to the camera, "Have you ever seen such cruelty!" her violation of theatrical illusion draws attention to the artifice of the film. Since the preceding beating is played with such transparent falsity, the whole scene signals the same message. Hedley Lamarr also addresses the camera directly in a scene during which he is supposedly racking his brain to think of a totally unsuitable sheriff for Rock Ridge. After mulling the problem over aloud, he says to the camera, "Where will I find such a man? Why am I asking you?" Again, the viewers are forcefully reminded that they are watching a film, not a real villain talking to himself about a real problem in a real office. As a consequence of this insistent self-referentiality, Korman's character is later allowed to say to his gang, "You will only be risking your lives, whilst I will be risking an almost certain Academy Award nomination for best supporting actor."

A more subtle form of self-referentiality involves the plan by which Sheriff Bart defeats Lamarr's gang. In the closest approximation that the film makes toward thematic significance, Bart convinces the townspeople to cooperate with the former slaves and Chinese laborers from the railroad crew in building a canvas-and-plywood simulation of Rock Ridge. The premise is that the villains will be fooled into accepting the artificial town as real until they can be surrounded and killed or captured. In one sense, the preposterous plan is an implausible joke; in another, it is an epitome of Brooks's film, with the viewers playing the part of Lamarr's gang. This is especially clear when the viewers get their first full shots of the completed project. Zooming in from a distance that reveals the two-dimensionality of the town—the unpainted backs of the flats, the supporting braces—the camera comes to rest on a restricted shot of the newly constructed main street. Then the camera pulls back on what appears to be an actual main street, complete with actual buildings and actual sagebrush. Brooks is effectually saying, "Look at the illusions I can create! See how real it all seems! See how easily you are fooled?"

Later, Brooks reverses the process to make a similar point. After Lamarr's gang have been suckered in by the movie-set town, the inevitable fight takes place between the townspeople and the villains. During this fight, however, the simulated buildings have "real" doors and "real" glass windows, which characters are thrown through. After this scene has continued long enough to ring changes on all the comic fight gags familiar from the John Wayne movies of the 1950s, the camera pulls back, this time revealing the roofs of the "real" Rock Ridge and then the roofs of the surrounding buildings, which turn out to be on the Warner Brothers lot. So, this is only a movie after all, and the "real" buildings are only illusions!

The camera then zooms in on another set in which Dom De Luise, outfitted in jodhpurs, beret, and megaphone, in the role of Buddy Bizarre, is directing a huge musical production number featuring dozens of male dancers in evening clothes—all of whom turn out to be homosexual. As with the earlier signifiers of Jewishness, the presumed homosexuality of all male dancers also signals SHOW-BIZ, something understood simultaneously only by insiders and by the entire viewing audience. Soon the fight scene from the main street of Rock Ridge spills over onto this set, ostensibly signaling a collision of the "pretend" world of the western and the "real" world of motion picture production. Since the actors from the two movies then fight, while retaining their film characters, the viewers must question how real anything they are seeing is.

This uncertainty continues as Lamarr/Korman escapes from the studio and jumps into a cab, saying, "Drive me off this picture!" The cab takes him to Grauman's Chinese Theatre, which is showing a film entitled *Blazing Saddles.* Bart/Little pursues him on horseback, mixing the roles of actor and sheriff. In fact, neither Korman nor Little is truly a western character in these scenes; but neither are they truly themselves. When they face each other in the theater lobby, their speech and behavior are as scripted as in their earlier scene in Governor LePetomane's office. In this way, Brooks keeps insisting on the viewers' awareness that *Blazing Saddles* is first and foremost a film.

The final evidence of this insistence is Brooks's refusal to accept an organically consistent form of closure. In fact, Richard Mitchell comments on this reluctance as the key to the overall work: "The film's ending (or endings) exemplifies most of its strengths and weaknesses. Brooks obviously had several different ideas on how to end the film. Instead of choosing among them, he simply shot them all" (187). Mitchell's observation is plausible. The film could end— or at least reach an appropriate climax—in the big fight scene involving Buddy Bizarre and his dancers, since Slim Pickens gets to punch out De Luise after saying, "Piss on you! I'm working for Mel Brooks." Some point about conflicting visions of film and reality could be established here, but the film continues, supposedly spilling into the studio commissary and a pie fight. Another conclusion concerning illusion and reality briefly emerges, possibly one evolving from the actor dressed as Adolph Hitler, but that possibility also evaporates when Lamarr escapes from the studio. The shoot-out in which Bart guns down Lamarr in the theater lobby might also have brought closure in a more conventional setting, but here it only sets up a self-referential joke. Lamarr falls to the floor of Grauman's next to the concrete square containing the signature and footprints of Douglas Fairbanks. Lamarr, or perhaps Korman, moans, "How did he do such fantastic stunts with such little feet?"

The illusion-reality resolution seems possible again when the sheriff and the Waco Kid reenter the theater to see the end of *Blazing Saddles*. Waco says, "I sure hope there's a happy ending! I love a happy ending!" The viewers are probably willing to settle for an ending of any sort at this point, since their usual expectations about film are being deliberately violated. *Deliberately* is the key term, as Mitchell recognizes in saying, "If *Blazing Saddles* is a flawed film, however, it is one that is deliberately flawed, for Mel Brooks knew exactly what he was doing" (187). The actual ending of the film carefully balances the alternatives that Brooks has been playing with in these later scenes and throughout the film. The sheriff returns to town and, instead of accepting a secure position based on the townspeople's gratitude, rides off in pursuit of further challenges. Rejoined by the Waco Kid, Bart gallops into the West. Such scenes reaffirm all the modes of closure dear to the western movie, but these scenes are balanced by others, including the townspeople's rejection of Bart's noble speech as "bullshit" and the Kid's embarrassing possession of a box of popcorn left over from Grauman's. All of these segments finally come together in a scene in which Bart and Waco dismount from their horses so that Little and Wilder can ride off into the sunset in a stretch limo.

In *Blazing Saddles*, Mel Brooks demonstrates that it is still possible to make a "western movie" in 1974, but he also demonstrates that to do so a film-maker must work as much against conventions as with them. The film reveals, furthermore, that success in both directions depends very heavily on the mediated experience of the audience.

Many of Brooks's later films follow the self-referential paths established in *Blazing Saddles*. As Nick Smurthwaite and Paul Gelder demonstrate—in their *Mel Brooks and the Spoof Film* (1982)— *Young Frankenstein* (1974), *Silent Movie* (1976), and *High Anxiety* (1977) make their self-referentiality especially clear by drawing attention to their places in the cinematic genres of horror films, silents, and Hitchcock thrillers. However, even the films by Brooks not rooted in "spoof" or parody, such as *To Be or Not To Be* (1984), reflect a self-conscious awareness of their status as created artifacts, rather than fictionalized slices of life. Historically, films as various as *Golddiggers of 1933*, *This is Spinal Tap*, and *The Muppets Take Manhattan* show that any film about another medium of entertainment inevitably attracts attention to the fact that film is also an entertainment medium. More perhaps than any other American film-maker, Mel Brooks depends in his films on the viewers' understanding of these basic truths. The point emerges with especial clarity in Brooks's *Spaceballs* (1987), a parody—or, as Smurthwaite and Gelder would probably argue, a "spoof"—of science-fiction films in general and of George Lucas's phenomenally successful *Star Wars* (1977) in particular. In fact, the particularity of the parody may very well turn out to be a weakness in the long run as the viewers' recollection of Lucas's original grows less distinct. Now, what *was* the name of that robot? What did they call those little creatures in monks' robes?

The parodic elements of *Spaceballs* are more accurately detailed even than those in *Blazing Saddles*. The words in the opening credits roll on the screen in the high-tech reverse invented for the Lucas film. Here, however, the establishing premises conclude with the sentence: "If you can read this, you don't need glasses." In an early scene, the double chignons over the ears of Princess Vespa (Daphne Zuniga) turn out to be the earphones of a space-age Walkman. The costumes in *Spaceballs* also closely echo the earlier film, as do many of the sets, particularly the dungeons of the Death Star. Brooks also reproduces many of Lucas's more striking visual effects. In the duel between the hero, Lone Star (Bill Pullman), and the villain, Dark Helmet (Rick Moranis), the weapons are called "schwartzes," but they look and sound just like light sabers. When Lone Star must accelerate to escape from Dark Helmet, he pushes his ship all the way up to "hyperactive," but the visual effect of exploding light particles closely resembles that generated by "hyperspace" in *Star Wars*.

To underscore its basic nature as film as well as parody, *Spaceballs*, also echoes many other popular films. The audience is reminded of some of these merely through passing allusions. Princess Vespa shoots "like Rambo," for example. A TV news program promises a review of *Rocky V*. When Snotty offers to "beam down" President Skroob (Brooks), the president agrees, saying, "What the hell, it works on *Star Trek!*" The television connection of the two previous examples probably intensifies their allusiveness, despite their brevity. There are more extensive references also, as to Indiana Jones. Probably because Harrison Ford starred in both *Star Wars* and the Indiana Jones films, Lone Star wears a battered leather jacket as part of his costume through much of *Spaceballs*. Furthermore, his wookie-like sidekick, Barf (John Candy), observes that the cave of

Yogurt (Brooks again) "looks like the Temple of Doom." Other brief references consist of musical allusions: the theme from *Jaws*, the "Colonel Bogey March" from *The Bridge on the River Kwai*, Strauss's "Thus Spake Zarathustra" from *2001*, and the theme from *Lawrence of Arabia*.

This last piece of music is played when Lone Star's spaceship runs out of gas and crash-lands in a desert, calling up visual memories of *Lawrence* as well as of *Star Wars*. This scene illustrates another form of echoic allusion used in *Spaceballs*. At several points in the film, Brooks shoots whole sequences in a style intended to remind the viewers of earlier films. To some degree, this is the effect created by the scene in which the *Jaws* theme underscores a painfully protracted tracking of the exterior of Dark Helmet's flying fortress. The same might be said of the scene in which Michael Winslow simulates the weird sound effects that define his role in the *Police Academy* films. The fact that Winslow is again wearing a uniform italicizes the reference.

A more reverberating echo occurs when Lone Star, Barf, the Princess, and her robot Dot Matrix (Joan Rivers) approach the "Everlasting Know-it-all" Yogurt for counsel and assistance. The visual and sound effects in the scene clearly conjure up memories of Dorothy's approach to the great Wizard of Oz. The following scene, in which a diminutive Brooks emerges from the giant statue of Yogurt, also recalls Frank Morgan's emergence from behind his curtain in the 1939 film. Another flash of déjà vu should occur when a Statue-of-Liberty-shaped head of a giant transformer crashes down from space onto a deserted beach. Two apes on horseback ride up to inspect the humans emerging from the head in a distinct—and fairly gratuitous—allusion to *Planet of the Apes*.

Even more gratuitous is a two-part sequence set in the space diner that Lone Star and Barf drop into for a quick bite. Since nothing happens in the diner that has any relevance to the overall plot of the film, the sequence must exist solely for it humorous potential, and this humor involves two extended references to other popular films. In the first, another diner patron, played by John Hurt, screams in pain and grabs his stomach, apparently suffering from something he ate. When his stomach erupts to eject a green special-effects monster, Hurt gasps, "Oh no! Not again!" The viewers must recall Hurt's role in *Alien*, or the scene becomes unintelligible as well as gratuitous. Since the credits define Hurt's role in the film as "John

Hurt," the purely allusive nature of the episode is confirmed. Then, totally ignoring Hurt's supposed misery, the camera follows the little green monster as it dons a straw hat and sings, "Hello, my honey! Hello, my baby!" while dancing out of the picture. Unless the viewers recall the Warner Brothers cartoon, *One Froggy Evening* (1955), the second half of this sequence would seem even more pointless than the first. But then, what true movie fan does not cherish some memory of the singing, dancing frog in the classic cartoon and all the misery he brought to the man who found him at the construction site? Clearly, Brooks expects his ideal viewer to be as immersed in popular film history as he is himself.

This expectation underlies the types of directly self-referential devices that Brooks adopts in *Spaceballs*. Some of these concern progression of the film's narrative. At one point, Colonel Sandurz (George Wyner) delivers an expository monologue to Dark Helmet concerning events crucial to the narrative's premises. Obviously, narrative coherence requires that Dark Helmet already be in possession of these facts, or he would not have embarked on the current mission. Thus it is certain, as Roland Barthes explains in another context, in his essay "Introduction to the Structural Analysis of Narratives," that the information can only be intended for the viewers. In recognition of this, Dark Helmet turns to the camera and asks, "Everybody got that?" The viewers' prior experience of film naturally has conditioned them to attend to plot exposition of this sort without question. Brooks's self-referential device forces this experience to become conscious and to provoke questions. One such question must be posed when Colonel Sandurz uses a remote control to switch off a TV wall screen and the entire film goes black. Dark Helmet tells him, "You turned off the whole movie." When Sandurz activates the remote control again, *Spaceballs* resumes, and yet the viewers must be more acutely aware than ever that they are watching images projected on a screen, not real human beings living in the future.

The sort of technical trickery involved in the scene featuring the remote control surfaces in other self-referential devices also. At one point, a camera dollying in for a close-up of Dark Helmet supposedly collides with him accidentally, knocking him backwards to the floor. Again, a technique that the viewers take for granted is brought to the conscious level through comic highlighting. Since Brooks uses a similar device in *High Anxiety*, when he has a dollying camera bump against a glass window, he must feel that this element of film-making calls for particular attention. Another quality of camera technique is italicized during the desert sequence in *Spaceballs* when Lone Star emphasizes the need for an early start before "that blazing sun gets overhead." The following shot of a blazing sun causes Barf to exclaim, "Nice dissolve!" Through such devices, anyone's willing suspension of disbelief would be seriously challenged.

In several moves beyond the technical, Brooks explodes the viewers' credulity altogether. In the duel between Lone Star and Dark Helmet, for example, the action carries the participants through the fourth wall of the set into the area occupied by Brooks's crew. A careless stroke supposedly injures the operator of the boom mike. When Dark Helmet blames the accident on Lone Star, consistency of character is maintained, but a flagrant violation of cinematic convention still takes place. In another scene, Dark Helmet's henchmen finally seem to have cornered the four principals in spite of their heroic leap through a dangerously closing steel door. The viewers must surely be disappointed that such derring-do has not secured the heroes' escape. Closer scrutiny reveals, however, that things are not as bleak as they seem, because the captain of the guards screams at his men, "You idiots! These are not them! You've captured their stunt doubles!" These devices serve multiple purposes for Brooks as well as for the audience. The viewers get the thrill of the stunt, the shock of the capture, and the delight of the escape. Brooks gets his characters out of a very tight spot so that his film may continue. Some influence from the later Muppet movies might be suspected.

All his own, however, is the highly self-referential scene in which Brooks helps his villains catch up with his heroes. Because it is so hard to maneuver in "ludicrous speed," Dark Helmet has lost the trail of Lone Star. Colonel Sandurz suggests that they view the videocassette of *Spaceballs, the Movie* to find out where Lone Star has gone. Luckily, Sandurz says, this casette is available owing to "a new breakthrough in home video marketing—instant casettes." Luckily also, the flying space station contains a "Mr. Rental" location that is stocked with all of Mel Brooks's movies. The camera lovingly and self-referentially pans all of these titles before settling on *Spaceballs*. The audience's subsequent viewing of the casette on the movie screen is surely an experience of hypermediation. The casette scene begins with the FBI warning against reduplication and then fast-forwards through scenes that the audience has already viewed.

When the casette comes into focus, it displays Sandurz and Dark Helmet watching a screen that shows them watching a screen, and so on, as on the Morton Salt box. Dark Helmet seems particularly impressed by this technology and alternately engages in small hand movements, watches these movements on the TV screen, and looks into the motion picture camera in puzzlement. When he asks Sandurz, "When does this happen in the movie?" self-referentiality reaches a distinctly advanced state.

Sandurz's reply pushes it even further: "Now! You're looking at now, Sir. Everything that happens now is happening now." In one sense, the scene creates a bizarre form of realism since Dark Helmet's puzzlement seems organically consistent with such a technological marvel. Since Dark Helmet is not a person, but a character played by Rick Moranis, there is another sense in which Brooks may be said to be perpetrating some sort of realistic illusion. On the other hand, reminders that film is repeatable, that films are available on casette, that casettes may be fast-forwarded and reversed—all point in directions entirely counter to realism. The final effect of this scene can only be a heightened awareness on the viewers' part that they are seeing something made, not something with an independent reality.

The emphasis on immediacy pushes this awareness further, toward some convictions already established for most viewers by television. "Everything is happening now," explains Sandurz, an explanation just as likely to have been offered by Garry Shandling, the Muppets, or the casts of *SCTV* or *SNL*. In other words, Mel Brooks's films ultimately provide viewers with the experience of "watching a movie," just as they are accustomed to "watching TV." Everything can be experienced here and now by switching on a screen. In fact, this is what President Skroob declares in *Spaceballs* when he says, "Now that I have my coffee, I'm ready to watch RADAR." Comedy is assuredly Brooks's main goal in his films, but an increase in his audience's awareness is an unavoidable byproduct of the kind of self-referential comedy he creates.

In his essay "Parody," Wes Gehring confidently associates Woody Allen with Brooks in terms of their shared experience as writers for Sid Caesar's *Your Show of Shows*. Surely Gehring is correct in this emphasis. Especially in his earliest films, Allen's disposition toward the medium closely resembles Brooks's, even though Allen manifests this disposition in somewhat less manic forms. In *What's*

*New, Pussycat?* (1965)—Allen's first screen experience—he received dual credit as actor and writer. His schlemiel role in this film clearly built upon the persona he had developed in his successful stand-up career, as Maurice Yacowar shows in his *Loser Take All: The Comic Art of Woody Allen* (1979). Yacowar also notes (29–33) some of the self-referential devices that Allen worked into the script, such as a guest appearance by Richard Burton, the allusions to films by Alfred Hitchcock and Federico Fellini, and the flashing title, "Author's Message," that runs under Peter O'Toole's sentimental paean to monogamy. Even in his first film, and even under the direction of Clive Donner, therefore, Allen revealed a distinct impulse to exploit the conventions of his medium.

Allen's next film, *What's Up, Tiger Lily?* (1966), confirmed these tendencies, not only in the parodic echo of *What's New, Pussycat?* in the title, but in the second film's very nature. As many readers may now have forgotten, *Tiger Lily* was actually a Japanese film entitled *Kagi No Kagi* that Allen recut to fit a new, broadly comic script of his own invention. Yacowar claims that the original Japanese thriller was already "a spoof of the James Bond films" (114). Thus any pretensions to realistic illusion must be discounted in advance. There are few such pretensions in Allen's script, which insistently draws attention to itself by means of irrational racial allusions, references to American popular culture, and one-liners of the sort that had been polished by Allen in his stand-up routines. In fact, the film does not even pretend that these Japanese actors are actual, living persons faced with real dangers. Rather, Allen openly assumes that the moving pictures on the screen are occasions for jokes. Significantly, he also assumes that the viewers know this. Why, after all, would anyone go to see *What's Up, Tiger Lily?* in the first place, except to see what Woody Allen was up to?

In order to characterize Allen's comic sensibility, Gehring and Yacowar both emphasize parodic dimensions of later films such as *Take the Money and Run* (1969), *Bananas* (1971), *Play It Again, Sam* (1972), *Everything You Always Wanted to Know About Sex* (1972), *Sleeper* (1973), and *Love and Death* (1975). As in the case of Brooks—and other directors such as Carl Reiner, Jim Henson, and Rob Reiner—Allen's use of parody and allusion in these films clearly reveals his awareness that he and his viewers participate in a rhetorical community of people acutely aware of "what goes without saying." This awareness is evident even when Allen strives for an effect other than comedy, as when obvious echoes of Ingmar Bergman resound inescapably throughout the deadly *Interiors* (1978). In happier achievements such as *Broadway Danny Rose* (1984) and *Radio Days* (1987), Allen's comedy may not involve direct parody of any specific film or film genre, and yet the general sense of SHOWBIZ permeating both films keeps signaling viewers that they are watching a screen rather than looking through an open window on life—or perhaps in the case of *Radio Days* of listening in on a party line.

The highly self-referential *Stardust Memories* (1980) offers particularly striking illustrations of Allen's attitudes toward his medium and his audience. As a self-confessed epigone of Ingmar Bergman and Federico Fellini, Allen might naturally be expected to consider films about making films to be legitimate projects. As inescapably a part of the highly mediated rhetorical community of contemporary America, Allen might be expected to approach such film-making in terms of the self-referential devices we have seen at work elsewhere, on television and in the work of Mel Brooks, for example. *Stardust Memories* fully meets such expectations.

The film presents the story of Sandy Bates, a Jewish, balding, highly acclaimed maker of comic films, whose romantic life is turbulent, whose professional life is unsettled, and whose current film cannot reach satisfactory closure. The story develops as Sandy, played by Woody Allen, agrees to attend a film festival gotten up in his honor at a seaside resort. He must be cajoled because, as was also the case with Woody Allen in 1980, Sandy seems torn between his own desire to make lugubrious, significant films (like *Interiors*) in the manner of Bergman and his fans' desire that he repeat the comic formulas (like *Bananas* and *Sleeper*) that he has grown bored with. Specifically, Sandy struggles with the heads of the movie studio, who want to replace the nihilistic ending of his film-in-progress with a more upbeat conclusion appropriate to an anticipated Easter release date. Whereas Sandy wants the film to end in a garbage dump, the studio heads want the film to end in jazz heaven. The very terms in which these endings are posed demonstrate that Allen assumes a great deal of mediated experience on the part of his viewers, that, for example, they will recognize the Bergmanesque echoes of the first alternative and the formulaic Hollywood mentality suggested by the second.

One of the most effective means by which Allen draws on this experience is his creation of fictional films, supposedly representing Sandy's past and present creative work, within his film. By borrowing some helpful vocabulary from Gerald Prince's *A Dictionary of Narratology* (1987), we may say that within the primary or "diegetic" narrative of *Stardust Memories,* Allen imbeds secondary or "metadiegetic" narratives. The viewers' first experience of *Stardust Memories,* following the credits, consists of a ticking clock, resonating through a train interior in which a character played by Woody Allen seems unhappy to be surrounded by an assortment of gloomy, Bergmanesque types—all apparently bound for some symbolic destination. Since viewers are unaware at this point that Woody is playing Sandy, another, fictional, actor-director, the initial impression probably is uncertainty as to whether Allen is making a comic parody of the nouvelle vague or a serious art film, perhaps a variation on *Interiors.* Since Woody struggles comically to escape from the train, the former assumption seems more likely. Before viewers can decide for sure, however, the train episode ends, terminating in shots of unexposed film and the noise of a projector. Viewers discover that the foregoing scene has been part of a film within the film and that they have foolishly taken as "real" what was only "a movie."

Similar dislocations occur throughout the work, especially during the film festival when the metadiegetic films are used to establish Sandy's previous artistic experiences. Since Sandy was an actor in these earlier films, as was his earlier lover, Dorrie, played by Charlotte Rampling, these scenes also help provide background for Sandy's current romantic situation. The dual role of Allen's friend Tony Roberts as both an actor in these metadiegetic films and as a friend of Sandy and Dorrie provides further congruence between the films and the fictional film-maker's life. By rapidly cutting between these levels—both filmed in black and white—Allen deliberately blurs his narrative shifts. As a result, he creates uncertainty in the viewer's mind as to what truly constitutes the "truth" about Sandy's life.

Metadiegetic films are not the only device through which Allen exploits his viewers' mediated experience, however. As the narrative approaches the point at which we might, on the basis of earlier films, expect closure, Allen seduces his viewers with a whole series of false climaxes. After Sandy and Daisy (another romantic interest, played by Jessica Harper) attend a screening of *The Bicycle Thief,* for example, their car breaks down. Any experienced film-goer probably anticipates several possible developments at this point—each promising some resolution of Sandy's crises. Instead, Allen has Sandy and Daisy encounter a group of Felliniesque UFO devotees, partying in a large field to music that strongly echoes Nino Rota's sound tracks for Fellini's films. Since Gordon Willis, Allen's usual cinematographer, films these scenes in imitation of the lighting and distorted, arty, camera angles used by Fellini in 8 1/2, the stylistic parallels clearly suggest that a resolution to Allen's film may occur along the avant-garde, modernist, lines pioneered by the filmmakers he admires. But these plausibly conditioned expectations turn out to be mistaken.

In a sequence of apparently unrelated developments, filmed in a variety of un-Felliniesque styles, the film subsequently approaches and withdraws from a dazzling variety of endings. First, Sandy encounters the UFO that the previous scenes appeared to render absurd and hears a voice that speaks in the mechanical tones familiar to viewers of low budget sci-fi films and Bugs Bunny cartoons. This voice encourages Sandy to give up his search for existential significance and settle for making comic films: "You wanna do mankind a real service?" Tell funnier jokes!" Before viewers can determine whether this is, after all, the point of Allen's film, a demented fan shoots Sandy. When a psychiatrist next provides a posthumous psychoanalysis of Sandy to the audience at the film festival, viewers may conclude that Allen's film is ending ironically with Sandy's problems unsolved.

Even this assumption is subverted. Sandy begins to argue with the psychiatrist's interpretations, suggesting that he is not dead after all. Since the other characters pay him no heed and seem unaware of his presence, it may seem that the film is veering off in the direction of the whimsical paranormal, perhaps some updated version of *Topper*. In confirmation, the "late Sandy Bates" testifies, while accepting an award, that he was led to affirm life, instead of seeking unattainable answers, by his happy memory of spending a Sunday morning in spring with Dorrie many years ago. Viewers are probably attracted to this engagingly framed and romantically heightened domestic scene, especially since it is underscored by Louis Armstrong's version of "Stardust" on the sound track. After all, past experience has conditioned most film-goers to associate theme music with a narrative climax.

Once again, a plausible narrative expectation turns out to be invalid. It evolves that this was all part of a dream of Sandy's, that he is not dead, and that he is in deep romantic trouble with Isobel for calling out Dorrie's name while unconscious. Clearly, *Stardust Memories* cannot end at this point. On a train very much like the one in the first scene, Sandy wins Isobel back by explaining the new ending he has conceived for his metadiegetic film. It will end, he says, with Isobel's giving Sandy "a big, wet kiss." When Isobel protests that such an ending would be too sentimental, Sandy replies, "It's the good sentimental," and she kisses him. Viewers may or may not be troubled by the fact that Isobel was not slated to appear in Sandy's film, but if they do not question this, they may feel that Allen's film is reaching some sort of conclusion when the train pulls out of the station in a shot that is familiar from many old movies.

Amidst such conjectures, viewers are probably startled to hear applause. Sandy and Isobel have been acting in a metadiegetic film, after all, one that has just ended on "a big, wet kiss" on a train. The applauding audience is not the crowd at the film festival, however, but another group composed of all of the actors in *Stardust Memories*. These characters troop up the aisle, toward the camera, commenting in mixed terms on the film they have just seen—on the film the viewers have just seen. When the actresses discuss "his" annoying habit of kissing with his mouth open, considerable uncertainty develops. Is "he" Sandy in his roles in the metadiegetic films? Is "he" Woody Allen in his role as Sandy? Or what? Allen refuses to provide certain answers. After these characters have exited, someone returns to the viewing room alone. As the sound track plays, "Easy to Love," either Sandy or Woody finds a pair of sunglasses, puts them on, and exits into the camera. The camera pans to the ceiling lights of the viewing room, and Allen's film ends.

Surely the viewer derives some sense of thematic coherence from *Stardust Memories*, probably something about the artist's ambivalent relation to his audience. Perhaps this theme might be stated in terms appropriate to films from the past such as *8 1/2, Lust for Life*, or even *Golddiggers of 1933*. Allen's shifts among the narrative levels in *Stardust Memories* make such apparent compatibilities moot, however. Any sense of tidy coherence in Allen's film must ultimately be recognized as the creation of the audience's "narrativity," to borrow a term from Robert Scholes, rather than of the film's thematic organicism. As Scholes explains, the audience's previous experience of film makes the quest for thematic significance inescapable. As film viewers, we will have our "meanings" tied up in a neat—or untidy—package at the work's end even if we must supply many of the missing parts ourselves. Allen's understanding of his audience's expectations permits him to escape the trap of facile narrative closure that is seemingly demanded by the viewers' expectations. By transforming what might otherwise seem to be narrative imperatives, he is able to make the sort of film he wanted without ponderously offending his audience. He is able to do so, however, only because he confidently—and correctly—assumes in his viewers a highly sophisticated awareness of film conventions.

Many contemporary reviewers, including David Denby, in *New York*, Alex Keneas in *Newsday*, Richard Schickel in *Time*, and Leonard Quart in *Cineaste*, agreed that *Zelig* (1983) develops many of the same themes explored in *Stardust Memories*, most especially Allen's ambivalence about success and popular acclaim. Moreover, all of these reviewers saw *Zelig* as the more sophisticated of the two, largely on stylistic grounds. In the *Christian Science Monitor* (21 July 1983), David Sterritt agreed that in this film Allen succeeded in "stretch[ing] the language of film" (16), and in *Magill's Cinema Annual, 1984*, Rob Edelman concluded similarly that "Allen has stretched the medium of cinema as far as he can" (476–77). The stimulus for this rare display of critical unanimity seems to be Allen's open acknowledgement and self-referential exploitation of a whole complex of cinematic conventions.

In the simplest sense, *Zelig* might be seen merely as a parodic documentary, as *Sleeper* is a parodic sci-fi film. Technically, at least, *Zelig* qualifies brilliantly on these grounds. The voice-over by Patrick Horgan is consistently case in the narrative present that is favored in historical documentaries, and the segments of the story presented as news film all end with humorous banalities that ring true to experienced viewers of *Movietone News* and *The March of Time*. Dick Hyman's original musical score sounds equally authentic. *Zelig* might in all these respects be merely what it purports to be: a documentary about the world-famous "human chameleon" of the 1920s and 1930s who just dropped out of sight around the beginning of World War II. Thus, even if the film is not an actual documentary about a real man named Zelig, it might be understood as an organically consistent narrative about an imaginary Zelig, somewhat like Frank Capra's film *Mr. Smith Goes to Washington* (1939).

Zelig's fictional biography is interwoven with authentic documentary footage, however, so that viewers are sometimes confronted not only with a comic parody but also elements of the real thing. The ticket-tape parade with which *Zelig* opens is obviously historical film of an actual parade down Broadway. The couple riding in the car are not real celebrities, however, but Leonard Zelig and Dr. Eudora Fletcher, two fictional characters played by Woody Allen and Mia Farrow. The still photograph of Eugene O'Neill shown later is probably familiar to many viewers, but the man standing beside O'Neill is Zelig. The same may be said of the famous photograph of Pagliacci: the body is Caruso's; the face, Zelig's. Surely the newspaper headlines announcing the stock market crash are authentic, as is the film of chaotic buying and selling. On the other hand, the film of Zelig sitting on a gurney in Manhattan Hospital cannot be authentic because his feet are pointing downward, as real feet cannot do.

Throughout the film, the technical wizardry of cinematographer Gordon Willis and film editor Susan E. Moore permits Allen to blend original material and documentary sources seamlessly. Even professional viewers were astounded. Quart explains in his review that "new footage was artificially aged by the use of fifty years old lenses and mattes to give the film the grainy flickering, poorly-lit quality of "Twenties' footage" (42). Edelman was impressed by the realistic sound quality, achieved by the use of "actual 1928 microphones" (478). Technical mastery obviously figures prominently in the message that Allen is sending in this film, and it must figure also in the viewers' reception of the message. Thus, the viewers' attention is frequently distracted from the story of the fictional characters to the operations of the director. When Zelig stands in the on-deck circle while Babe Ruth takes batting practice, the question is not how did Zelig get into the Yankees' training camp, but how were these shots of Zelig cut into the original film? Allen must have been anticipating such questions about his work. As early as *What's Up, Tiger Lily?* it is clear that self-referentiality figures prominently in his conception of what film can do.

We may see this self-consciousness in the important segment of *Zelig* depicting Dr. Fletcher's psychiatric treatment of the central character. Since *Zelig* is a movie, the viewers need to see film of what happened during these sessions. Since this movie purports to be a documentary, there has to be some explanation of how this film happened to be available. The narrator's highly technical account of this is comic in itself—especially when reinforced by shots of the huge but supposedly inconspicuous spotlights and microphones arranged about the famous "white room"—but the principal joke involves Allen's concern with how to get information across on film. In a later scene, Allen makes this joke more subtly. The subject here is Zelig's increasing depression, which is thoroughly anatomized by the narrator over a long piece of film supposedly showing Zelig, sitting alone in a corridor and smoking. Why anyone recorded this scene on film in the first place is left to the viewers to figure out. What they probably decide is that Allen filmed the scene to make them ask this very question.

Another device italicized in the film is the effort to establish documentary authenticity by calling on the memories of "witnesses," as Warren Beatty had recently done in *Reds* (1981). To establish a realistic atmosphere, Allen films older actors—Ellen Garrison, Sherman Loud, and Elizabeth Rothschild—in full color as they reminisce in the 1980s about their youthful experiences as Fletcher, her cameraman Paul Deghuee, and her sister Meryl. The visual contrast with their younger depictions, in black and white, by Mia Farrow, John Rothman, and Stephanie Farrow is effective, especially since the older actors' lines seem consistent with their characters in the past.

On the other hand, Jean Trowbridge, who plays the role of Dr. Fletcher's mother in the 1980s, speaks lines totally inconsistent with the supposed intent of the documentary. Dr. Fletcher's mother says that her daughter never wanted to be a psychiatrist in the first place, that she was always an unpleasant and difficult child, and that her father was equally difficult in addition to being a drunkard. Obviously, a real documentary-maker would edit out this segment since it runs counter to the direction of the film as a whole. Mrs. Fletcher's memories are funny enough, but their final purpose must be to signal Allen's presence self-referentially rather than to develop Fletcher's character thematically.

The same is true of the testimony given by the actual "witnesses," including Susan Sontag, Irving Howe, Saul Bellow, and Bruno Bettleheim—also filmed in color. In the light of Irving Howe's recent book, *The World of Our Fathers* (1976), it is amusingly predictable that he sees Zelig as the illustration of some facet of Jewish historical experience. Susan Sontag's comments about Zelig's intellectuality are also comically appropriate. In both cases, though, the most profound joke is self-referential. Viewers are forced to wonder: Is that really Howe or just an actor playing a role? If that really is Sontag, why would she agree to appear in this comedy? Is Woody Allen really so influential that Saul Bellow wants to appear in one of his films? Significantly, the direction of all these questions is toward Allen and away from Zelig.

It is important to recognize that these celebrity cameos result in dislocating customary responses to film. When viewers cannot tell how "real" something on the screen is supposed to be, they are jarred into a rhetorical situation requiring increased alertness to all kinds of conventions. In *Zelig*, Allen makes such demands on his viewers, not only through these cameos, but also through his use of a film within his film. Although Allen makes far more sophisticated use of the technique in *Stardust Memories* and *The Purple Rose of Cairo*, he also disorients his viewers' expectations with a metadiegetic film in *Zelig*. Supposedly made by Warner Brothers at the crest of Zelig's popularity in 1935, *The Changing Man* is a romanticized, Hollywood version of Zelig's life. Since the viewers have come to know the "real" Zelig and Fletcher, they cannot help but recognize how inauthentic the acting and the actions are in this Hollywood depiction. Unlike his practice in *Stardust Memories*, Allen here creates a jarring conflict of tone between his two levels of narrative. Thus, whenever Allen's film moves from the story of Zelig to *The Changing Man*, there is a corresponding challenge to the viewers' credulity.

The most effective shift occurs late in the film when Zelig and Fletcher flee Nazi Germany to pursue their love in the United States. Having watched Farrow (as Fletcher) wave to Allen (as Zelig) at a huge Nazi rally, we see Garrett Brown (as Zelig) wave back in *The Changing Man*. Perhaps a momentary confusion attacks some viewers, but Brown's style of performance is so much more theatrical than Allen's that any uncertainty must be brief. The viewers' situation is complicated, however, when the voice of the older Fletcher states over Brown's scene that this movie version was inaccurate. In the next shot, Garrison, as the older Fletcher who is filmed in color in her 1980s living room, says that the actuality was much more dramatic than the movie showed. Supposedly captured German documentary film then follows, depicting the lovers' thrilling escape from the Luftwaffe. This film looks realistically grainy, but the sound track consists of the sort of bogus, *Schweinhund* German used in cheaply produced Hollywood war films. In such scenes, the documentary about Zelig becomes so intertwined with *The Changing Man* that viewers cannot tell which is the "real" story. The most likely discovery is that neither story is "real," that both of them are equally *movies*.

This mediated consciousness is a strength in *Zelig* which is too little recognized even by admiring critics. David Sterritt's compliment to Allen for "stretch[ing] the language of film," for example, was based on his assumption that he and Allen shared a perception of contemporary America as a "culture hooked not only on video games and microcircuits, but on foggy concepts like 'human potential' and psychiatry" (16). We must question whether the simplistic "culture shlock" abhorred by Sterritt, and many of Allen's other fans, could sustain the rhetorical community needed for effective artistic communication even in a popular film such as *Zelig*. Is it not more likely that the common body of mediated reference constituting contemporary American culture supplies richness rather than paucity? If so, then Norman Brooks's imitation of Al Jolson's "I'm Sitting On Top of the World" provides more than period flavor to Allen's film. Such songs—and other artifacts such as the actual documentary footage of Bobby Jones, Fannie Brice, and Jack Dempsey— are not just attendant circumstances of events in American culture but the culture itself. By the same token, documentary films are not substitutes for American history but history themselves. At least they must be part of Woody Allen's history or he would not have been able to make *Zelig*.

Allen's immersion in this culture is unquestionable, despite an attraction to European film styles and occasional laments about his upbringing, such as his confession to Caryn James, "I had no cultural background whatsoever, and I mean absolutely none" (22). What Allen means, of course, is that he was not taken regularly to the ballet and opera as a child and that his parents did not raise him on ponderous books like the ones Alvy Singer presses on Annie Hall. On the other hand, Allen's deeply American acculturation is evident throughout his films. Not to repeat the examples previously cited, we might simply mention the fond reconstruction of radio experience in *Radio Days* (1987) and the deus ex machina in *Hannah and her Sisters* (1986) through which Mickey Sachs solves his existential crises by watching the Marx Brothers in *Duck Soup*. Perhaps the most interesting illustration of these attitudes is *The Purple Rose of Cairo* (1985).

*The Purple Rose* centers on Cecilia (Mia Farrow), a mousy depression-era hash-house waitress who is married to a coarse, womanizing, wife-beating sponger named Monk (Danny Aiello). Unsurprisingly under these circumstances, Cecilia seeks escape from reality in the formulaic romantic films offered weekly at her neighborhood theater, the Jewel. The contrast between these films and Cecilia's real life emerges clearly in the opening scene, which shows Cecilia dreamily contemplating a poster advertising this week's offering, an obviously escapist B-movie called *The Purple Rose of Cairo*. Her imaginative trance deepens as Fred Astaire sings on the sound track, "Heaven, I'm in heaven." Suddenly the fantasy is shattered as a letter falls to the pavement from the marquee overhead. Fred's voice fades. Back in real-life New Jersey, Cecilia is urged by the theater manager not to miss this week's feature. "Cecilia, you're gonna like this one," he says. "It's better than last week's, more romantic." Immediately Allen cuts to a hard, angry woman sitting in a diner. "Miss, I wanted oatmeal *before* my scrambled eggs," she says to a still dreamy-eyed Cecilia, who is now wearing her waitress's uniform. Here in the first few minutes of Allen's film, viewers are clearly warned that the movies are not real life.

If any doubt lingers, Monk repeatedly expresses the contrast for his wife and Allen's viewers. When Cecilia begs Monk to accompany her to the first night's showing of *The Purple Rose*, he refuses, saying, "Cecilia, you like sitting through that junk. Me, I'm gonna shoot crap, O.K.?" Clearly, Monk rejects the premise that popular films can transform and illuminate everyday experience. Just as clearly, Cecilia has different expectations, and so she goes to the Jewel alone to share vicariously in the devil-may-care highlife of beautiful people such as playboy Larry Wild, the countess, and "explorer-poet-adventurer" Tom Baxter "of the Chicago Baxters." Allen's viewers must also reject Monk's unimaginative criticism. After all, if they are watching Allen's *Purple Rose* in the first place, they do not share Monk's conviction that all movies are "junk."

Fantasy is clearly the preferable alternative for Cecilia because, within his color film, Allen has created a brilliant replica of a 1930s black-and-white musical, down to the lighting, set design, and tuneful sound track by Dick Hyman. Thanks to Gordon Willis's photography, Allen's parody captures with stunning accuracy what Lawrence O'Toole called "the pearly tones of an actual film from the period" (63). Fred and Ginger would feel right at home in these art deco surroundings, as Arlene Croce shows in *The Fred Astaire &* *Ginger Rogers Book*. Because she has seen so many films of this sort, Cecilia also feels at home, and—for the same reason—so do Allen's viewers. In such films, characters drink champagne, find love, temporarily lose it, and then live happily ever after. Therefore, real and fictional viewers may expect the same for Tom Baxter, Copacabana chanteuse Kitty Haynes, and—by extension—for Cecilia.

Escape into the black-and-white *Purple Rose* is easy for both types of viewers because Allen smoothly cuts from color shots of Cecilia and the other patrons of the Jewel, to shots in which the theater in color frames a screen showing the black-and-white *Purple Rose*, to shots in which the black-and-white film fills the whole field of vision. Viewers thus can watch exactly the same romantic comedy that Cecilia is watching at exactly the same moment she sees it and feel a comparable if not identical sense of optimism. The viewers' shock is comparable to Cecilia's when Allen transports them directly from the black-and-white Copacabana to the dismal color of the apartment in which Monk is flagrantly courting the sexual favors of a gross neighbor named Olga. This contrast between film and life so disturbs Cecilia that she packs her bags to leave an obviously failed marriage. The shaken viewers can only applaud her decision. Against this applause, Monk again articulates the unimaginative, realistic attitude: "You won't last! You'll see how it is in the real world." Alas, Monk is right. Cecilia has no money, no skills, no wealthy friends, no prospects, no real hope. She soon returns to further abuse and humiliation.

It would seem that only movies can provide Cecilia with some means of escape. This turns out to be literally true when the pith-helmeted Tom Baxter steps off the black-and-white screen into the drab, but full-colored Jewel theater. He has been watching Cecilia watch him through five showings of *The Purple Rose*, he says, and she has won his heart. His plan is to leave the film, take Cecilia away with him to Egypt, and live happily ever after. Viewers probably anticipate some difficulties on the way to romantic fulfillment, but other films of this sort have preconditioned them to expect that the difficulties can be overcome. If a millionaire and a struggling hoofer from the chorus can find true love, a waitress and a fictional character may do the same. Surely desire must triumph over reason to create such hopes, but the alternative, in which Cecilia returns to her life with Monk, is by this point cinematically unacceptable.

Just in case a love affair between Tom and Cecilia might seem too incredible, Allen ingeniously turns the unlikely romance into a triangle by bringing Gil Shepherd, the actor who played Tom Baxter in *The Purple Rose,* from Hollywood to New Jersey. Gil's mission is to entice his creation back onto the movie screen, but he also seems smitten with the star-struck Cecilia. Allen has Jeff Daniels play these two parts with just enough differentiation to convince willing viewers—as well as Cecilia—that Gil might be a "real" rival to the fictional Tom. Whichever of the two heroes wins Cecilia's hand, he would be a marked improvement over the repulsive Monk. Allen's viewers may therefore still hope for the happy ending that is conventional in this genre.

Allen weighs the two suitors on scales composed entirely of the viewers' previous film experience. When Gil takes Cecilia on a date, they act like Dick Powell and Ruby Keeler—or Peter Lawford and June Allyson—performing two peppy musical numbers in a quaint little shop operated by a twinkly piano-playing, gray-haired lady (Loretta Tupper). Then the two reenact a love scene that Cecilia has memorized from Gil's earlier formula film, *Dancing Doughboys.* Perhaps Cecilia will choose to live happily ever after in Hollywood with Gil. Tom counters by taking Cecilia with him into the black-and-white world of the screen for the night of her life. Dozens of similar scenes echo through Allen's striking night-clubbing montage of the Harlequin Club, the Hot Box, the Club Harlem, and the Latin Quarter, each with appropriate music for dancing. If Cecilia ends up on the silver screen with Tom, the resolution would be equally attractive and equally consistent with the premises of the film and the desires of the viewers.

As things turn out, after raising the prospect of two emotionally satisfying resolutions, Allen denies his viewers both. Cecilia sends Tom back onto the screen, and we learn that he will be destroyed along with all the prints of this film. Having persuaded Cecilia to reject Tom, Gil has abandoned Cecilia and returned to Hollywood. He was only acting after all. Monk is the only man in Cecilia's future, because, as he says, "It aint the movies. It's real life." As Allen's viewers well know, in real life, waitresses from New Jersey more often end up with men like Monk than with Gil Shepherds or Tom Baxters. In deference to the cynical objectivity demanded by contemporary audiences, Allen must allow Monk and the depression to win out over Tom and the Copacabana.

Along the way to this somber conclusion, however, Allen creates a dazzling black-and-white image of perfection to shine on the screen once more and to appeal to the Cecilia lurking inside all experienced film-goers—and film-makers. Consequently, after he has punctured her romantic illusions, Allen closes his film with Cecilia seated once more in the Jewel theater, her pathetic suitcase and ukelele on the seat beside her, as she stares in rapture at Fred and Ginger dancing on the screen in *Top Hat*. The sound track plays, "Heaven, I'm in heaven," and Cecilia begins to smile. As he fades to black over the intimations of this faint smile, Allen affirms the vitality of his medium, romantic film comedy, even in the face of a plot that appears to repudiate it.

By rejecting both the banal happy endings of conventional film comedy and the apparent inconclusiveness beclouding *Stardust Memories*, Allen succeeds in transcending the gap between desire and actuality, popular art and life. Unlike *Stardust Memories*, this film does not serially propose and reject incompatible conclusions. Instead, it suspends the positive and negative, the real and imaginary, in a purely cinematic form of ambiguity. Of course, Cecilia must eventually leave the theater and return to Monk—a happy ending in no one's view. Even this somber reflection does not cancel the earlier positive impression, even for Pauline Kael. Although real life often demands either/or choices, Allen has accorded such equivalent solidity to New Jersey and the silver screen that we can balance the double vision of Cecilia gloomily anticipating her return to Monk and imaginatively dancing with Fred Astaire. In his interview with Caryn James, Allen says about this ending, "The ambiguity may be good luck, something that came from the healthy growth of that film" (27–28). Surely "good luck" can have played a very small part in such a brilliantly conceived and crafted film. On the other hand, "healthy growth" is clearly apparent, especially a growth in Allen's understanding of how popular culture provides the common community of reference and an occasion for self-reference.

WORKS CITED

Barthes, Roland. "Introduction to the Structuralist Analysis of Narratives." In *Image/Music/Text*, translated by Stephen Heath, 79–124. New York: Hill & Wang, 1977.

Croce, Arlene. *The Fred Astaire & Ginger Rogers Book*. New York: Outerbridge, 1972.

Denby, David. Review of *Zelig*. *New York*, 18 July 1983, 51.

Eames, John Douglas. *The MGM Story: The Complete History of Fifty Roaring Years*. New York: Crown, 1975.

Edelman, Rob. Review of *Zelig*. In *Magill's Cinema Annual, 1984*, edited by Frank N. Magill, 473–78. Englewood Cliffs, N.J.: Salem, 1984.

Friedwald, Will, and Jerry Beck. *The Warner Brothers Cartoons*. Metuchen, N.J.: Scarecrow, 1981.

Gehring, Wes D. "Film Comedy." In *Humor in America: A Research Guide to Genres and Topics*, edited by Lawrence E. Mintz, 91–108. Westport, Conn.: Greenwood, 1988.

———. "Parody." In *Handbook of Film Genres*, edited by Wes D. Gehring, 145–65. Westport, Conn.: Greenwood, 1988.

Howe, Irving. *World of Our Fathers*. New York: Harcourt, 1976.

James, Caryn. "Auteur! Auteur!" *The New York Times Magazine*, 19 Jan. 1986, 18+.

Kael, Pauline. Review of *The Purple Rose of Cairo*. *The New Yorker*, 25 Mar. 1985, 104+.

Keneas, Alex. Review of *Zelig*. *Newsday*, 15 July 1983, sec. 2, p. 3.

Mitchell, Richard. Review of *Blazing Saddles*. In *Magill's Survey of Cinema: English Language Films*, edited by Frank N. Magill, 1:184–87. 1st ser. 4 vols. Englewood Cliffs, N.J.: Salem, 1980.

O'Toole, Lawrence. Review of *The Purple Rose of Cairo*. *Macleans*, 11 Mar. 1985: 63.

Prince, Gerald. *A Dictionary of Narratology*. Lincoln: University of Nebraska Press, 1987.

Quart, Leonard. Review of *Zelig*. *Cineaste* 13, no. 2 (1984): 42.

Schickel, Richard. Review of *Zelig*. *Time*, 11 July 1983; 67.

Scholes, Robert. "Narration and Narrativity in Film." *Quarterly Review of Film Studies* 1 (1976): 283–96.

Sennett, Ted. *Your Show of Shows*. New York: Macmillan, 1977.

Smurthwaite, Nick, and Paul Gelder. *Mel Brooks and the Spoof Film*. London: Proteus, 1982.

Sterritt, David. Review of *Zelig*. *Christian Science Monitor*, 21 July 1983, 16.

Yacowar, Maurice. *Loser Take All: The Comic Art of Woody Allen*. New York: Ungar, 1979.

CHAPTER 5    **Jim Henson and Rob Reiner**

Kermit's Dad Meets

Rob Petrie's Son

In his captivating book *Of Muppets and Men*, Christopher French
documents the degree to which Jim Henson, the creator of the Muppets, was creatively formed by television. Henson's first success
came during the mid-fifties on local television in Washington, D.C.,
with a puppet program called *Sam and His Friends*. Next, Henson's
creation Rowlf the Dog appeared regularly on the Jimmy Dean variety show, which was broadcast nationally in the mid-sixties. It was
on the Public Television program *Sesame Street*, beginning in 1970,
however, that Henson and his puppets first attracted substantial
attention from the public. The syndicated *Muppet Show*, beginning
in 1976, was a natural consequence of this TV celebrity, as was *The
Muppet Movie* in 1979. It should be no surprise, then, that *The
Muppet Movie* and its successors, *The Great Muppet Caper* (1981)
and *The Muppets Take Manhattan* (1984), reveal many of the same
forms of self-referentiality apparent in television productions.

First of all, *The Muppet Movie* was written by the two head writers of *The Muppet Show*, Jerry Juhl and Jack Burns, and was produced
by Henson. As on *The Muppet Show*—and on television variety
shows in general—guest stars figure prominently in the film. Significantly, most of these stars also made earlier appearances on the TV
show. These include: Madeline Kahn, James Coburn, Milton Berle,
Edgar Bergen and Charley McCarthy, Bob Hope, and Cloris Leach-
man. Dom De Luise falls into this category also. His role as a Holly-

wood agent lost in the swamp serves as a precipitating factor in the plot, and it confirms the film's self-referentiality by reference to Hollywood as "The Dream Factory" and "The Magic Show," as well as through the character's name, Bernie, probably a veiled allusion to *The Muppet Show*'s principal talent booker, the agent Bernie Brillstein. Another familiar guest star, Steve Martin, probably gets the plummiest comedy spot in the film when he plays an offensive waiter in the style that he brought to a high degree of refinement earlier on *Saturday Night Live*. Finally, Paul Williams was an early guest on the TV show and was earlier engaged in the film project as composer of the musical score, along with Kenny Ascher. Other guest stars in the film, who did not appear on *The Muppet Show*, include television personalities Telly Savalas, Carol Kane, Richard Pryor, and Big Bird, along with film actors Elliott Gould, Orson Welles, and Mel Brooks. If appearances on talk shows can be admitted as television credentials, then these actors too may be seen as TV "celebrities," and thus as prime candidates for guest shots on TV-mediated films.

The self-referential elements in *The Muppet Movie* are not confined to echoes of television, however. Beginning with its very title, this film draws attention to itself primarily as a work of cinema, not television. The film's structure makes this clear. As on the TV show, the film has a framing structure dependent on Statler and Waldorf, the crusty, old, cynical, humanoid Muppets who ridicule the performances of all the others. In the film, these two travel to the art deco movie lot of World Wide Studios in a thirties-style limousine to watch the premiere screening of *The Muppet Movie*. At the studio, they join an audience composed of the cast of the TV show, some of whom do not appear in the feature film-within-a-film. In the previous chapter, we used the term *metadiegetic* to refer to such secondary narratives. We could therefore say here that, at a crucial point in the Muppets' metadiegetic film, the projector supposedly breaks because it has been manhandled by the Swedish Chef, a TV Muppet who does not figure in the metadiegetic film. When this happens, the Muppets interact according to their TV personalities until everything has purportedly been sorted out. The actual film audience then watches the picture on the screen shift from the viewing room back to the metadiegetic film, which at this point involves some nature-documentary footage of the Grand Canyon and other natural wonders of the West. The overall movie concludes back in this same viewing room with the Muppets commenting on the metadiegetic film and praising the performances of the Muppet audience members who appeared in it. Surely, the actual audience is being reminded that the metadiegetic film is only a "movie," an art form, and not real life.

Because of the odd conflation of players and roles that is basic to the Muppet formula, this reminder is hedged around with all sorts of ironic italics. Gonzo and his chicken, Camilla, who are lovers in the metadiegetic film, sit lovingly together in the viewing audience. Floyd and Janice, two members of the Electric Mayhem band, seem as attached to each other in the audience as they are in the metadiegetic film. Miss Piggy is clearly an actress, however, interested in the adulation of fans and the attention of the photographer, rather than in continuing as the eternally loving life partner of Kermit, which she seems to be at the conclusion of the metadiegetic film. Kermit also seems to be more the supervisor that he was on *The Muppet Show* than the rising performer he seems at the conclusion of the metadiegetic film. In other words, Muppet actors are sometimes playing actors and sometimes playing roles. However, since they are always puppets—human beings playing the roles of animals and humanoids—the levels of artificiality are particularly complex. Whatever the case, the actual viewer cannot escape far into *The Muppet Movie* without being reminded of its basic nature as film.

Often the reminders come by way of allusion. The structure of the metadiegetic film, for example, recalls the hundreds of movies in which the hero gradually accumulates a gang, member by member, as in *The Magnificent Seven* and *The Wizard of Oz*. Here, Kermit sets off for Hollywood alone, to be joined successively by Fozzie Bear, the Electric Mayhem band, Gonzo and Camilla, Jack the Monster, Miss Piggy, and Rowlf. The film's stereotypical success story and its unsophisticated love plot surely are intended to provoke similar recollections of formula films, as is Kermit's showdown with Doc Hopper in the main street of a western ghost town. The camera angles from behind and beneath Doc Hopper (Charles Durning) and the amazing reverse angles through Kermit's legs richly echo this film genre during the potential shoot-out scene. Some more specific allusions have a similar, if more pointed, purpose. The white dinner jackets and military uniforms on the customers in James Coburn's oddly Mediterranean El Sleezo Cafe cannot help but remind the initiated film-goer of Rick's Cafe Americaine in *Casablanca*, just as

Miss Piggy's fantasy of running romantically through a meadow in slow motion should call up memories of *Elvira Madigan* (or at least of a shampoo commercial). All of these allusions point in the same self-referential direction. To function with complete success, however, the allusions must depend very heavily on the viewer's prior experience of popular films.

The same might be said of the film's more ostentatious forms of self-referentiality. When Kermit is hurled into Paul Williams's upright piano by a ceiling fan, he turns to the camera and says, "I hope you appreciate that I'm doing all my own stunts." Williams then mugs surprise into the camera. When Elliott Gould is about to announce the winner in the Bogen County beauty pageant, Charley McCarthy says sarcastically to the camera, "You're not gonna believe who the winner is, folks." As usual, Bergen quiets Charley, here by saying, "Come now, Charley, it's their movie!" The winner, unsurprisingly, turns out to be Miss Piggy, but then, it has to be Miss Piggy if the plot is to go forward, and go forward it does.

This is true at an even more crucial point in the plot. At a later stage, it seems impossible that Kermit will get to Hollywood in time for his audition. The station wagon that the gang providentially extracted from Mad Man Mooney (Milton Berle) has finally died, stranding them in the desert with scant hours remaining. Just when all seems lost, the Electric Mayhem arrive in their band bus. Dr. Teeth explains that they read the screenplay that Fozzie left with them earlier in the picture and realized that Kermit needed to be rescued. They have arrived to help him realize his destiny, that is, to help the plot reach the happy ending for which it seems destined.

This ending is one of the most interesting of the self-referential elements in *The Muppet Movie*. After a variety of complications and coincidences that exist only in formula films, Kermit gets to audition for Lou Lord (Orson Welles). Before Kermit can sing a note, Lord realizes his star potential and offers him a contract, fame, and fortune. This ending is assuredly happy, but it is too precipitous to provide the audience complete satisfaction.

When a huge production number starts to build, however, the desired satisfaction seems just around the corner. The premise of the number is that a film about the plot of the metadiegetic film will now be made. The Muppet participants in the metadiegetic film scurry about a sound stage, singing, painting sets, and moving props. It seems that they are to be stagehands as well as actors in a musical reprise of "The Rainbow Connection," the song that Kermit sings to open the metadiegetic film. The set is a symbolic rendering of the plot of the metadiegetic film, with different flats representing different stages in the plot. This effect is reinforced as the Muppet actors allusively repeat lines from the metadiegetic film to one another. In a real sense, this musical number can bring satisfactory closure to Henson's film since it welds all the elements of the metadiegetic film together into a single artistic structure.

The writers then choose to remind us that the story of Kermit's success is only a metadiegetic film, not the whole story of *The Muppet Movie.* Thus, the production number disintegrates into a shambles when Gonzo destroys the newly built set while reenacting an earlier scene in which he ascended into the sky by means of helium balloons. With the disappearance of the set, the anticipated closure also disappears. All is apparently not lost, however, since the Muppets then sing a song with the lyric, "Life's like a movie. Write your own ending," while a rainbow beams down on them through a hole in the roof of the wrecked soundstage. When "THE END" appears on the screen, the actual audience may be willing to accept this slightly more self-referential conclusion as a form of emotionally appropriate closure.

Jack the Monster immediately breaks through this closing title onto the stage of the viewing room in which the Muppet audience is sitting. "THE END" is not the ending after all, and the postfilm activities among the Muppets then ensue. Ultimately, Animal must fill the whole screen to say, "Go home! Go Home! Bye! Bye!" In other words, no conclusion to the metadiegetic film may bring appropriate closure to *The Muppet Movie.* Since this is a film about making and viewing films, it can only be concluded by stopping, by not showing or watching any more—film's equivalent to turning off the TV set and going to bed.

*The Great Muppet Caper* and *The Muppets Take Manhattan* exploit generally the same repertoire of self-reflexive devices employed in *The Muppet Movie.* Guest stars from the Muppets' TV show appear in both films: John Cleese, Peter Ustinov, Liza Minnelli, Brooke Shields, James Coco, and Linda Lavin. Other familiar television performers also play parts of varying prominence: Diana Rigg, Jack Warden, Peter Falk, Dabney Coleman, Joan Rivers, and Art Carney. Christopher French reports in *Of Muppets and Men* that guest appearances on *The Muppet Show* were highly sought after as a result of the program's first-year success. The eagerness of such well-known actors to appear in the three films surely confirms French's judgment and probably accounts for the participation of personalities such as Charles Grodin, Gregory Hines, Vincent Sardi, and Mayor Ed Koch. Again, it is likely that any of these faces might be more familiar to the viewing audience on the basis of their television appearances than from their primary careers, and so their non-television status need not be counted against them.

Since the principal authors of both films, Tom Patchett and Jay Tarses, earlier wrote scripts for television sitcoms such as the *Bob Newhart Show* (1972–78) and the *Tony Randall Show* (1976–78), their use of guest crossovers is perfectly understandable. Their Emmy award in 1972 for a *Carol Burnett Show* script and their creation of the self-referential *Buffalo Bill* TV series, starring Dabney Coleman (1982–83), further testify to their immersion in the traditions of television. Their collaborators on *The Caper*, Jerry Juhl and Jack Rose, previously wrote for *The Muppet Show*. Jim Henson directed *The Caper*, and his right-hand man, Frank Oz, the alter ego of Miss Piggy, directed *Manhattan*. Throughout both films, then, hovers a faint ghost of television.

As in the first Muppet film, there continues to be a great deal of parody and allusion to formula films. For example, *The Muppets Take Manhattan* clearly relies on the audience's knowledge of Hollywood musicals. Since the film's premise is that a group of talented kids want to take their original show to Broadway, the most obvious antecedents are the Mickey Rooney/Judy Garland series made by MGM. The staging of the musical numbers and the costuming, however, recreate a 1930s look that probably derives more immediately from the Dick Powell/Ruby Keeler musicals produced by Warner Brothers. Especially in her first entrance during the musical number "Together Again," Miss Piggy's black-and-white-check costume and her jaunty beret echo the perkier side of Ruby Keeler. The musical formula film is also the inspiration for this film's use of stage space. As in films such as *42nd Street* and *Golddiggers of 1933*, the Muppet musical, *Manhattan Melodies*, involves production numbers supposedly taking place on a proscenium stage but actually depending on enormous spatial sweep, sophisticated overhead photography, and close-ups that would be inaccessible to any theater audience.

Classic movie musicals also shape two key scenes in *The Caper*. In the first, the dance floor of the Dubonnet Supper Club becomes the presumed setting for a Busby-Berkeley-style production number that would actually require a very large soundstage to mount. In the second, a fashion show becomes the occasion for an Esther-Williams-style water ballet. This fashion show also italicizes another convention of the movie musical. When Miss Piggy substitutes for another—human—model to show off a bathing suit, the members of the audience gasp with amazement at her beauty and applaud wildly, despite the fact that Piggy is surrounded by absolutely gorgeous women. Since similarly implausible scenes appear in most formula musical films, the veiled allusion should attract the viewer's attention to the transparency of the convention. Charley McCarthy could appear in another cameo to say, "You'll never guess who will be considered fairest of them all, folks!"

*The Great Muppet Caper* also echoes other formula films in the plot device by which Kermit mistakes Miss Piggy, the receptionist, for Lady Holiday (Diana Rigg), the fabulously wealthy fashion designer. (Perhaps, since Kermit and Fozzie Bear are playing identical twins, any sort of mistaken identity might be forgiven.) As the title stipulates, the film also parodies the "caper" genre, familiar through paperback thrillers such as the Parker series by Richard Stark (actually written by Donald E. Westlake), television programs like *Mission Impossible*, and films like *The Great Escape* and *Topkapi*. Late in the Muppet film, Henson constructs a very impressive segment in which he intercuts a caper masterfully designed by Charles Grodin with a farcical anticaper masterminded by Kermit. Grodin's gang of fashion models carefully tick off the equipment on their list—computer program, stopwatch, detonator, harpoon gun—in shots intercut with Kermit's gang's checklist—whoopie cushion, plastic vomit, peanut butter. The members of Grodin's gang respond with "Check!" to each item; Kermit's report each item as misplaced, broken, lost, or eaten. The effect is highly comic and brilliantly parodic. It is also extremely self-reflexive in placing these scenes within such a familiar film context.

As in *The Muppet Movie*, both of the later films directly call attention to the medium. While climbing the outside of John Cleese's house in *The Caper*, Miss Piggy announces, "Next time they want stunts, they get a double!" In the same film, Diana Rigg makes a very unnatural speech during her first meeting with Miss Piggy. When Piggy asks, "Why are you telling me all that?" Rigg replies, "It's plot exposition. It has to go somewhere." Later, Miss

Piggy throws Peter Ustinov out of his truck into some garbage cans. Oscar the Grouch emerges from one of them. When Ustinov asks, "What are you doing here?" Oscar replies, "A very brief cameo." Ustinov mugs at the camera, "Me too!"

This film resembles the first in being framed self-referentially also. The opening credits roll over a scene of Kermit, Fozzie, and Gonzo in a hot-air balloon. The Muppets read the credits aloud, comment on their length, and ask questions: "Kermit, what does 'B.S.C.' stand for?" The closing credits end on a full-screen Gonzo, who is holding a flash camera. He says to the viewers, "Wait! Hold it right there! Don't go home yet! Say, cheese!" Then a flashbulb erupts, and Gonzo says, "I'll send you each a copy!" The effect of this device is less like switching off the TV than the ending of the first film, but it still suggests a resistance to closure that cannot help but emphasize the artificiality of the entire process.

In *The Muppets Take Manhattan*, some of the more obvious devices are abandoned, and yet self-referentiality significantly colors the film. In *The Caper*, Henson, the director, occasionally makes technical allusions to earlier films, as when he concludes the water ballet sequence with Grodin and Kermit superimposed in the upper corners of the screen, each framed in a heart-shaped shot. Oz, the director of *Manhattan*, concludes his film with the recently married Kermit and Miss Piggy romantically rocking in a crescent-moon swing against an obviously theatrical background, as Judy and Mickey might have done, or Ruby and Dick, or Jeanette and Nelson. Oz also deliberately exploits other cinematic clichés, beginning with the opening sequence in which the credits are projected across familiar aerial photography of Manhattan, which segues into the Westchester countryside, then New England, then a small town, then a campus with the identifying sign "Danhurst College," then a collegiate Gothic building, then a stage, and then Kermit. If it all looks familiar, it should. Also familiar are the Muppets who fill out the wedding scene later in the film. Here, the self-referentiality transcends even that of the viewing room scenes in *The Muppet Movie*, since the cast of this metadiegetic film is augmented not only by the cast of *The Muppet Show* but also by the Muppet regulars on *Sesame Street*: Big Bird, Burt and Ernie, Cookie Monster—the whole gang.

Overall, the series of Muppet movies attests to an advanced degree of self-consciousness on the part of the films' creators. Throughout the series, the writers and directors seem acutely aware that they are making films not TV shows, an awareness often revealed by means of outrageously self-referential jokes. And yet, they seem aware also of their roots in television, most especially of the sense that, as Gerald Mast has shown in his *Film/Cinema/Movie*, television is an equivalizing medium, a process that establishes equality among otherwise disparate forms of experience (100–105). Since it is basic to the Muppet formula that puppet animals and puppet humanoids may interact on an equal footing with one another, with puppet monsters, and with human actors, this form of television awareness seems especially plausible.

This form of TV consciousness is probably responsible also for the assumptions that these film-makers reveal about their audience's mediated experience. The famous guest stars who are sprinkled throughout the series of films can operate effectively only when the viewers recognize them. It is crucial to understand that, in the case of the Muppets' guest stars in particular, this knowledge would be derived primarily from television. In fact, it is through television that a viewer would have learned about the Muppets in the first place. As we have seen, the use of parody and allusion in the Muppet films also presumes that the audience has a sophisticated knowledge of popular cinema history. Ultimately, this familiarity is essential to a full appreciation of the Muppet films. The more the viewers know about the plots, stars, and techniques of old movies, the more likely they are to comprehend the various levels of references made in the Muppet films. Such comprehension is inseparable, furthermore, from the awareness that the Muppet films are simply films, an awareness continually reinforced through techniques of self-referentiality.

The rhetorical community for whom these references are accessible may perhaps be estimated from the statistical data included in the obituary notices that followed Henson's premature death in May 1990. An AP wire story judged that about half of all American children between 3 and 5 sometimes watch *Sesame Street*. Clearly an enormous audience is being acclimated daily to a highly mediated system of reference. Nor are American children the only postulants to the community. Garner's obituary notice claimed, "By the late '70s, *The Muppet Show* was the most popular television program on the globe, with an audience of more than 235 million people in 100 countries" (1D). Surely an immense community accustomed to Henson's kinds of references and self-references must be assumed. In fact, it was most probably Henson's communion with these people and their children that made the Muppets such a colossal success in the first place. Henson produced television programs for people accustomed to watching television, and his films were infused with the same spirit.

As a motion picture director, Rob Reiner was also strongly influenced by television, perhaps even more so than Jim Henson. As in the cases of Mel Brooks and Woody Allen, Sid Caesar constituted a prominent part of this influence. Rob's father, Carl, not only appeared on *Your Show of Shows* as second banana to Caesar but—as David Marc establishes in *Comic Visions: Television and American Culture*—often functioned without screen credit as head writer. When Brooks, Allen, and Neil Simon developed comic ideas for the show, therefore, these were often filtered through Carl Reiner before being pitched to the tyrannical Caesar. Eventually, changing tastes brought about the decline of TV variety shows, and Carl had to discover a new comic outlet. Unsurprisingly, he dreamed up a sitcom about Rob Petrie, head writer of a comedy-variety show starring a tyrannical comedian named Allen Brady. Like Carl Reiner, Rob Petrie wrote in Manhattan but lived in the suburbs with his wife and son. Rob's son was names Ritchie; Carl's son was named Rob. Rob's son disappeared at the end of *The Dick Van Dyke Show,* but Carl's son went on to star on the influential TV sitcom *All in the Family* (1971–79), to make a guest appearance in a *Saturday Night Live* sketch featuring the Killer Bees, and to direct numerous motion pictures, including the highly self-referential *This Is Spinal Tap* and *The Princess Bride.*

*This Is Spinal Tap* (1984) is a highly mediated enterprise in many ways, and intentionally so. First of all, the film is a parody, generally of the documentary-film style and the techniques of cinema verité, and specifically—as Richard Porton observes—of "rockumentaries" such as Martin Scorsese's *The Last Waltz* (1978), an account of the last days of The Band. The film also relies heavily on a cast trained in television, including Christopher Guest, Harry Shearer, and Paul Shaffer from *Saturday Night Live.* Other easily recognizable TV personalities such as Howard Hesseman, Patrick MacNee, Fred Willard, and Ed Begley, Jr., also appear, as do future *SNL* cast members Dana Carvey and Billy Crystal. Television also influences the film in the sense that many of the camera angles and production values are borrowed technically from music videos. Finally, the subject matter of the film—life on the road with a rock band—is a mediated account of a purely mediated experience. Rob Reiner is, of course, completely aware of these resonances, and he draws strength from all of them.

The film immediately establishes its mediated status by opening with medium shots of Director Marty DiBergi, played by Director Reiner, explaining the origins of his fascination with Spinal Tap, a band called by many, "one of England's loudest." In this scene, DiBergi/Reiner's tone of TV "sincerity," so inappropriate to his foolish remarks, inevitably signals to viewers familiar with *SCTV* and *Saturday Night Live* that this will not be a documentary but the parody of a documentary. It is as if Bill Murray were sincerely expressing his deep respect for Frank Sinatra.

As was the case with its televised ancestors, technical accuracy is scrupulously maintained in this filmed parody. During an early sequence, for example, DiBergi interviews some of the band's followers in a voice-over. By intercutting questions and answers so that they sometimes overlap, Reiner creates a gritty form of cinematic "realism," as he does also in many of the scenes set backstage or in hotel rooms on the road. Cinematic realism is also the intended effect of the hand-held camera shots of the band on and off stage, particularly in a brilliant sequence, supposedly set in Cleveland, in which the band members cannot find their way from their dressing rooms to the stage. As the rockers wander through a backstage maze of corridors, the camera shoots them sometimes from the front, sometimes from behind, always with an unsteady air of urgency and dislocation. The scene is wonderfully comic, particularly as the band members stop repeatedly to ask directions from a maintenance worker, played by Wonderful Smith, and yet these very camera shifts signal Reiner's presence behind the scene. If the band were really lost, and DiBergi were really filming them live, his cameraman would be lost too and could not set up to capture the musicians' blind approaches.

The same might be said of the presumed outtakes shown behind the closing credits. Viewers have seen these characters before, sometimes in these same settings, but the questions DiBergi poses have no relation to any previous action. They have obviously been contrived to afford the actors an opportunity for comic improvisation, a fact confirmed when the actors—especially Michael McKean or Christopher Guest—give an unfunny answer and then follow up with something a little funnier. Remember, Reiner keeps saying, this is a comedy, not a documentary.

Reiner's disclaimers may be necessitated by the accuracy of his parody, particularly the portions of the film devoted to parodying rock documentaries. Since Spinal Tap has been operating, with varying membership, for seventeen years, Reiner must simulate historical footage of its earlier avatars. Two pieces are particularly convincing. In the first, the band—then called the Thamesmen—is shown on a black-and-white British television show called *Pop, Look, and Listen.* Dressed like early Beatles or the Dave Clark Five, they perform their first hit, "Gimme Some Money." The band's principal members—David St. Hubbins (Michael McKean), Nigel Tufnel (Christopher Guest), and Derek Smalls (Harry Shearer)—actually look young and innocent in this alleged TV film, not jaded and haggard as they do in the documentary's present. In another piece of historical footage, they appear on the American television show *Jamboreepop* a few years later in full color. Color television vividly reproduces the musicians' flower-power costumes and the two go-go dancers performing The Swim in the background. The revolving image shots in this sequence brilliantly recapture television's efforts in those days to come to terms with psychedelia. The music and lyrics of "Listen to the Flower People" do the same for the midsixties "Mersey Sound." Derek Smalls even mouths "We Love You" into the imaginary TV camera. As a member of his generation, Reiner apparently needed no refresher course to reconstruct this vivid parody. Those with less retentive memories could consult *My Generation* on VH-1, the music video channel aimed at older listeners.

Simulated TV film is only one of the devices by which Reiner elicits his viewers' enormous backlog of television experience. During the opening sequence, for example, DiBergi says that he gave up several lucrative opportunities to direct TV commercials in order to make this film. He had so many offers because of his previous successes: "That little dog that chases the covered wagon underneath the sink? That was mine." Like DiBergi, the actual writers of *This Is Spinal Tap* (Guest, McKean, Shearer, and Reiner) move easily between TV and motion pictures, a fact emphasized both by Richard Porton in *Magill's Cinema Annual, 1985* and by Robert Christgau and Carola Dibbell in their review for *Village Voice.* Reiner's TV credentials have already been established, Guest and Shearer came from *Saturday Night Live,* and McKean was in the original cast of

*Laverne and Shirley,* a show starring Reiner's ex-wife, Penny Marshall. Obviously, these writers know how television works. Perhaps this common TV experience lies behind David St. Hubbins's profound remark in *Spinal Tap:* "It's such a fine line between stupid and clever."

Further evidence of the TV influence follows the closing credits. Like other directors formed by television—Brooks, Allen, and Henson—Reiner is sometimes reluctant to bring traditional cinematic closure to his work. Thus, after milking the alleged outtakes for a few more jokes, Reiner presents a music video of the band's song "Hell Hole." This is followed by a parodic TV advertisement for an album of Spinal Tap hits entitled *Heavy Metal Memories,* "eighteen years of nerve-damaging music." As we might expect after the earlier examples, this piece is flawlessly accurate. As the announcer, Shearer maintains the balance of authority and mania familiar in such promotions; the couple used to dramatize the romantic possibilities of the music are suitably slick and mindless; and the crawling list of song titles is simultaneously stupid and plausible. Especially when viewed on video tape, this joke advertisement is practically indistinguishable from the real thing. Perhaps for this reason, the ad is followed by a running text: "For anyone who thought the preceding Greatest Hits commercial was real, IT WASN'T, The aforementioned record does not exist, Neither does SPINAL TAP." As Christgau and Dibbell point out, the last point is not completely true. The actors did appear on *Saturday Night Live* and a few other TV shows to sing some of their songs, largely as a promotional device for the film. In this respect, "real life" can be used as effectively as parody to satirize the whole issue of merchandising across media boundaries.

The video for "Hell Hole" also draws effectively on the viewers' mediated experience by exploiting many conventional devices of music videos: split screen, bizarre camera angles, slow motion, computer colorization, simulated concert performances, and supposedly wacky dramatizations. The writers have obviously watched their share of MTV, and they assume their viewers have done the same. Earlier performance footage of the band—especially doing their revolting song "Big Bottom"—surely derives from the same experience.

The concert version of "Rock and Roll Creation," though, is probably the most effective demonstration of how thoroughly mediated these writers are. In a style that echoes the most pretentious qualities of a number of rock bands—Yes, Led Zeppelin, Electric Light Orchestra—Spinal Tap performs all the usual concert shtick in an overwrought set that presumably symbolizes the origins of the universe. The chief props are three clear plastic pods from which David, Nigel, and Derek are to emerge, play, and return. However, Derek's pod will not open. Stagehands break out hammers, crow bars, acetylene torches, but nothing works until the number is over. Then Derek bursts forth as the other two reenter their pods. Although the actors carry off the physical humor well enough to entertain the musically naive, the joke is obviously intended primarily for viewers who have suffered through similarly pretentious performances in music videos and at concerts.

In this respect particularly, *This Is Spinal Tap* operates within a highly mediated rhetorical community. The whole idea of parodying rock-and-roll documentaries could occur only to writers who were immersed in film and rock music and confident that an audience existed that was composed of viewers who were similarly immersed. Thus, it becomes possible to sustain a running joke about the cover for the band's new album *Smell the Glove*. Writers and viewers alike must understand the adolescent misogyny animating much heavy-metal music to see the humor in an album cover photo of a naked women on all fours wearing a dog collar and sniffing a glove. When representatives of the label object to this cover as sexist, the same community can appreciate the humor involved in the revised cover, which is totally black in tribute to the Beatles' *White Album*. This joke might also appeal to Joan Didion, who used the same title for her 1979 collection of essays.

The script often expects viewers to draw on considerable mediated experience. For example, Frank Drescher's characterization of Bobbi Fleckman, handler of artists' relations at Polymer records, sends out acutely comic messages, but only to viewers with some previous sense of how the music industry operates. The same might be said of Paul Shaffer's very funny depiction of Artie Fufkin, Polymer's ineffectual promotion man in Chicago. As in the many rock and country songs that exploit the artists' careers as subject matter, communication takes place only when both sides are similarly informed. In *This Is Spinal Tap*, the writers count on such information when the band attempts a dismal a cappella rendition of "Heartbreak Hotel" at the grave of Elvis Presley. In the same way, June Chadwick's character, Jeanine Pettibone, has little significance if viewers do not see parallels between her role in the breakup of Spinal Tap and Linda McCartney's in the demise of the Beatles. In some concert footage, Jeanine even beats a tambourine out of time in Linda's trademark style. In short, *This Is Spinal Tap* is a movie about making movies about rock-and-roll celebrities, written by and for people with enormous quantities of mediated experience.

In *The Princess Bride* (1987), Rob Reiner makes similar assumptions about slightly different elements of this community's experience. Whereas *Spinal Tap* was based on music, Reiner's later film is based on William Goldman's 1973 popular novel, entitled in full: *The Princess Bride, S. Morgenstern's Classic Tale of True Love and High Adventure, The "Good Parts" Version.* In both cases, furthermore, Reiner's original sources have been further mediated through his own and his viewers' experience of film. Reiner's *The Princess Bride* derives as much from swashbuckling films starring Douglas Fairbanks and Errol Flynn as from Goldman's novel, but then, Goldman's novel is heavily influenced by these films also, as his subtitles suggest. Again, an artifact of contemporary popular culture may be seen to operate within a rhetorical community based on a complex layering of mediated experiences.

As in *Spinal Tap*, media hipness is assumed. The film opens with a TV child actor, Fred Savage, in the role of The Grandson, playing a video baseball game while recovering from a cold. Another TV actor, Peter Falk, in the role of The Grandfather, arrives to entertain the boy with a reading of Morgenstern's story of "fencing, fighting, torture, revenge, giants, monsters, chases, escapes, true love, and miracles." If the familiar faces do not alert the viewers to the artificial nature of this enterprise, the narrative menu must.

Other familiar TV personalities surface later. Christopher Guest appears again, this time in the role of the evil Count Rugen. Billy Crystal, who had a small part in *Spinal Tap* as the boss of a troupe of mime waiters, here has a juicy comic role as Miracle Max, a magician whose borsht-belt dialogue features such references as the MLT sandwich, "mutton, lettuce, and tomato, sliced thin, with the fat cut off." His crone, Valerie, is played with equally broad comedy by Carol Kane, familiar to TV audiences from *Taxi*. French wrestler André the Giant plays the role of Fezzik the Giant. In a review for

*Time*, Richard Corliss also comments on the roles of Peter Cook and Mel Smith, whom he plausibly assumes to be familiar through BBC TV imports.

One tonal effect of television on the film is the consistently anachronistic dialogue. As in Mel Brooks's movies, everyone talks like a bicoastal media personality. When Westley, the hero (Cary Elwes), duels with Inigo Montoya (Mandy Patinkin), their badinage seems to conjure up the ghost of James Garner's Maverick. Chris Sarandon's Prince Humperdinck turns down an invitation to watch Count Rugen torture Westley by saying, "I've got my country's 500th anniversary to plan, my wedding to arrange, my wife to murder and Gilder to frame for it. I'm swamped!" Burt Reynolds could hardly do it better.

Naturally, the primary source of mediated references is the history of film. When Princess Buttercup (Robin Wright) jumps from a high window into the arms of Fezzik, she falls in slow motion, as characters do in movies not in life. Real life has little to do with most of the acting in the film either, especially that represented by the starry-eyed lovers, Westley and Buttercup. In his review for *Magill's Cinema Annual, 1988*, Richard Strelitz compliments the film's melodramatic villains, Count Rugen and the dastardly Vizzini (Wallace Shawn), on the same grounds. As Anne Bilson observed in her March 1988 review for *Monthly Film Bulletin*, this ostentatiously broad acting allows Reiner and Goldman, author of the screenplay, to "have their cake *and* eat it" (87). As we have seen in considering *Moonlighting*, such a desire can be fulfilled more frequently in art than in life.

But Reiner does seem to get his just deserts, to succeed in making the kind of film that he keeps claiming to be no longer possible. For example, the outdoor scenery used early in the film to establish the countryside of Florin is breathtakingly real, as are the horrible cliffs Westley must climb in pursuit of the kidnapped Buttercup. The plateau at the top of the cliff, however, is so obviously a soundstage that no child would be fooled, especially a child who had watched much television. And yet, Reiner intends the two settings to function as parts of his film.

Consider as a further example Mark Knopfler's musical score, which is sometimes melodic and stirring—as when Buttercup is kidnapped—and sometimes corny and obvious—as when Buttercup is first introduced as a princess or when Westley's hand finally emerges from the pit of deadly quicksand. Given Knopfler's successful musical career, both as a soloist and as part of Dire Straits, the original and effective music is not surprising. Given Reiner's strong sense of film history, neither is the cornball. It is the kind of music usually written for studio swashbucklers of the 1930s. As Joseph Gelmis wrote in *Newsday* (25 July 1987), the challenge facing Reiner and Goldman was not so much how to make a thriller that would fool the audience but how to maintain a "double vision" on the present film and its historical antecedents. *The Princess Bride* is a film about romantic adventure, but it is also a film about films about romantic adventure.

This intention is apparent in the film's use of narrative dislocations, almost in the style of Woody Allen's *Stardust Memories*. In Reiner's film, the framing narrative, concerning The Grandfather and The Grandson, is filmed in full color and is set in the latter's realistic bedroom. The principal narrative, the metadiegetic film about Westley and Buttercup, is also filmed in full color but set in the fairy-tale world of Florin. Since the two narrative levels have few resemblances beyond color, even rapid cutting of the sort exploited by Allen would do little toward muddying their contrasts. Switches are effected, however, by means of Peter Falk's voice as he supposedly reads Morgenstern's tale aloud. Initially, the viewers glide easily from the sick boy's bedroom into the tale by means of the narrative fade-outs long conventionalized in Hollywood films. When Westley and Buttercup first kiss, however, the viewers are jolted back to the bedroom by Savage's protesting whine, "Is this going to be a kissing book?" When the setting immediately follows the voice back to the bedroom, viewers have their first slight dislocation. Falk threatens to stop reading. Savage agrees to keep listening. The setting returns to Florin, but the kiss has ended, and the adventure can resume.

Here is a great strength of Reiner's film and also of Goldman's novel. In the latter, the narrator often interrupts Morgenstern's narrative to comment on his material or to advise the reader how to respond. Early in the novel, a typical comment on Morgenstern's technique suggests that "maybe it was just the author's way of telling the reader stylistically that 'this isn't real; it never happened'" (42). There is no *maybe* about it in Reiner's case, and yet he still intends to provide his viewers with all the thrills available in adventure films, "to let them have their cake *and* eat it," as Bilson says.

Surely this is the effect of the scene in which Buttercup leaps overboard to escape from her kidnappers, only to find herself surrounded by man-eating "shrieking eels." As an obviously cheap special-effects eel approaches the camera with its jaws agape, Falk's voice says, "She doesn't get eaten by the eels this time," and the scene shifts back to the boy's bedroom. Since no one could believe in such phony eels in the first place, there is no point in Goldman and Reiner's trying to write around them. Why not just raise the suggestion visually and move on to other things? Surely it is a bonus for the viewers to be complimented on the sophistication that would permit them to see through such special effects. It is also a bonus for the film-makers to finesse a problem in this way so as to let the narrative proceed.

Later, more complex sequences operate similarly. When Prince Humperdinck comes out on a balcony to announce that he has married Buttercup, we hear The Grandson's interruption: "You read that wrong. . . . If she didn't marry [Westley], it wouldn't be fair." Back in the bedroom The Grandfather responds, "Who says life is fair? Where is that written," and the scene returns to the balcony. It soon evolves that this scene is part of Buttercup's nightmare, and so the viewers may expect that she probably will marry Westley sooner or later. In the novel, the narrator also breaks in upon this episode to recall how much it disturbed him as a child and to focus the reader's response: "Interruption, and hey, how about giving old Morgenstern credit for a major league fake-out. I mean, didn't you think for a while at least that they really were married? I did" (202). As with the shrieking eels, the story provides the audience with a thrill that need not be absorbed organically into the narrative. In fact, neither episode can be organically absorbed without changing the basic nature of the tale as a romance. Through Falk's speech, however, the film has established a crucial distinction between romance and reality. In a romance, as in a certain sort of film, we may have the world as we would wish it to be. In everyday life, we must accept the only world available to us, the world in which little boys catch colds, grandfathers get old and die, and few people find true love.

Having acknowledged this distinction, the film is then free to ignore it. After Prince Humperdinck has subjected Westley to the fearsome torture machine, for example, Fezzik discovers Westley's body and announces that he is dead. Savage's voice breaks in: "What does Fezzik mean, he's dead? . . . Westley's only faking, right?" Back in the bedroom, The Grandfather says that Westley really is dead and that the Prince has won, a clear recognition of the ways of the world. Back in the pit of despair, however, Inigo Montoya proposes that they bring Westley back to life by purchasing the services of Miracle Max. After considerable comic byplay, Max restores life to Westley—and shape to the romantic adventure.

On other occasions, equally preternatural events are absorbed into the narrative without any interruptions from The Grandson. While searching for Westley, Inigo and Fezzik cannot discover the hidden entrance to the pit of despair. Inigo prays to his father's ghost and discovers the secret through some sort of ESP. After Inigo has been stabbed, apparently to death, by Count Rugen, he brings himself back to life by recalling his vow to revenge his father's death. He grows stronger each time he says, "Hello, my name is Inigo Montoya. You killed my father. Prepare to die!" Eventually, he slays Rugen. Actually, such events are no more real or unreal than the eternal love between Westley and Buttercup, or the country of Florin, or the band called Spinal Tap. Reiner is making movies, not life, and he gives his audience credit for knowing this.

Richard Strelitz concludes his review of *The Princess Bride* by observing, "There is much to be said for a system that allows such films to be made" (288). While applauding this assertion, we might add that the "system" involves not only the economics of Hollywood but also the rhetorical community of reference shared by Reiner, Goldman, and their audience. To be even more accurate, however, we should emphasize the places of Mel Brooks and Woody Allen in this community. Without their mediated experiences, these film-makers would probably languish in the kind of creative paralysis suggested by Ben Jonson's remark, quoted earlier in relation to *Moonlighting:* "A man cannot invent new things after so many" (113). Instead of lamenting their involvement in a contemporary aesthetic problem, which can be traced back at least 350 years, these film-makers transcend it by acknowledging their awareness of what has gone before and by acknowledging their audience's probable awareness of these same sources. By openly espousing self-referentiality, they are able to keep on making movies.

Bilson, Anne. Review of *The Princess Bride*. *Monthly Film Bulletin*, Mar. 1988, 87.

Brown, Les, ed. *The New York Times Encyclopedia of Television*. New York: Times Books, 1977.

Christgau, Robert, and Carola Dibbell. Review of *This Is Spinal Tap*. *Village Voice*, 6 Mar. 1984, 52.

Corliss, Richard. Review of *The Princess Bride*. *Time*, 21 Sept. 1987, 74.

Didion, Joan. *The White Album*. New York: Simon and Schuster, 1979.

Dunne, Michael. "Donald E. Westlake." In *Critical Survey of Mystery and Detective Fiction*, edited by Frank Magill, 1700–1706. Pasadena, Cal.: Salem, 1989.

Finch, Christopher. *Of Muppets and Men: The Making of the Muppet Show.* New York: Knopf, 1981.

Garner, Jack. "Bacteria Infection Fatal to Henson." *The (Nashville) Tennessean*, 17 May 1990, 1D+.

Gelmis, Joseph. Review of *The Princess Bride*. *Newsday*, 25 Sept. 1987: 3, 5.

Goldman, William. *The Princess Bride: S. Morgenstern's Classic Tale of True Love and High Adventure, The "Good Parts" Version*. New York: Harcourt, 1973.

Johnson, Ben. *Timber: or, Discoveries*. In *Criticism: The Major Texts*, edited by Walter Jackson Bate, 112–16, Enlarged ed. New York: Harcourt, 1970.

Marc, David. *Comic Visions: Television Comedy and American Culture*. Boston: Unwin, 1989.

Mast, Gerald. *Film/Cinema/Movie: A Theory of Experience*. New York: Harper, 1977.

Porton, Richard. Review of *This Is Spinal Tap*. In *Magill's Cinema Annual, 1985*, edited by Frank N. Magill, 484–88. Pasadena, Cal.: Salem, 1985.

"'Sesame Street' Creations Are Seen Across the Globe." *The (Nashville) Tennessean*, 17 May 1990, 5D.

Strelitz, Richard. Review of *The Princess Bride*. In *Magill's Cinema Annual, 1988*, edited by Frank N. Magill, 285–88. Pasadena, Cal.: Salem, 1988.

CHAPTER 6 **Rock Music**

Here I Am, up on the Stage

Popular music today clearly has developed out of some aesthetic assumptions institutionalized during the romantic period of the late-eighteenth and nineteenth centuries. Robert Pattison's brilliant critical study, *The Triumph of Vulgarity: Rock Music in the Mirror of Romanticism,* proposes many striking parallels between this earlier cultural period and today's music. As Pattison plausibly explains, the parallels exist because: "For the great mass of Westerners, Romanticism is not an historical past, but a vivid present with all its power experienced fresh. Rock is the living expression of this vulgar Romanticism. In rock the days forecast by Shelley and Whitman have been accomplished. Who would have thought it? The poets really are the unacknowledged legislators of the world" (86).

Because Pattison is more concerned with the effects of a subversive mass culture on traditional society than with the rhetorical operations of self-referential art forms, many of the arguments he pursues are irrelevant to the purposes of this discussion. Highly relevant, though, is Pattison's emphasis on romanticism's consistently postulated equation between speaker and experience. Other critics have proposed such an equation to be characteristically "lyric,"—typical of self-expressive poetry—especially if such poetry has recognizably musical qualities. In other words, highly personal lyric poems are often like highly personal song lyrics. Both are supposedly rooted in the personal experience behind the speaking or singing voice, and both are often highly self-referential.

Even poets writing long before the dawn of romanticism exploited this avenue of self-expression. Before launching into an extended poetic narrative in his *Aeneid*, published in the second decade, B.C., Virgil worked himself into the fabric of his first line: *"arma virumque cano."* In translating the poem into English, C. Day Lewis promoted the self-reference from the third word to the first: "I tell about war and the hero" (13). The story is the main focus in the poem, of course, but the listener or reader is reminded that the poetic story did not write itself. The artist's creative role is advertised through a subtle self-reference.

In avowedly lyric poems, the self-references can become much more pronounced. Shakespeare's Sonnet 65, proposes that his lover may defy the ravages of "sad mortality" only by living on in the speaker's verse: "That in black ink my love may still shine bright" (14). Sonnet 18 makes the same point more immediately, that is to say, more self-referentially:

> Nor shall Death brag thou wand'rest in his shade
> When in eternal lines to time thou grow'st.
> So long as men can breathe or eyes can see,
> So long lives this, and this gives life to thee. (11–14)

The poem clearly identifies itself as a poem through the word *lines*, and the author clearly identifies himself through his arrogant claims toward literary immortality. In terms of how this tradition will manifest itself in late-twentieth-century popular music, however, the key term is *this*. Shakespeare's Sonnet 18 says to its reader, "You are reading this poem right now at this minute," just as self-referential television programs later on say, "You are watching this TV program right now," and self-referential rock lyrics say, "You are listening to me sing right now," perhaps even, "right now up on this stage" or "right now in this very video that you are watching right this second."

Sometimes the lyric of a popular song will signal an artist's presence through a simple self-reference. In James Taylor's "Fire and Rain" (1969), a striking instance of this singer's experiences of "fire and rain" is presented as follows: "Susanne, the plans they made put an end to you." Lost love, emotional confusion, a sense of manipulation by larger forces—all these elements of romantic angst are clearly present in the lyric. However, when the singer continues, "So I went out this morning and I wrote down this song. / I just can't remember who to send it to," the listener is being told that these feelings are being mediated. Since the listener must be aware at some level that the song is probably issuing from a mechanical device, whether at home, in the car, or in a stadium, the disclaimer may be understood as an organic—and prudent—element of the song.

Something similar occurs near the beginning of Randy Newman's "Rednecks" (1974) when the singer announces, "I went to the park and I took some paper along / And that's where I made this song." The cases are only "similar" since the character singing Newman's song is a fictional persona clearly distinct from the composer, unlike Taylor's "Sweet Baby James" character. To dramatize the differences, we need only look at the explanation provided for composing the song. Newman's redneck has been motivated not by lost love but by seeing Lester Maddox interviewed on television by "some smart ass New York Jew." From the singer's perspective, it was unsurprising that this northern liberal laughed at Maddox and that "the audience laughed at Lester Maddox too." By piling the name *Lester Maddox* on top of such tabooed terms as *smart ass* and *New York Jew*, Newman clearly separates himself from the singer on a linguistic level, and this distinction affects even the listener who has had no previous experience of Newman's satiric approach on this album, *Good Old Boys*, or elsewhere. Such a listener must quickly realize that Randy Newman is not speaking in his own person in this song. The lyric also signals subtly that no one else is speaking either, that this is a "song," not a true confession by an actual person.

Newman's self-referential lyric devices are often filtered through his fictional personae. "My Life Is Good" (1983), for another example, focuses on the lavish life-style of a successful musician nicknamed "Rand," but the gross emotional insensitivity depicted in the lyrics obviously belongs to a fictional character and not to the creative composer. Even this character's presence is mediated somewhat when he says that his illegal-alien maid of all work "wrote this song for me." And a fine song it is, full of lush instrumentation and musical variety! The accompanying lyric reinforces this music-business aura by referring to "some young associates of ours" who are making a flying visit to L.A. in order to sample some "real good cocaine." The singer also mentions "some kind of woodblock or something" and "this new guitar we like." The crowning evidence of this speaker's successful life in the music business is his introduction of Mr. Bruce Springsteen as "a very good friend of ours." According to this name-dropper, Springsteen once said to him, "Rand, I'm tired / How would you like to be the Boss for awhile?" A nasty, almost frightening picture of musical celebrity emerges in the song, an effect easily attributable to the satiric bent that caused Newman to write "It's Lonely at the Top," supposedly for Frank Sinatra. The picture is authorized, though, as much by the listener's recognition of the inside references as by Newman's creation of them. This recognition stems, moreover, from the listener's mediated exposure to the business rather than to first-hand experience of cocaine and woodblocks.

One of Billy Joel's earliest successes was also based on a lyric persona who shared some of the composer's musical experiences and yet afforded a measure of distance. According to Bob Shannon and John Javna's fascinating book *Behind the Hits: Inside Stories of Classic Pop and Rock and Roll*, Billy Joel's "Piano Man" (1974) was based on his stint in 1971 as a Los Angeles piano-bar performer billed as "Bill Martin at the keyboards" (155). For this reason, the bartender in the song calls the piano player Bill, not Billy, and the lyric describes Bill's lack of success in the present tense of 1974, not in the past of 1971. Other details straddle the autobiographical lines more ambiguously, avoiding blatant self-identification while creating a distinctly self-referential tone. The singer's descriptions of his sordid working conditions have this effect. His piano is tuned for a tinny, carnival sound, and his microphone always carries the unmistakable odor of beer. The piano man's devotion to his music can transcend these limitations, however. He plays with such feeling that the patrons always tip him generously, amazed that such a talent is performing for a bunch of alcoholic losers. These details sound authentic, and Joel's singing and piano-playing on the recording fit the lyric so appropriately that the listener can only assume some degree of personal experience. Perhaps Billy Joel did not do exactly what the piano-player in the song did, but the listener must accept this recording as in some sense a personal disclosure.

Even less autobiographical discounting is required by Rick Nelson's "Garden Party" (1972). The story of Nelson's rejection by the crowd at Richard Nader's oldies reunion is today fully recounted in Shannon and Javna's *Behind the Hits* (149). At the time of the song's composition, most rock fans would probably have known already that the Madison Square Garden audience wanted to hear nothing but Ricky's earlier hits. Even without the external testimony of rock historians or first-hand recollection, the lyric explicitly states that the fans came to hear "all the old songs" and even refers directly to one of these early hits by mentioning "Mary Lou." According to the lyric, Nelson was willing to accept such nostalgia as perfectly legitimate. He says that the audience were entitled to get what they paid for: "I thought that's why they came." In light of this sweet reasonableness, presented in Nelson's typically laid-back vocal style, the listener feels compelled to sympathize when the singer complains about the fans' refusal to hear any new material. The lyric then economically establishes Nelson's newer country-and-western emphasis by noting that the rejected song was "'bout a honky-tonk," confident that the sympathetic listener will catch the reference without elaboration. As with so much self-referential rock music, the dominant emotion is melancholy, perhaps self-pity, and as is the case with much music of this sort, a texture of specific detail drawn from the music business establishes the listener's position as an understanding insider.

An interesting development of these themes occurs in Starship's "We Built This City" (1985). The lyrics at first seem much less straightforward and consequently less self-referential than the foregoing examples, especially the cryptic line, "Marconi plays the mamba," which puzzled many radio listeners at the time. Decoding becomes easier in the repeated line from the chorus, "We built this city on rock and roll." Any experienced listener can easily establish the autobiographical parallels. The city is San Francisco, and the "building" took place when the music scene flowered during the late 1960s in such places as the Fillmore. This, of course, means that "we" must be understood as, not Starship, but the Jefferson Airplane, of which Starship's lead vocalist, Grace Slick, was the catalyst. As in the case of Don Mclean's much more complex "American Pie" (1971), such an act of interpretation must produce increased involvement on the listener's part, and the elegiac mood—"Don't you remember?"—also establishes a community of memory between performer and listener. Of course, this community is based upon the references to the music business contained in the songs themselves.

In such songs, the listener is allowed, or encouraged, to participate vicariously in the joys and sorrows of the business. The level of participation naturally varies, extending from cursory notation to quite elaborate delineations. Very little specific information is provided in Grand Funk's "American Band" (1973), beyond the fact that the band has been "out on the road for forty days" and has most recently played in Little Rock. Since the song's primary purpose is to glorify the kind of sensual highlife available to anyone with comparable youth, health, and enthusiasm, the self-references to rock music are more or less incidental.

Even in Barry Manilow's hit "I Write the Songs" (1975), there is little elaboration of the details of show business beyond the claim, "I put the words and the melodies together." Again, the lyric can get by on minimal specificity, but probably for different reasons. The composer of "I Write the Songs," Bruce Johnson, told Shannon and Javna (71) that he composed the lyric with Brian Wilson of the Beach Boys in mind, but Wilson was uninterested in recording the song. Since Manilow's image as singer and public figure has always been so different from Wilson's, one might expect the substitution of one performer for the other to create a misfit that would prevent any sort of self-referentiality. However, Manilow was well known to pop music audiences as the composer of numerous hit songs—including a famous commercial for McDonald's—and so it is probable that the lyric came across as autobiography, rather like Billy Joel's references to piano-playing.

A final illustration, chosen from this rich pool, is James Taylor's "Hey Mister That's Me up on the Jukebox" (1971). This title exemplifies the implied but undeveloped self-referentiality present in the lyric. Since the song's overall intention is to create a feeling of bluesy alienation, little more detail is required beyond the mention of "this sad song," for when characterizing the singer as a "lonesome picker," Taylor's emphasis is primarily on the first term, not the second. A listener need have relatively little mediated experience of the popular music business to comprehend the sentimental emotional messages of such songs. Of course, the more closely the listener is willing to identify this message with James Taylor the composer, in addition to James Taylor the performer, the more effectively the self-references may communicate.

This tendency toward pathetic musical autobiography is so universally practiced that it even provided subject matter for more than a week's worth of "Doonesbury" strips by Garry Trudeau. In the series, reprinted in *Doonesbury's Greatest Hits*, rock star Jimmy Thudpucker's efforts to make a significant new album are supposedly frustrated by materialism. Whereas Thudpucker wants to sing songs only about Morris Udall's presidential platform, his producer insists on including at least one "dues song." Thudpucker says, "Listen, I'm sick of songs by rockers who whine about how they had to *suffer* on their way to the top," but the producer reminds him: "It's in your *contract*, Jimmy! One per album!" Probably few experienced listeners would disbelieve this stipulation, except perhaps to question its understatement.

Two songs by Jim Webb fit these requirements particularly well, but in the process they illustrate somewhat different textures of self-referentiality. The first song, "Tunesmith," was recorded by Johnny Rivers on *Rewind* (1967), an album relying heavily on material by Webb and characterized overall by a melancholy tone of self-pity. Because "all [his] friends are gone," the singer is "all alone at the break of day." He has achieved fame only to discover that "there's nothing to it." Thus, when the singer says that he is "married to the road," he might possibly be misapprehended as a successful but alienated traveling salesman. When he goes on to explain his failed romantic life by saying, "I belong to my songs," however, the listener must understand the singer's suffering to be the result of his artistic commitment to the music business, the same business to which Webb and Johnny Rivers were committed. When the singer asks in the chorus, "But who sings a song for the tunesmith," listeners are being invited to extend their sympathies in three directions.

Webb's other song on this subject, "If You See Me Getting Smaller," was recorded in 1977 by Waylon Jennings on his album *Ol Waylon*, another appropriately melancholy setting for Webb's sentiments. The relevant differences between the two songs—aside from the personae of the performers—involve the degree to which Webb allows his self-referentiality to become specific. This singer is also sad and isolated—even the train he travels on is "wet and lonely"— but there is no doubt that the cause of his misery lies in his life as a musician. This is expressed most clearly in a portion of the lyric dealing with the welcoming crowd "standing in the rain" at a train station in Philadelphia. Even though this crowd is composed of the singer's loyal fans, his self-absorption focuses instead on his "borderline career." There may be some mild irony in that phrase, as there may be in the singer's reference to himself as "a madman full of beer." The emotional distance usually attending irony is very slight here, however, especially when filtered through Waylon Jennings's tearful rendition.

Not only is the music business the cause of this singer's suffering, it is also the source of his specific imagery, as when he describes his touring entourage as "a four-piece band and a charter bus." The purpose of such references to the life of a musician is to afford the listener a sense of community with the singer, based on a mutual recognition of specific, albeit commonplace, details. Elsewhere in the lyric, Webb extends a more demanding and more flattering invitation by describing the ups and downs of the singer's career as: "Down, down, and out, brother,/Up! Up! and away!"—the latter an allusion to one of Webb's most successful songs. Song lyrics are often used in this way to deepen the sort of communication that takes place among composer, singer, and audience.

An acute analysis of this transaction appears in "A Listener's Guide to the Rhetoric of Popular Music" (1986), by Robert L. Root, Jr. Like most commentators on rock lyrics, however, Root does not fully recognize the contribution of self-referentiality to this communication process. "Lodi" (1969), a Creedence Clearwater Revival song by John Fogerty, can add further clarification. In a slight switch on the familiar formula, the singer in this song is not weary from the rigors of the road. On the contrary, although he "came into town, a one-night stand," his "plans fell through," and so, seven months later, he's "stuck in Lodi again." Any listener might empathize on the basis of his or her own failed plans, and thus communication between singer and listener is probable.

The lyric determines that the empathy run in only one direction, however, by emphasizing the singer's extreme dissatisfaction with the progress of his musical career: "The man from the magazine said I was on my way. / Somewhere I lost connections, I ran out of songs to play." This failure is more significant and galling, the lyric insists, than the disappointments that might attend some other career. Lest the listeners resent this strong implication of superiority on the singer's part, the lyric solicits their empathy through images that resemble Joel's in "Piano Man." The last chorus begins: "If I only had a dollar for every song I've sung, / Every time I've had to play while people sat there drunk." The second line especially identifies the disadvantages of the music business in terms that cannot be easily converted to the listener's own life. Most of us do not have to ply our trades in front of crowds of drunks. The lyric may thus come as a revelation to the listener who has undoubtedly been a member of such a crowd in the past. The lyric cushions the shock by anticipation, however, by earlier saying about such disappointments, "I guess you know the tune." In this way, the lyric flatters the listeners into complicity by assuming a mutuality of experience before turning toward extreme acts of self-referentiality.

John Cougar Mellencamp's lyrics are similar in often promising an insider's view of the music business. His "Pop Singer" (1989) encourages the listener to recognize ethical distinctions between the careers of the Mellencamp-like singer and those of most other performers. Since the song was accompanied by a cleverly mounted video, these distinctions could be easily drawn. In the video, Mellencamp and his backup singers appear in costumes echoing those worn in most formula videos. By using overly familiar settings and camera shots to film the performers, the video strongly supports the claim that Mellencamp's singer is doing something significantly different from what a "pop singer" does. By exploiting this double-barreled approach, the song could flatter a wide audience on its perceptiveness while still engaging in advanced self-promotion.

A more subtle example is Mellencamp's song "Serious Business" from his album *UH-HUH* (1983). This lyric depicts a minidrama in which a music-business executive offers an inexperienced singer all sorts of sensual blandishments: a swimming pool, food, sex with either gender, even long-distance calls on a "French telephone." The singer, sensing corruption, confesses himself out of his moral depths and seeks to escape, only to be told, "Son / This is serious business / Sex, violence and rock and roll." The song ends with the singer apparently trapped in this silken prison. One effect is an implication that the listeners have penetrated the shell of the music business to the festering vice they have always assumed to lie within. Another is a sense of emotional authenticity. If a member of the music community, a "pop singer," says this is the way things are "out there," then it must be true. A third effect is the listener's involvement in the singer's and song writer's self-referential whining.

The final chorus in particular shows this self-absorption at its worst, as the singer translates his struggles in the music business into a passion play. He invites an unnamed force, perhaps the industry moguls, perhaps the insatiable fans, to "put me on the cross for all to see." Since being seen by as many people as possible is probably the goal of any professional entertainer, this fate might not seem too horrible at first hearing. The singer therefore introduces another New Testament reference to emphasize the bitterness of his suffering: "Let those people throw stones at me." Nothing in the lyric or in Mellencamp's performance of the song suggests a trace of irony in these hyperbolic sentiments. Apparently, Mellencamp is serious.

For a rock persona to get away with comparing himself to Jesus Christ, considerable rhetorical ingenuity is required. In Mellencamp's song—and in most other self-referential musical lyrics—the transaction involves first disarming the listener's normal judgment through flattering implications of shared experience. The more specific the insider references here, the better. Then, when the singer depicts his own suffering in extreme emotional terms, listeners are encouraged to recognize the expression of a shared experience because they clearly "know the tune." Once listeners can be convinced that a self-referential lyric analogically represents their own lives, no emotional statement can be too extreme. Who, after all, sees his own life in terms of understatement?

Like Mellencamp—but for a much longer period—Neil Young has invited listeners inside for a look at what goes on in the business. His 1983 song "Payola Blues," written with Ben Keith and recorded with the Shocking Pinks, solicits the listener's involvement first through use of the tabooed word *payola* in the title and then through dramatized scenes in which the singer successfully bribes disc jockeys to play his music. The song's dedication to Alan Freed and its reference to "a brand new record company / New manager too" contribute further to the listener's sense of a privileged place in the circle of rock music literati. These last details also reveal the heightened form of self-referentiality already familiar from our discussion of Rick Nelson's "Garden Party." Most people listening to this song by Neil Young would already know—or could immediately guess— that he had changed record labels and was working with a new band and pursuing a different musical direction.

Most informed listeners would probably also recognize the accuracy of the song's chorus—"No matter where I go, / I never hear my record on the radio"—since none of Young's records were major popular successes during this stage of his career. Assuredly, there is additional flattery in the implication that the listener is more discerning than the mass audience represented by the disc jockeys. In the light of James Henke's 1988 *Rolling Stone* interview with Young, the lyric later acquired additional layers of self-reference. According to Henke, Young's relations with this "new record company," Geffen, eventually degenerated to a point at which the label sued Young for refusing to make the sort of commercial music that might be played "on the radio" (69). Although rock lyrics often reach great heights of self-referential excess, they are not necessarily without any autobiographical authenticity, it would seem.

Another song, "Prisoners of Rock 'n' Roll," from *Life*, Young's 1987 album recorded with Crazy Horse, involves a similar rhetorical situation, but the communication strategy is more complex. Unlike most of the songs we have considered, there is some hint of humor and self-directed irony in "Prisoners of Rock 'n' Roll." Probably some of the lyric sincerely presents Young's feelings about playing with Crazy Horse: "We don't want to be watered down / Takin' orders from record company clowns." On the other hand, the total context of the song as lyric and performance reveals the title as a comic exaggeration, more suggestive of Randy Newman than of John Cougar Mellencamp. There is probably great truth also in some other lines, especially in light of Young's unhappy relations with Geffen: "We never listen to the record company man. / He'll try to change us and ruin our band." All of this perhaps sincere information is presented in a style of false naivety, however, both lyrically and in terms of the band's stripped-down arrangement. This singer is not a threatened innocent like the singer of Mellencamp's "Serious Business." He is a more sophisticated performer, adopting the persona of a young musician who might actually say, "When we're jammin' in our old garage / The girls come over, and it sure gets hot."

Such a musical character might also conceivably say, "That's why we don't wanna be good." On the other hand, so might Neil Young. In the *Rolling Stone* interview, Henke describes Young as a singer with "a wavering relationship to pitch" (65). Even Young's sincerest partisans would probably agree with this description. Rawness is an attribute not only of the sound created by the band Crazy Horse but also of Young's style as a singer, a fact known both by the composer and his listeners. In "Prisoners of Rock 'n' Roll," Young uses this shared musical secret, along with the other insider references, as a form of rhetorical bonding with his listeners, thereby allowing him to indulge in very advanced self-references without sacrificing communication.

As Young's song reveals, humor is not totally incompatible with self-referentiality. "The Cover of *Rolling Stone*," recorded by Doctor Hook (1972), is an excellent case in point. This lyric establishes a community of insider hipness, partly by referring to rock phenomena such as groupies, but mostly by its title, which even the marginally informed listener would recognize as representing success in the music business. This aura of realism is furthered through emotions that listeners would probably accept as plausible and similar to their own, most especially the brilliant line "Gonna buy five copies for my mother." In consequence of this carefully woven texture of plausibility, the way would probably be open for the lyric to indulge in considerable self-indulgent whining.

A listener enlisted already by these details might lend a sympathetic ear to a singer complaining about such a difficult pursuit. As R. Serge Denisoff points out in *Tarnished Gold*, "Only 17 new artists per year, it is believed, ever record a Top 40 hit, while in the same year 23 persons are statistically likely to be struck dead by lightning" (38). Since *Rolling Stone* publishes twenty-six issues per year, most fans would probably recognize Doctor Hook's odds as comparably and lamentably slim. The song does not plunge into miserable self-indulgence, however. For one thing, the composer, Shel Silverstein, is a fine comic talent. For another, Ray Sawyer sings the lyric with a comic edge that keeps the listener's sympathies at bay. Surely, that is why Sawyer was chosen to sing the song rather than the mellifluous Dennis Locorriere, who sang lead on all of the band's other hits. Finally, as in the case of "Prisoners of Rock 'n' Roll," the boozy, garage-band arrangement refuses to succumb to the more somber implications of the lyric. Though avowedly self-referential, "The Cover of *Rolling Stone*" involves listeners in a shared laugh at the attitudes of some rock performers. Significantly, the same comic devices make clear that the actual artists behind the song are not to be confused with the performers depicted. Any resemblances are "purely coincidental."

This is very much the tone adopted in Joe Walsh's "Life's Been Good" (1978). Walsh's rock star persona is as materially gross as the singer in Randy Newman's "My Life is Good." He has a fabulous mansion that he has never seen, a Maseratti that "does 185," an office with "gold records on the wall." He goes to parties, "sometimes until four." He says about his fans, "They send me letters, tell me I'm great." He is, in short, the stereotypically successful "pop singer."

He is, however, less morally gross than Newman's character. As in traditional dramatic monologues written by poets such as Robert Browning, the singer in Walsh's lyric reveals qualities to the listener that he does not himself recognize. What he reveals is that he is a fool rather than a villain. He tells us, "I live in hotels, tear out the walls. / I have accountants pay for it all." Listeners probably will not identify with the singer upon hearing this, but they probably will not reject a character who seems so confused and inept. In the same vein, the singer cannot enjoy his Maseratti because his license was revoked. He stays so late at parties because "it's hard to leave when you can't find the door." Vices abound in this singer's character— violence, alcoholism, pride—but he seems too naive to exploit his vices and too foolish even to recognize them. This lack of awareness is Walsh's chief stroke of characterization. The singer says uncomprehendingly, "It's tough to handle this fortune and fame. / Everybody's so different; I haven't changed." Perhaps he has not. Perhaps he has always been an oaf, but if so, he has always been an innocent one. Only such an innocent could summarize this bizarre account by saying, "Lucky I'm sane after all I been through." Walsh, on the other hand, is not innocent. On the contrary, as this lyric demonstrates, he is a considerable poetic talent. As a result he may write critically about the business he knows best without obviously directing his listeners' attention to his own experiences. Once again, a slight comic twist allows self-referentiality to function without the stigma of self-indulgence.

Life on the road has probably elicited more self-referential rock songs than any other element of the music business. Some are almost celebratory, in the manner of "We're an American Band" by Grand Funk and the far more detailed "What's Your Name" (1977) by the Lynyrd Skynyrd Band. This lyric, by band members Gary Rossington and Ronnie Vanzant, stresses the freedom from social restraints and conventional responsibilities afforded by a mobile life conducted within a protective shield of money and sensual comfort. The singer is driven to the concert hall in a limo, performs on stage, finds "a little queenie," takes her back to the motel, plies her with champagne, and enjoys a night of sexual indulgence. The next morning, he says goodbye to the groupie, offers to find her a taxi, and says that he hopes to see her again next year when the band passes through Boise, Idaho.

The singer's life is not without minor difficulties. For one thing, an obviously southern singer finds himself in Boise. For another, the police say that the band cannot drink in the motel bar because of a fight between one of the crew and a motel guest. For a third, the singer must rise early and take a bus to the next stop on the tour. On the other hand, Boise turns out to be great fun, the band can drink champagne up in their rooms, and the hard-driving arrangement gives no sign that these musicians on tour feel unappreciated or alienated. Perhaps the "little girl" whose name has slipped the singer's mind might feel exploited, but the singer feels just fine. In fact, he encourages the girl to adopt an attitude of sexual equality like his own: "Shootin' you straight, little girl, / Won't you do the same." He tells her further, "There aint no shame," a point specifically related to sex in the song's dramatic context, but more generally to the life of a touring musician.

Upbeat songs about life on the road are distinctly in the minority, however. More typical is the long monologue with which Jackson Browne introduces his 1978 version of Maurice Williams's perennial favorite, "Stay." The dramatic situation in which Browne will ask the listener, rather than his girl, to "Stay, just a little bit longer" involves a singer addressing the audience at the end of a concert. With just a piano as accompaniment, the singer describes the striking of the concert set by his "roadies." This part of the story is presented persuasively through specific imagery: amps, trusses, "slammin' doors and foldin' chairs," a waiting tour bus. The listener surely must feel privileged to get such a detailed look at a concert from the inside. Immediately exploiting this rhetorical communion, Browne involves the listener in some melancholy reflections about the roadies: "They're the first to come and the last to leave / Working for the minimum wage." The listener can only sympathize with the oppressed roadies and admire Browne for his generous sympathies. This emotional involvement also opens the way for Browne's elaborate self-references. These begin simply enough with the remark that "the sound of slammin' doors and foldin' chairs" is an experience that the usual concert-goer will "never know." Thanks to this lyric, the listener now does know and should feel sorry for the singer who must deal nightly with such melancholy events.

The sounds are not the worst of it, by any means. Soon the band will get on the bus and "drive all night and do the show in Chicago / Or Detroit." The singer cannot remember because, on an extended tour, "These towns all look the same." The listener should not envy the singer, then, for traveling to exciting places and making lots of money. According to this singer, life on the road is nowhere nearly as exciting as the Lynyrd Skynyrd band claims. Actually, "We just pass the time in the hotel rooms and wander around backstage." Having solicited this much sympathy from the listener, the lyric returns to accumulating the specific details that can authorize more. By this time, the song's arrangement has moved beyond the solo piano to include a drum and synthesizer background more consistent with a story about a touring rock group. The imagery establishing the tour bus is also consistent: "eight-tracks and casettes . . . stereo . . . magazines . . . truckers on C.B. . . . Richard Pryor on a video." Such specificity surely leads listeners to believe that this is the way it is on the band bus. The listener is right there, riding tediously along with Jackson Browne and his band, "thinking about the ones we love" and ironically envying dentists and secretaries who can wake up tomorrow morning in their own beds in their own towns.

These suffering artists out on the road are the ones who truly need love and sympathy, and so the lyric sadly appeals to the audience: "People, stay, just a little bit longer." This segue into the Williams oldie is supported by the arrangement's turning toward a more emphatic rock beat, thus suggesting, on one level, that the whole introductory monologue has been only a clever musical ruse, perhaps Jackson Browne's version of Bobby Short. On a more significant level, however, the monologue has been a dead-serious exercise in self-referentiality. Whatever the pretended purpose of the story,, the actual effect has been to summon the listener's sympathy for the successful singer-composer on the basis of his very success. Here is self-referentiality of a very advanced form.

Probably the most fully realized example of the self-referential road song in Bob Seger's "Turn the Page," written in 1972, as he tells the concert audience on his *Live Bullet* album (1976), that is to say, written prior to his national success with *Night Moves* (also 1976). Significantly, Seger continued to perform the song long after the circumstances in which it originated changed for the better. The lyric, as we have come to expect, is filled with specific details, including the "lonesome highway / East of Omaha" and the "echoes from the amplifiers / Ringing in your head." As in other self-referential lyrics, the purpose of such detail is to establish a community of shared experience with the listener. This community is reinforced, as is often the case, through a contrived use of the second-person pronoun *you*. A listener cannot help feeling flattered by an implied pronomial inclusion in the experience of feeling "a million miles away" when standing "out there in the spotlight." The lyric also reminds the listener realistically of how "the sweat rolls out your body / Like the music that you play." Honored by this inclusion, the listener is probably proud to be part of a selfless, generous, sweat-producing act of creation. Perhaps the listener might also feel a little self-pity about having to work so hard, even if vicariously. Surely Seger's doleful rendition and the wailing saxophone in the background of the arrangement would support such feelings.

The most intense act of identification is created earlier in the lyric, however, when the singer, acting as "you," "walk[s] into a restaurant / Strung out from the road," only to encounter stereotyping and hostility from ignorant rednecks who ask, "Is that a woman or a man." Clearly, these people can never be part of "you" since they do not understand—as the listener does—the symbolic importance of Seger's expressively long hair. That Seger is always pictured as heavily bearded further stigmatizes the rednecks' position and easily secures deeper identification from the listener. Who, after all, has never been falsely judged by ignorant outsiders? This identification with the singer-composer as part of an elite of musical originality is brilliantly used to mask the extreme self-promotion of the song overall.

Not only is "Turn the Page" a song by a rock star about being a rock star, it is even rendered in the first person, at least in the frequently repeated chorus that provides the song's title: "There I go, turn the page." This image brilliantly conveys how repetitious life might be "on the road again." As a result, it may enlist even the sympathy of listeners who have truly boring jobs that do not reward them nearly as handsomely as show business can. Perhaps to prevent any resentment on the part of listeners who might fasten on the issue of financial remuneration, the lyric also introduces a slight note of self-mockery: "Here I go playing star again." Use of the word *playing* is probably intended to soften the egotism of the following *star*, but little softening actually takes place. Even if this singer does not see himself as the sort of "star" epitomized by Frank Sinatra—or Neil Diamond, or Chubby Checker—he still finds his personal experience as a performer riveting enough to merit extended presentation to a crowd of strangers. He is at least a "star" in his own mind and consequently, he assumes, of intrinsic interest to others.

Since his listener's submersion in the mediated world of popular music has probably reached a very advanced degree, such assumptions may be valid. Because of the tabloid nature of so much media reportage, the singer may also be correct in assuming the greatest interest to lie in how much he has suffered out on the road. If so, then the opportunities for self-referential popular music may well have ripened to the point at which even John Cougar Mellencamp's vision of rock star as savior may become acceptable. Perhaps we have finally become ready to accept the popular bumper-sticker notion that "Elvis Died for Our Sins."

WORKS CITED

Denisoff, R. Serge. *Tarnished Gold: The Record Industry Revisited.* New Brunswick, N.J.: Transaction, 1986.

Henke, James. Interview with Neil Young, 1988. In *The Rolling Stone Interviews: The 1980s,* 65–72. Introduction by Kurt Loder. New York: St. Martin's, 1989.

Pattison, Robert. *The Triumph of Vulgarity: Rock Music in the Mirror of Romanticism.* New York: Oxford University Press, 1987.

Root, Robert L., Jr. "A Listener's Guide to the Rhetoric of Popular Music." *Journal of Popular Culture* 20, no. 1 (1986): 15–26.

Shakespeare, William. *Sonnets.* Edited by Douglas Bush and Alfred Harbage. The Pelican Shakespeare. Baltimore: Penguin, 1961.

Shannon, Bob, and John Javna. *Behind the Hits: Inside Stories of Classic Pop and Rock and Roll.* New York: Warner, 1986.

Trudeau, G. B. *Doonesbury's Greatest Hits.* New York: Holt, 1978.

Virgil. *The Aeneid.* Translated by C. Day Lewis. New York: Doubleday/Anchor, 1952.

CHAPTER 7 **Country Music**

My Life Would Make

a Damn Good Country Song

The forces that have led to increasing self-referentiality in other popular art forms have also influenced the development of contemporary country music, even if some members and critics of the Nashville music community have denied these influences. Some of this denial is probably based on self-interested image-making. For example, when Ed Benson spoke on behalf of the Country Music Association in a *U.S. News & World Report* article devoted to a sudden increase in the popularity of country music (21 June 1982), he unsurprisingly told Harold Kennedy that "the essence of country music, at its best, lies in its lyric integrity, and that hasn't changed. It still deals with the real experiences of life—love and work, temptation and failure" (55). One might assume, on the basis of Benson's testimony, that country songs do not deal with the life and presumed hard times of music professionals, as rock-and-roll music often does.

Even more disinterested commentators often encourage such assumptions. In an historical essay published in the *South Atlantic Quarterly* (1985), Kent Blazer acknowledges that "Post-World-War-II country music may not be genuine folk culture," but he goes on to claim that "it is almost surely less distant, less manipulated and shaped by external forces and is closer to grass-roots feelings than most cultural media" (25). Careful examination of a wide sampling of country songs shows just the opposite to be the case.

One form of highly mediated expression, perhaps peculiar to country music, consists of songs incorporating references to song writing in their very titles. Willie Nelson's "Sad Songs and Waltzes" from his 1973 album *Shotgun Willie* is a sad song because of Nelson's tearful vocal and the wailing, almost Hawaiian, steel-guitar background, but it is also a sad song because it says it is. The premise behind the lyric is that a singer would like to strike back at his faithless lover by writing a hit song about her betrayal, but he cannot get even because "sad songs and waltzes / Aren't selling this year." The song provides an interesting demonstration of the old rhetorical principle of apophasis, by which an orator establishes a point while claiming not to do so. It also clearly demonstrates that country music can be as self-referential as any other popular medium.

So does "Public Domain" by Bob Livingston. This song, performed by Jerry Jeff Walker on his album *Ridin' High* (1975), is couched in the second person and thus purportedly directed toward the listener. However, its true subject surfaces in the first line of the chorus, "Don't be concerned if the song sounds familiar," and in the last, "It's all just public domain." Surely the object of these references is to establish a connection between traditional western cowboy music, most of it now in the "public domain" in terms of copyright, and the song now being sung. We may not know who wrote "I Ride an Old Paint," but we can easily discover the "Public Domain" was written by a living, working artist. This fact is signaled also by the lyric's reference to financial exploitation by moguls who "promised me points" but failed to provide any "loot."

One more example, "Pick up the Tempo" by Willie Nelson, must suffice to illustrate this mode. In this song from *Phases and Stages* (1974), the lyric draws parallels between the singer's existential style of "living too fast" and his musical style of playing country music up tempo. The two sides of the parallel are obviously of unequal importance to the singer and composer, however. While the existential excesses are briefly handled—"Some people are saying that time will take care of people like me"—the musical side receives much more specific treatment, as when the lyric complains, "The singer ain't singin' / And the drummer's been draggin' too long." Because this song permits considerable self-reflection, again while seeming not to, it is unsurprising that it also appeared on Walker's *Ridin'*

*High* as well as the sound-track album from Nelson's highly self-referential film, *Honeysuckle Rose* (1980).

Many more country songs follow the strategies adopted by their rock siblings in advertising their character within the lyrics rather than in their titles. "All the Gold in California" from the album *Straight Ahead* (1979) by Larry Gatlin warns against unwarranted optimism about West Coast success and thus might seem to the extremely unwary listener to be a type of musical *Grapes of Wrath*. It soon becomes clear, however, that the "gold" refers as much to record sales as to riches. The chorus concludes: "It don't matter at all where you played before/California's a brand new game." As in rock songs like Bob Seger's "Turn the Page," the lyric flatteringly includes the listener in its self-absorption through the pronoun *you*.

This device also operates in a similar song by Gary P. Nunn, "London Homesick Blues," which begins, "When you're down on your luck and you ain't got a buck." The listener is clearly invited to commiserate with the singer in terms of a common experience, the blues. Significantly, these blues have been brought on not by poverty or failed romance but by frustration over an unsatisfactory musical venue. The weather in London is cold, the people are not Texans, and "the only friend I got / Is a smoke and a cheap guitar." As listeners, we are being asked to accept that this is a song about writing songs, not the actual testimony of someone who is truly suffering right now, right in front of us. The song's nature as a performance is reinforced when the singer says that the English are jealous of his boots, "the prize / Some people call 'manly footwear,' " an allusion to Merle Haggard's famous "Okie from Muskogee," which is another cry from the heart.

These assumptions are evident in Nunn's rendition of this song on Walker's album *Viva Terlingua!* (1973). Whenever the lyric mentions Texas, the live audience erupts in clamorous shouts and whistles, as they do during the chorus beginning, "I want to go home with the armadillo." Obviously the audience is responding enthusiastically to a performance, not to a confession. Since this recording was adopted as theme music for *Austin City Limits*, a slickly mounted PBS performance series, it is increasingly difficult to accept claims such as Kent Blazer's that country music is "closer to grass-roots feeling than most cultural media." Probably closer to the truth is what Irving Azoff of MCA told Chet Flippo for an article in *People*

*Weekly* (21 May 1984): "Nashville is just another wing of the music industry" (137).

Another reason to see country music as part of the larger popular entertainment industry lies in the phenomenon of the musical crossover. As Harold Kennedy explains in his *U.S. News* article, Kenny Rogers transformed himself from an over-the-hill pop singer into a fabulously successful country artist without substantially changing his singing persona. Convincing evidence might be gathered from one of Rogers's greatest country hits, "She Believes in Me" (1977), written by Steve Gibb, from the album *The Gambler*. The song's premise is that the singer's dedication to his "little songs" causes him to neglect the woman who waits for him every night, crying softly. This situation is remarkably similar to that described in countless rock songs, including "Beth," a 1976 hit for Kiss on their album *Destroyer*. A country twist may be glimpsed in the fact that the singer created by Gibb-Rogers sees himself primarily as a writer, who must "fumble with a melody or two," rather than as a member of a band, who must stay out till all hours rehearsing for a performance. In any case, this singer is avowedly dedicated to the music business, a commitment that has brought him—even more than the waiting woman—considerable suffering.

The same might be said of the couple depicted in Bob McDill's song "Amanda," performed by Waylon Jennings on his *The Ramblin' Man* album (1975). Amanda's misfortune has been to love this singer instead of becoming "a gentleman's wife." The singer's fate has been to spend his life on the road as a country musician so that "now [he's] over thirty and still wearing jeans." Jennings's vocal, though perhaps not as doleful as Rogers's on "She Believes in Me," definitely solicits the listeners' sympathy for this singer as a suffering artist. McDill's lyric suggests an alternative to this approach—and perhaps an ambivalence concerning the whole issue of self-referentiality—in the lines: "It's a measure of people who don't understand / The pleasures of life in a hillbilly band." As with rock songs, however, the pleasures of the music business are seldom the principal focus of self-referential country songs.

Many striking examples appear in the work of Kris Kristofferson, a doleful composer if there ever was one. Kristofferson's song "The Pilgrim: Chapter 33" (1970), for example, is a major downer when taken simply as the account of a derelict, "wasted on the sidewalk /

in his jacket and his jeans." When the chorus observes that "He's a poet, (he's a picker)," listeners are encouraged to interpret the character's suffering as somehow symbolizing that of the composer/performer. This connection surely must have inspired Willie Nelson in his rendition of the song on *Willie Nelson Sings Kristofferson* (1979) since, as John Morthland maintains in his *Rolling Stone* review (21 February 1980), it is the only animated cut on the whole album (56–57). As in the case of the cross-fertilization between Nelson and Walker mentioned earlier, like spirit calls out to like.

Interaction among talents such as that represented by the Nelson/Kristofferson album often—and understandably—produces self-referential performances, since listeners as well as artists tend to view the operation as an arranged performance. Thus, Willie Nelson has also recorded with Waylon Jennings, Leon Russell, and Merle Haggard, to mention only his more country colleagues. The key examples of this procedure, however, are *Wanted! The Outlaws* (1976), with Willie, Waylon, Jessi Colter, and Tompall Glaser; and *Highwayman* (1985), with Willie, Waylon, Johnny Cash, and Kris Kristofferson. These two albums, jam-packed with self-referential songs, may be understood to constitute the two historical poles of the "outlaw" movement, as I argue in my article "I Fall Upon the Cacti of Life! I Bleed!: Romantic Narcissism in 'Outlaw' Cowboy Music" (1988).

One song on *Highwayman* is especially pertinent to the issues we are here investigating: Johnny Cash's "Committed to Parkview." Coming after many public disclosures concerning the drug- and alcohol-abuse of all four performers on the album, this song about a famous Nashville addiction-withdrawal facility could not avoid autobiographical resonances if it wanted to, especially when rendered in Cash's quavery singing voice. Beyond its probable self-references to Cash and his fellow highwaymen, the song is self-referential simply in its highly specific references to the Nashville country music scene. One patient thinks he is Hank Williams. One is the neglected child of a music superstar. Several are song writers. Everyone seems somehow connected to the industry, both "those who never made it [and] those who did and now are through." Furthermore, all of these people have been so bruised psychologically that, either voluntarily or by force, they have been "committed to Parkview." The lyric dramatizes this condition by describing a typical day in the life of the singer, who is also a patient. It beings at 6:30 in the morning, drags on through breakfast, and peaks when "they give me my injection / And I go back to sleep." Surely Cash's song paints a grim picture, as grim perhaps as any drawn by Kristofferson, but part of the effectiveness just as surely derives from the singer's pretense of sharing with the listener an insider's view of the business.

Much self-referential country music shares this strategy with rock songs such as Billy Joel's "Piano Man" and John Cougar Mellencamp's "Serious Business"—for example, Waylon Jennings's "Are You Sure Hank Done It This Way," from his album *Dreaming My Dreams* (1975). In this song, the singer establishes a tone of insider reference through highly specific images: "rhinestone suits and new, shiny cars," "one-night stands," and the "five-piece band / Lookin' at the back side of me." The rhetorical implication is that the listener is as familiar with these elements of the business as the singer is. For that reason it is needless to supply old Hank's last name or to explain that "speedin' my young life away" refers as much to taking amphetamines as to racing from one one-night stand to the next. Country music listeners may be expected to know, or think they know, that Hank Williams was a notorious substance abuser, just as rock fans are expected to recognize the hints about high living in Mellencamp's song. In both cases the intention is to engage the listeners' sympathies through a flattering supposition of equivalent experience.

Another song by Jennings, "Bob Wills Is Still The King," creates a similar rhetorical compact, although its ingredients are less stark. On *Dreaming My Dreams*, the song is introduced by a monologue in which Jennings says that he wrote it "on a plane between Dallas and Fort Worth," thereby touching off a Texaphile response as ringing as the one Gary P. Nunn elicits with "London Homesick Blues." Here the community is based on the audience's shared enthusiasm for the "music / That we call Western swing," especially as performed by Bob Wills and the Texas Playboys. Without the context of so many other self-referential popular songs, we might consider this reference to be aimed simply at providing the same type of lyric specificity as Austin and the Red River in other lines. On the contrary, details of the latter sort serve merely to supply a realistic context for the references to Wills, the Grand Ol' Opry, and Willie Nelson. This is not a song about place, even though the singer declares that he is "proud to be from Texas." It is rather a song about music, in particular the kind of music produced by Waylon Jennings. That is why the lyric tells us that the singer "grew up on . . . Western swing" even before it declares that "Bob Wills is still the king."

Country songs need not dwell egotistically on the actual composer or performer to exploit the listeners' membership in this musical community. Jimmy Buffett's song "Brand New Country Star," from his self-referentially titled album *Living and Dying in 3/4 Time* (1974), probably draws some autobiographical resonance from Buffett's own frequent crossovers between pop and country music. Because the lyric comically focuses on a character called "he" rather than "I," however, listeners are encouraged to accept the song as a commentary on the business rather than on the performer. The "he" of this song is an especially promising singer because "He can go either country or pop." The listener is assumed to recognize the commercial advantage of such versatility and thus to understand why the character has abandoned the "sequined suit" that "Are You Sure Hank Done It This Way" would lead us to expect. By the same token, although the new star "rides around in a Lincoln Continental," he avoids the stereotype of Jennings's song by having "No steer horns on his car." Buffett's song makes little claim to seriousness or pathos, but it relies just as much on the listeners' familiarity with the country music business as the songs that make such claims.

Travis Tritt's "Put Some Drive in Your Country" from his album *Country Club* (1990) is another self-referential country song that avoids pathos. Tritt's lyric quickly establishes the same sort of community with the audience as the Jennings song about Bob Wills: "Well, I was raised on country classics like Roy Acuff and George Jones." The assumption is that the members of Tritt's audience can quickly call up similar musical memories. Because Tritt comes from a younger generation than Jennings, or even Buffett's new star, his memories also include "Waylon and Ol' Bocephus." Significantly, neither of these singers is identified more fully, in order to increase the listeners' contribution to Tritt's community of reference. The final element needed to confirm this community is a reference to Duane Allman. These musical allusions combine to authorize Tritt's musical self-definition: "I made myself a promise when I was just a kid. / I'd mix Southern rock and country, and that's just what I did." By explaining his musical roots, the singer can both justify his form of music and distinguish it from its antecedents. The song thus becomes its own advertisement.

Tritt's lyric also says that he gets excited whenever he hears "that outlaw stuff on my car radio," thus placing the singer within one of the largest rhetorical communities of contemporary country music and, perhaps, borrowing additional legitimacy thereby. As noted above, the arrival and development of the outlaw movement can be pinpointed historically. In his 1984 article in *People Weekly*, Chet Flippo also identifies some economic consequences: "The drastic change—that is to say, the commercial change [in country music]—began early in 1976 with *Wanted: The Outlaws*. That was the first Nashville album to go platinum" (135). Given the mediated environment in which the American popular entertainment industry flourishes, we might have some reasonable expectations about how this sort of commercial success would affect the self-referentiality of country music, and we would be correct.

When Pete Axthelm arrived early on in Austin to report on the phenomenon for *Newsweek* (12 April 1976), he quoted Jerry Jeff Walker's wife Susan, who was already disturbed about the effects of mediated image-making: "If you need a lot of publicity men to make you look real and crude, then you ain't crude" (79). Her misgivings proved prescient when Willie Nelson appeared on the cover of *Newsweek* (14 August 1978) and when Willie and Ol' Waylon mopped up at the Grammy awards in 1979. Obviously, declaring himself to be an outlaw might be a wise business decision for a country singer, at least in public-relations terms. In 1978, Michael Bane devoted an entire book, *The Outlaws: Revolution in Country Music*, to interviewing these singers and composers and recounting their successful careers as musical nonconformists.

No wonder David Allen Coe wanted to sneak on board the gravy train with songs like his "Willie, Waylon and Me" (1977). Especially in the telling lines, "While in Texas the talk turned to outlaws / Like Willie and Waylon and Me," it is clear that Coe would gladly settle for even a junior partnership in the corporation. How powerful this influence was may be glimpsed in Alanna Nash's profile of Lacy J. Dalton for *Stereo Review* (November 1980). Although Dalton did not record with Willie or Waylon or write songs about them, she still feels the mediated power of the concept: "They like to play up the idea that I'm an outlaw, that I'm hard and tough. . . . But I'm not" (68). Even after the *Highwayman* album (1985) was appearing in the cut-out barrels in record stores, the term continued to maintain its significance, as in Jay Cocks's article for *Time* (25 July 1988) on the new wave in country music: "All those outlaws of the past decade, those rebels against the deep-shag song-writing of mainstream Nashville, have become the '8os Establishment" (69). For a country musician to pose as an outlaw, then, constitutes a self-referential statement about the music business; it is not a historical statement about the West.

One of the most successful songs of the outlaws, Ed and Patsy Bruce's "Mamas Don't Let Your Babies Grow up to Be Cowboys" from the album *Waylon & Willie* (1978), clearly establishes this distinction. The lyric of this frequently recorded song recounts the unhappiness of an unconventional male who prefers freedom to commitment because "he's just different." Little in the song substantiates that he is a cowboy beyond his costume—"Lone Star belt buckles and old faded Levis"—and the fact that sooner or later "he'll probably just ride away." More significant is an inclination to present his lover with "a song [rather] than diamonds or gold." Clearly this preference has little to do with breaking horses or herding cattle—or rustling or gunfighting.

This outlaw is neither a cowboy nor a criminal, as is evident in a crucial line in the chorus: "Don't let 'em pick guitars and drive them old trucks." Probably modern cowboys would use trucks rather than horses for transportation, but so would good old boys in general; the only cowboys habitually to sing and play guitars were the ones in the entertainment business. This is the testimony of a real cowboy, "Jack" Thorp, in his collection *Songs of the Cowboys:* "I never did hear a cowboy with a real good voice; if he had one to start with, he lost it bawling at cattle, or sleeping in the open, or tellin' the judge he didn't steal that horse" (16). The pretense to authentic western experience in the Bruces' song is slight. They know, and Willie and Waylon know, and the listeners know, that this is a song about the trials of a life in country music.

Another document in this musical history is "My Heroes Have Always Been Cowboys" by Sharon Vaughn, sung by Waylon Jennings on *Wanted! The Outlaws.* As in the case of "Mamas," the lyric devotes little attention to specific details of western outlaw life, the only likely exceptions being: "high-ridin' heroes" and "old worn-out saddles." In another parallel to "Mamas," the Vaughn / Jennings drifter is likely to forsake his lover "with the words of a sad country song." He may be a country singer, but he surely is a composer since he laments that by "pickin' up hookers instead of my pen/I let the words of my youth fade away." As is usually the case in country music, melancholy is the predominant tone, but its source here should be recognized as the difficulties of the music business rather than the rigors of cowboy life or the disappointments of love.

These factors are developed even further in "Cowboy" Jack Clement's song "Let's All Help the Cowboys (Sing the Blues)," from Jennings's *Dreaming My Dreams.* This song makes no gesture toward the West other than through the word *cowboy.* The musical dimension is paramount in the title and in lines such as: "He plays the mandolin and other things" and "But she has ears to hear a different tune." Even leaving aside the western issue, the song barely concerns the lost love suggested in the latter example. When he is alone, this cowboy does not cry; he "takes his lonely pen in hand." Perhaps his romantic failures are not so disappointing after all, since they provide material for new songs: "Cowboys have to fall in love, get hurt, and all that bit / Let their hearts hang out so they can write you all a hit." We need not question the emotional quality of this song. The singer is probably begging for the listeners' sympathy as much as he might be if he were the victim of a cheating heart. However, this appeal is justified on the basis not of his ethical integrity as a lover but of his commitment to his art.

Furthermore, in asking cowboys to "sing the blues," the lyric mixes two modes of experience, the western and the urban. In linking cowboys to the contemporary phrases "all that bit" and "hearts hang out," it anachronistically mixes two historical periods. Only in the world of popular entertainment, the world in which Nashville producers and music entrepreneurs may be called "cowboy," can all these elements operate on an equivalent plane of reference. As Patrick Carr suggests in his article on Clement for *Country Music* (November 1974), the falsity of the general milieu can probably be understood to excuse any minor breaches of historical or cultural decorum.

This larger world of mediation is responsible for another immensely popular sample of outlaw music, "Luckenbach, Texas (Back to the Basics of Love)," by Chips Moman and Bobby Emmons, from *Ol' Waylon* (1977). Like the equally successful "Mamas," this song was intended as a duet for Waylon and Willie. Since the chorus begins, "Let's go to Luckenbach, Texas, with Willie and Waylon and the boys," self-referentiality is manifest.

In addition to these references to the intended performers, the song also locates itself in the wider world of country music by mentioning, "Hank Williams' pain songs, Newbury's train songs, and 'Blue Eyes Crying in the Rain.'" As with the songs by Jennings and Travis Tritt mentioned earlier, the failure to identify Newbury more fully or to explain the presence of another hit song's title contribute toward drawing the listeners more securely into the community of insiders. It is implied that they all know who Mickey Newbury is and why he might qualify to be a fellow traveler of the outlaws. They also may be expected to recognize the title of Willie's first big crossover hit, from *Red Headed Stranger* (1975). They may even recognize Luckenbach, Texas, as the scene of Jerry Jeff Walker's album *Viva Terlingua!* and the occasion for his maudlin testimonial to Hondo Crouch, Luckenbach's leading citizen, on *A Man Must Carry On* (1977). In any case, the listeners will understand that the song has nothing to do with actual cowboys but rather with those who would prepare for a trip to Texas by going out to "buy some boots and faded jeans." That "faded" surely raises the whole issue of pretense to a new level!

The last document in this history should be the appropriately titled "The Last Cowboy Song" by Ed Bruce and R. Peterson. This lyric avoids explicit identification with the outlaw movement until the last lines. Until that point, the lyric expresses self-referentiality only in its title and in its observation, "The voices sound sad as they're singing along." Otherwise, the song is a narrative about a cowboy in spirit who was born too late and is thus condemned to "clerk in a market / On weekends, selling tobacco and beer." The lyric calls up in contrast the days of Wyatt Earp "when fences weren't there" and when this character could have lived the life of a real cowboy. The authenticity of this vision may be called into question by the lyric's references to mediated interpretations of the West by Frederick Remington and Louis Lamour, but the cowboy in question—true or false—is assuredly not a member of the Grand Ol' Opry or the Austin music scene. The song's closest connection to the others that we have been examining occurs at the end, in a context surely demanded by its inclusion in the *Highwayman* album: "Me and Johnny and Waylon and Kris sing about him / And wish to God we could have ridden his trail."

In its specific identification of the performers, this lyric points toward another distinct form of self-referentiality in country music.

Most American popular music entails the listeners' familiarity with its performers. In the absence of this awareness, listeners are condemned to some form of elevator music. At a minimum, the quest for information about performers necessitates the disc jockey's list of names following "thirty minutes of uninterrupted music that *you* want to hear." In more elaborate forms, this curiosity is satisfied through the mixture of musical and personal details found in *Rolling Stone* interviews, *Entertainment Tonight*, and MTV *Music News*. In other words, the ingrained habit of associating performers with songs can be tied for better or worse to the mediated cults of musical stardom.

In country music these industry-wide trends seem to become exaggerated. Reporting on the twelfth annual Nashville Fan Fair for *People Weekly* (27 June 1983), Dolly Carlisle observes that "when it comes to star worship, nobody does it better than country music fans" (103). Her impression is based largely on the existence of fan clubs for country singers, which are composed of adult—often middle-aged—listeners. Carlisle plausibly sees this as a "unique symbiotic relationship binding country music folk and their followers." As supporting evidence, she quotes the testimony of singer Lee Greenwood: "Country music fans want a chance to touch and have a personal relationship with their favorite artist" (104). The uniqueness lies in the fact that such desires can easily be satisfied through events such as Fan Fair and through the traditional willingness of country musicians to talk to fans and sign autographs. The contrast with the Rolling Stones' experience at Altamont seems pertinent and definitive. As a consequence of this symbiosis, country songs often presuppose a degree of personal intimacy with listeners that is rare or nonexistent elsewhere in the entertainment industry (perhaps with the exception of talk shows).

Country music often shares with the talk shows an inclination toward personal revelation, especially of the shameful or scandalous variety. Merle Haggard's "Reasons to Quit" from *Poncho & Lefty* (1982), his duet album with Willie Nelson, is a cardinal example. By assuming a dual persona, the lyric can include both Merle and Willie in confessions such as "We keep smokin'. We keep drinkin'," and such boasts as, "Laughin' at the price tag that we pay." Perhaps any two singers—Randy Travis and George Strait, for example—might sing these lines with equal authority, but the middle-aged Nelson and Haggard are clearly the antecedents when the lyric says, "We keep roarin' down the fast lane / Like two young men feeling no pain."

Self-referentiality enters the song also through references to heavy drinking. A lively account of Haggard's roistering habits can be found in Bryan Di Salvatore's unprecedented *New Yorker* profile, "Ornery" (12 February 1990). Willie Nelson's credentials as a hard drinker appear in many places but most amusingly in the remark quoted in the 1978 *Newsweek* cover story by Pete Axthelm: "I don't know why I drink so much tequila. . . . It sure makes me drunk as hell. Come to think of it, that's why I drink it" (55). In other words, both men's reputations as heavyweight boozers should be assumed as parts of their professional personae, almost as well known to fans as song titles or characteristic costumes. Thus, when Haggard says, "I need to be sober. / I need to write some songs that will rhyme," he may refer to himself and to Willie too.

The self-promoting mixture of confession and bragging evident in "Reasons to Quit" surfaces in many other country songs. A recent example is Steve Earle's "The Other Kind" from his album *The Hard Way* (1990). Earle's carefully developed persona as a country rocker serves to authorize his description of himself as unconventional. Although "There are those who break and bend," presumably by producing records according to country or rock formulas, Earle's singer is proud to say, "I'm the other kind." This independence has its drawbacks, rendered in this song as an inability to carry on a lasting love affair, but these problems are adequately compensated by the singer's artistic integrity.

While Earle's self-promotion comes across largely through implication, David Allen Coe's "Longhaired Redneck," from his album of the same name (1976), takes a more direct route. Beginning with the first line, the singer brags about his outcast state: "Country DJ's know that I'm an outlaw. / They'd never come to see me in this dive." In these lines, Coe claims association with the more famous outlaws, compliments his listeners on having greater discernment than the industry professionals, and reinforces his persona as a marginal figure in the Nashville music scene. These rhetorical intentions operate throughout the song. At one point, the singer brags that "Johnny Cash helped get me out of prison," simultaneously referring to a criminal past presumably already known to the listeners and tagging along on Cash's more famous coattails. This criminal reputation has long formed a crucial part of Coe's persona, as Larry L. King reported in *Esquire* as long ago as 1976. In "Long-haired Redneck" Coe uses his tough-guy image to threaten a dissatisfied member of his barroom audience, thus providing listeners another opportunity to join Coe in a sense of shared musical values. It would surely be possible for Coe or Earle to write songs about the rigors of the music business in general, but the more intimate community of country music encourages a form of self-referentiality much closer to actual, or perhaps mediated, self-exposure.

Nowhere is this clearer than in the career of Hank Williams, Jr. As Williams observes in his song "Family Tradition," members of the country music industry have traditionally claimed that they belong to "a real close family." For the performer that people in Nashville call "Hank, Jr.," the claim is literally true since his father's name still carries iconic significance in country music. As we have seen, songs such as Waylon Jennings's "Are You Sure Hank Done It This Way" can borrow rich antecedents musically by referring to the songs of Hank Williams and autobiographically by alluding to his hard-rolling style of living. If this is so for singers who share with Hank Williams only their professional allegiance to Music City, U.S.A., imagine how powerful the appeal must be to a man caught in what Hank, Jr.'s song calls, "my unique position."

Throughout his career Hank, Jr., has relied on his musical patrimony and exploited its well-known symbolism to create his own self-references. As a singer and instrumentalist, Williams is probably superior in every way to David Allen Coe, and yet they have followed similar strategies in their songs, both in referring to more established country stars and in trading self-referentially on their own—often over-dramatized—life experiences. This is especially clear on *Hank Williams, Jr.'s Greatest Hits* (1982), an album containing nine songs written by Hank, Jr.—including "Family Tradition," "Women I've Never Had," and "All My Rowdy Friends (Have Settled Down)"—and one, "Kaw-Liga," written by his father. As his willingness to record a (very effective) rendition of "Kaw-Liga" testifies, Hank, Jr., is in no hurry to sever himself from this "family tradition," despite occasional laments about the burdens of his famous name.

In "Women I've Never Had," for example, the singer justifies his unconventional behavior by saying, "I was just born the son of a singer of songs," a rationalization that might have come from any of the "outlaws," except for the phrase "the son of." The same might be observed about the entire song "Family Tradition," whose references to drinking and smoking dope could easily have been written by Willie Nelson or Jerry Jeff Walker. Nelson or Walker might also be the object of the question, "Why must you live out the songs that you wrote?" However, when Hank Williams, Jr., sings the line "I am very proud of my daddy's name," the familial piety usual in country music takes on a peculiarly inside musical resonance.

Hank, Jr., also engages in the more familiar sorts of autobiographical references used by performers with less famous musical ancestors. In "Family Tradition," he refers to the 1973 automobile accident that almost took his life and brought about the dark glasses and beard that became part of his professional persona. In "All My Rowdy Friends," he truthfully acknowledges that he has seen his name in newspaper headlines not only in connection with his accident but with other, rather scandalous shenanigans. The subject of this song is the inevitable slowing down that comes to male roisterers with the beginnings of middle age: earlier bedtimes, more nights at home, more trouble coping with hangovers. Unlike many listeners in the same age group, however, Hank, Jr., is sharing these sobering experiences with George Jones, Waylon Jennings, Johnny Cash, and Kris Kristofferson, rather than with the boys at the office or at the City Cafe. Since the earlier excesses of these famous performers have been so thoroughly reported by newspapers, television, and fan magazines, celebrity actually becomes a source of intimacy, and Williams's listeners can be expected to enter vicariously into the personal situation described in the song.

As in many other songs of this kind, especially those written by Willie Nelson, the listeners' vicarious participation will be rewarded with a sense of insider hipness. George Jones and Johnny Cash are fully named in Williams's lyric, but listeners may be trusted to recognize the couple named Waylon and Jessi and the movie star named Kris without any further identification. As privileged insiders, the listeners can then also be trusted to share Hank, Jr.'s private experience, to lament the passing of his youthful highlife, perhaps to wish they could offer their own companionship—male or female—for a night on the town. In this respect, the "real close family" embraces friends as well as relatives.

The songs of Willie Nelson provide especially vivid illustrations of how this family-community functions. Nelson early established himself as spokesman for the outlaws, granting interviews and recording duet albums. He also created an annual Fourth-of-July picnic and music festival in his own name. Perhaps even more pertinently, Nelson starred in two films that offered thinly disguised fictionalizations of his own life: *Honeysuckle Rose* (1980) and *Songwriter* (1984). Most relevant of all, however, are the many songs written by Willie, sung by Willie, about Willie. A simple case is "Shotgun Willie" from the album of the same name (1973). The subject of the song is the difficulty of making a record, the supporting cast are the musicians usually called Willie's "family," and the second word of the lyric is *Willie*. The listeners are told that "you can't make a record / If you ain't got nothing to say," and their mediated experience very likely leads them to agree, but, of course, Willie does have something to say, as this song demonstrates. The significant development is that the listeners have helped him to say it, by agreeing to be parts of his self-referential community or "family."

Other songs call for more active audience participation. "Me and Paul" from *Yesterday's Wine* (1971) requires the listeners to supply the last name of Nelson's long-time drummer, English, to fill out the title. Although this is a slightly harder assignment than supplying "Williams" in the many songs referring to "Hank," Nelson's fans would surely be able to do so. They would also be able to recognize Kitty Wells and Charley Pride, the other members of the "package show in Buffalo" at which Willie and Paul "drank a lot of whiskey." As a reward for filling in these blanks, the listeners can vicariously experience the musical career of their idol: the heartache of being unappreciated in Nashville, the frustration of waiting backstage during a long show, the disappointment of performing in a place that "ain't geared for me and Paul." In one sense, the rhetorical strategy of this song is not very different from that of Billy Joel's "Piano Man" or Jackson Browne's "Stay." The listeners are given an inside look at the singer's experience as compensation for allowing the singer to indulge in self-pity. In another sense, Nelson's lyric presupposes listeners who are much more deeply informed about the performer and much more engaged in his life.

The same may be said more emphatically about "Devil in a Sleepin' Bag" from *Shotgun Willie*. Whereas a careful reader of liner notes might discover that Paul's last name is English, no assistance is provided the listener who does not recognize that "Devil" is Paul's nickname. I would not know so myself if I had not read it in Michael Bane's *The Outlaws: Revolution in Country Music* (142). The knowledge is very helpful, however, in putting the lyric's narrative into context. The "we [who] were headed home to Austin" are Willie's band, and "Connie and the kids" are Willie's biological family (at that time), not his musical associates. As in "Me and Paul," such knowledge brings the listeners the right to share Willie's experiences on the road. Most of these might be familiar from many other songs. The tedium of traveling on a bus, for example, might be gathered from Bob Seger or Jackson Browne. Neither of those performers—or their rock contemporaries—would be likely to write another part of this lyric: "I just got back from New York City. / Kris and Rita done it all." Again the last names are taken for granted, as is the sense of musical community. Just as TV viewers would need no last names to recognize Lucy and Desi or Ozzie and Harriet, so Nelson's fans do not need to hear "Kristofferson and Coolidge" to feel their "unique symbiotic relationship" to Willie.

Though to a lesser degree than Willie Nelson, Waylon Jennings has also engaged in this species of self-referentiality. By associating himself with Nelson on record and by authorizing Willie to speak for "Me and ol' Waylon" at the 1979 Grammy Awards, Jennings showed himself fully conscious of the outlaw movement's mediated character. Thus, in "Bob Wills Is Still the King," Jennings reminds his listeners that Texas is the home of Willie Nelson as well as of western swing. With this fact established, he may affirm that Willie would "be the first to tell you / Bob Wills is still the king." Aside from assuming that the listeners will accept the excellence of Texas swing, this lyric also assumes that the listeners will accept Waylon's authority to speak on behalf of his friend and associate, Willie Nelson. Surely this is a fair assumption, as the Grammies showed its converse to be. The point to be made is that this assumption can be used to authorize advanced degrees of self-referentiality. Two songs from Jennings's *"I've Always Been Crazy* (1978) demonstrate this point vividly.

In "A Long Time Ago," the singer begins: "I don't look the way the average cowboy singer looks." Although this could be said about many performers, it could certainly be said about the long-haired, bearded Waylon of 1978. The next line also might apply more broadly but, in light of what Jennings's fans had surely read and heard about him, probably points to the composer/singer himself: "I'll admit I've taken things I never should have took."

When he sings, "Don't ask me who I gave my seat to on that plane," however, the case is closed. This can be no one but Waylon who, on "the day the music died" in 1959, gave up his seat on the doomed airplane to the Big Bopper. The lyric assumes this to be common knowledge among Waylon's fans, since "I told you that a long time ago." Even if the listeners did not happen to hear Waylon's first-hand testimony, "You can read a different story in a lot of different books." The lyric is accurate in this respect. One useful account is "Waylon Jennings' 'The Last Tour': A New Journalism Approach" by R. Serge Denisoff in *Journal of Popular Culture* (1980). That the lyric takes this advanced mediation for granted is highly significant. Jennings as composer accepts that his professional life lies in the "public domain" and that it is equally available to him and his listeners. He can elliptically say, "Me and old Willie, lordy, we been sold and bought. / I guess y'all heard about some kind of system that we fought," and presume that the listeners will fully understand the self-reference.

Similar autobiographical assumptions operate in "Don't You Think This Outlaw Bit's Done Got Out of Hand," an account of Jennings's August 1977 arrest for narcotics possession. It is clear from the outset that this is a self-referential performance. Having said that he supports the police, the singer announces, "This song's about the night they spent protectin' you from me." A hint of humor, even self-mocking humor, comes through here and will continue to color the song, as when the singer asks, "Was it singin' through my nose that got me busted by the man?" The lyric goes on to fill in specific details of the arrest: "The cars pull up. The boys got out, and the room filled up with law." The lyric also reiterates Jennings's claim of innocence, already familiar to devoted readers: "They got me for possession of something that was gone."

Mostly, as can be guessed from the title, the song wryly anatomizes the mediated celebrity inseparable from the outlaw movement: "Someone called us outlaws in some old magazine. / New York sent a posse down like I ain't never seen." The singer apparently feels that this media attention was excessive. On the other hand, Jennings expresses this feeling in a song that he intends to copyright and record for a major record company. He furthermore addresses this song to a highly involved community of listeners who already know most of the facts of his arrest, due in large part to the activities of the posse of journalists from New York. A considerable degree of self-referentiality seems to be ultimately inseparable from a career in country music.

Like their rock analogs, country songs sometimes focus on the performing aspects of the music business: nights on the road, unsympathetic fans, bad financial deals made in pursuit of success. The self-referentiality in country music often differs, however, in focusing on song writing rather than on performing. To mention only a few examples, Willie Nelson's "Sad Songs and Waltzes," Bob Livingston's "Public Domain," and Steve Gibb's "She Believes in Me" look at the country music business primarily from the perspective of a struggling composer. Just as rock music entices the listeners into a community of shared value by stimulating a fantasy of rock stardom, so country songs often proffer the equally alluring fantasy of writing a hit song. When Tom Cruise's character, Joel Goodsen, dances before his mirror in *Risky Business* (1983) while lip-synching Bob Seger's "Old Time Rock & Roll," he acts out a fundamental dimension of contemporary rock consumerism. The comparable experience for a country music fan must be vicarious participation in a singer/composer's struggle to fulfill Jack Clement's imperative to "write you all a hit."

As in so many other cases, Jerry Lee Lewis may be used to supply the climactic illustration. In a typically self-referential performance on his album *Odd Man In* (1976), Lewis begins by reminding his listeners of what they probably know already: "Well, I've took enough pills for the whole damn town." With a characteristic substitution of his whole name for the expected pronoun in Donnie Fritts's lyric, the singer continues, "Jerry Lee Lewis has drank enough whiskey to lift any ship off of the ground." After recounting several other Gargantuan excesses and insisting that he has turned over a virtuous new leaf, the singer concludes: "My life would make a damn good country song."

This line, which supplies both the title and chorus for this song, surely would cause experienced listeners to nod in agreement. In fact, Jerry Lee's life has made a number of damn good books, including *Jerry Lee Lewis: The Killer's Story* by Tania A. Lefebvre, *Hellfire: The Jerry Lee Lewis Story* by Nick Tosches, and *Great Balls of Fire: The Uncensored Story of Jerry Lee Lewis* by Myra Lewis and Murray

Silver, not to mention a recent movie starring Dennis Quaid, *Great Balls of Fire* (1990). Perhaps songs such as "My Life Would Make a Damn Good Country Song" lead listeners to think the same about themselves, and perhaps this is the key to the community of self-referentiality sustaining contemporary country music.

## WORKS CITED

Axthelm, Pete. "Songs of Outlaw Country." *Newsweek,* 12 Apr. 1976, 79.

———. "Willie Nelson: King of Country Music." *Newsweek,* 14 Aug. 1978, 52+.

Bane, Michael. *The Outlaws: Revolution in Country Music.* New York: Doubleday/Dolphin, 1978.

Blazer, Kent. "Pictures from Life's Other Side: Hank Williams, Country Music, and Popular Culture in America." *South Atlantic Quarterly* 84 (1985): 12–26.

Carlisle, Dolly. "Loretta, Dollie, Conway & the Rest Greet the Faithful at Nashville's Annual Fan fair." *People Weekly,* 27 June 1983, 103–5.

Carr, Patrick. "Swinging Cowboys!! It's Jack Clement! The Anatomy of a Nashville Legend." *Country Music,* Nov. 1974, 42–46.

Cocks, Jay. "Trippin' Through the Crossroads." *Time,* 25 July 1988, 68–71.

Coppage, Noel. "Music Man Waylon Jennings." *Stereo Review,* Oct. 1980: 92.

Denisoff, R. Serge. *Tarnished Gold: The Record Industry Revisited.* New Brunswick, N.J.: Transaction, 1986.

———. "Waylon Jennings' 'The Last Tour': A New Journalism Approach." *Journal of Popular Culture* 13, no. 4 (1980): 663–71.

Di Salvatore, Bryan. "Ornery." *The New Yorker,* 12 Feb. 1990, 39+.

Dunne, Michael. "'I Fall Upon the Cacti of Life! I Bleed!': Romantic Narcissism in 'Outlaw' Cowboy Music." *Studies in Popular Culture* 11, no. 2 (1988): 22–39.

Flippo, Chet. "Inside Country." *People Weekly,* 21 May 1984, 134+.

Kennedy, Harold. "America Sings Along with Country Music." *U.S. News & World Report,* 21 June 1982, 54–55.

King, Larry L. "David Allen Coe's Greatest Hits." *Esquire,* July 1976, 71+.

Lefebvre, Tania A. *Jerry Lee Lewis: The Killer's Story.* Paris: Editions Horus, 1980.

Lewis, Myra, with Murray Silver. *Great Balls of Fire: The Uncensored Story of Jerry Lee Lewis.* New York: Quill, 1982.

Morthland, John. Review of *Willie Nelson Sings Kristofferson. Rolling Stone,* 21 Feb. 1980, 56–57.

Nash, Alanna. "Lacy Dalton: The Hottest New Country Ticket Going." *Stereo Review,* Nov. 1980, 66–68.

Thorp, N. Howard "Jack." *Songs of the Cowboys.* With variants, commentary, notes, and lexicon by Austin E. Fife and Alta S. Fife. New York: Clarkson N. Potter, 1966.

Tosches, Nick. *Hellfire: The Jerry Lee Lewis Story.* New York: Delacorte, 1982.

## CHAPTER 8

**Music Videos**

Advertisements

for Themselves

In her perceptive study *Rocking Around the Clock: Music Television, Postmodernism, and Consumer Culture*, E. Ann Kaplan shows that music videos have been around for some time, although pioneering videos by artists such as David Bowie originally served merely as promotional devices for albums. Only with the establishment of MTV on 1 August 1981, did the video begin to take on the self-justifying autonomy that it now maintains. With twenty-four hours of air time demanding to be filled with videos every single day, MTV established an immediate need for more, and more complex, music videos. MTV quickly encountered competition from cable programs such as *Night Flight* and *Night Tracks* and the NBC network show *Friday Night Videos*, as R. Serge Denisoff explains in his 1986 music history, *Tarnished Gold: The Record Industry Revisited* (369–72). Denisoff also reports that Ted Turner launched an entire music video network, the Cable Music Channel (CMC), in 1984 to compete with MTV. As everyone knows, MTV eventually overwhelmed its rivals, but the whole competition significantly increased the possible outlets for music videos.

The development of video outlets with different music formulas opened the field even further. In 1983, two cable channels were established to broadcast country music videos: The Country Music TV Network (CMTV) and the Nashville Network (TNN). The Black Entertainment Network (BET) soon offered still another opportunity, especially for videos featuring the black jazz and soul artists who were admittedly under-represented on MTV. When VH-1 was spun off MTV on 1 January 1985 to attract mellower viewers uninterested in the spandex/heavy-metal bands featured on the parent network, the field attained its present contours.

Today, the determined viewer may watch music videos of almost any sort around the clock. Judicious use of a VCR can carry on this video-watching even while the human viewer is sleeping or working. To test this proposition, I set my own VCR to watch twelve hours of music videos between 29 August and 1 September 1990. Four hours of MTV were recorded between 1:00 A.M. and 5:00 A.M. to capture a maximum of videos and a minimum of entertainment news, contests, and comedy. For similar reasons, I set my machine to watch VH-1 from 9:00 A.M. through 1:00 P.M. To get four hours of videos from TNN required three stints split between mornings and evenings and spread over two days because of the network's more varied format. Then, instead of flipping through two or three videos while waiting for something else to come on another channel, as is usually my approach to this medium, I watched the whole twelve hours in several sustained sittings. The experience produced several reflections, the principal being that music videos are highly self-referential.

Interesting conclusions about music videos are not unprecedented. In an essay entitled "Metaphor, Metaphysics, and MTV," Sue Lorch finds in music videos a contemporary, mediated form of metaphysical poetry. A more taxonomic approach by Joan D. Lynch results in her identification of three types of videos in her essay "Music Videos: From Performance to Dada-Surrealism": videos that reproduce concert performances, those devoted to fictional narratives, and those experimenting with film techniques. In "Music Video and the Spectator," Marsha Kinder also divides videos into three types, based on performance, narrative, and "dreamlike visuals." Dean Abt expands the categories to four in his "Music Video: Impact of the Visual Dimension," by proposing that many videos use some combination of these approaches.

E. Ann Kaplan's more sociopolitical inquiry yields five types: romantic, socially conscious, nihilistic (performance), classical, and postmodernist. By means of a highly scientific sampling method, H. Stith Bennett and Jeff Ferrell also discover five slightly different varieties of video in their amusingly titled essay "Music Videos and

Epistemic Socialization": politics, romance, motion (cars), conversation, and persona shift. While each of these perceptive viewers may contribute substantially to our understanding of the content or structure of videos, none, it seems to me, has sufficiently recognized or explained the self-referentiality of this popular art form.

The most obvious of these self-references occur in videos about making videos. Probably the Ur-video of this kind was made for "Easy Lover," a 1984 duet by Phil Collins and Philip Bailey. As part of the video, but before the actual singing starts, Collins plausibly adopts the role of the more experienced performer to tell Bailey that they are going to film "a video about making a music video." Some predictable shtick about makeup and costumes ensues as backdrop for the vocal duet, but also some actually funny shots of Bailey supposedly trying to teach Collins to move with soul. In all, the video for "Easy Lover" succeeds in being highly entertaining. Because it is admittedly a video about a video about a video about a song, however, it is noteworthy that the plot situates the viewers at several removes from any pretended live performance. Subsequently, similar video structures have appeared in connection with songs from all segments of the musical spectrum, thus probably testifying to some essential property of the genre.

The aspiring country group Pirates of the Mississippi, for example, support their remake of Hank Williams's song "Honkytonk Blues" with a video, broadcast on TNN during my viewing experiment, that illustrates most of the devices familiar in this sort of self-referencing. The picture is sometimes in full color as the band performs the song on stage. Sometimes it switches to black and white as the band members examine a monitor to see how previous shots in their video look. Sometimes only the viewer can see this monitor, a fictional experience of a fictional event. Sometimes the screen is filled with computer-colorized black and white, so the viewer can only be witnessing a cleverly filmed scene, not even a simulated live performance. Such technical gimmickry emphasizes that videos are created art forms, not reproductions of real experience. This is the intention also behind the jumpy cutting in this film and the zoom shots into the expectant, often mugging, faces of the band members. One other self-referential device deserves mention. Before the band appears, the screen is filled with a sign saying, "Seat Belts are Required While Viewing This Video." No viewer can relax into suspended disbelief under such technical bombardment.

Although the music appeals to different musical tastes, the video for REO Speedwagon's "Live It Up," broadcast on MTV, draws on similar technical devices. There is, first of all, a disclaimer sign: "Viewer of this video voluntarily assumes all risk and danger incidental to its viewing including, but not limited to, injury due to very high decibel levels, occurring prior to, during, or after viewing. Repeated viewing may cause slurred vision and profuse sweating." This sign appears repeatedly, for varying lengths of time, during the course of the film, thus emphasizing the modular construction present in videos but not in life. Various shots of clapper-boards serve a similar purpose. At one point the screen is filled for several seconds—long enough to read it—with a clapper-board reading: "Production: REO SPEEDWAGON / Scene: GIRL RUNNING / Director: MARK REZYKA / Camera: DANIEL PEARL / Date: 7-1-90." A shot of a beautiful girl running immediately follows. No matter how deeply they wish to believe in this video, viewers cannot fail to realize that it is only a film made months ago, in discrete segments, by media professionals with names (and, most likely, bank accounts, families, and subscriptions to periodicals). By flashing briefer clapper-board shots throughout the film—most notably one entitled "beauty shot" over a closeup of Kevin Cronin—the video continually reinforces this conclusion.

Though less visually creative, the video for Bon Jovi's "Bad Medicine," (unsurprisingly) also broadcast on MTV, creates a similar impression. The chief difference between this video and the two already mentioned is that "Bad Medicine" is framed by a narrative featuring Sam Kinison and a group of Bon Jovi fans. Acting in his angry comic persona, Kinison asks the band whether their new video will be innovative or just "the same video slop" filled with "glamour rock pretty boys [who] get on camera and dance around." According to Kinison, videos of this type always use the "same lighting angles, same camera angles." When the band members admit that they have pretty much planned on making a formula video of this sort, Kinison encourages the fans—most of whom are beautiful and scantily clad females—to grab their own video cameras and go to work. The ensuing video consists mostly of the predictable performance shots, but these are intercut with shots of the "fans" and their video cameras. Often these shots are followed by rapid cuts to oddly framed or slightly blurred shots of the band. Although the video probably contains little true originality in the way of lighting or camera angles, the use of self-referential devices permits Bon Jovi to get away with still another heavy-metal performance video. The whole operation is authorized, however, by the rhetorical convention shared by makers and viewers that this is how music videos actually are made.

Another, even more interesting, framing narrative surrounds David Lee Roth's video "Just a Gigolo / I Ain't Got No Body" (1985). In this story, Roth works as a video jockey on a program entitled *Dave TV.* In this role he is surrounded by a clown-like TV crew and some equally exaggerated and grotesque music-business types. As an escape from this routine, he fantasizes making his own video. Naturally, Roth stars in this video, using the persona of Diamond Dave that he cultivated following his break with Van Halen. As Diamond Dave, he passes from sound stage to sound stage through various backstage sets filled with extras in bizarre costumes. The implication seems to be that an anachronistic musical performance like this tribute to Louis Prima requires video support from some form of visual excess.

At no time is there any pretense that the viewer is encountering an unmediated musical performance. In fact, the video reveals its creativity primarily through its identification with other music videos popular at the time it was made. Roth successively encounters sets on which actors simulate the video performances of Michael Jackson, Cindy Lauper, Richard Simmons, Billy Idol, Willie Nelson, and Boy George. As in other art forms, allusion here serves the dual purpose of establishing a community of reference with the audience and of acknowledging the present example's place within the medium. At the end of the fantasy video, Roth even alludes to his own video "California Girls" by imitating the simulated tap dancing he used to bring a charming naivety to the earlier work. Here, a video is an advertisement for itself.

Such intertextual self-referencing is not unusual in music videos. The video for Fleetwood Mac's "Skies the Limit," broadcast on VH-1, is an excellent case in point. Although the lyrics suggest the familiar theme of love's ups and downs, the video makes clear that the song is actually about how the band has triumphed over adversity to confront the unlimited future of the title. This point is established visually by cutting between the present video performance and films illustrating earlier Fleetwood Mac hits. Viewers cannot, therefore, believe that the music they are hearing is being simultaneously performed.

The presence of mediation is signaled also by shifting between color and black-and-white film, by the use of clapper-boards to identify shots, and—as is often the case in videos—by the band's multiple costume changes, especially those by Stevie Nicks. There are also narrative framing devices, such as Nicks's arrival in a limo and the band's exits from various concert stages. Most unusual among these devices, is a frame at the beginning and end of the video in which Mick Fleetwood recites a poem, obviously concerning his own career: "Still a boy with a dream / and eyes full of fun. / I've been through the mill / and made it, with just / two sticks and a drum." Fleetwood's sing-song delivery of the poem and his famous ocular mugging are probably intended to soften the blatant self-referentiality of the poem and of the video overall. Surely, no one is fooled by all this. "Skies the Limit" is another self-advertisement.

The video for "Invisible Touch" by Genesis, broadcast on both MTV and VH-1, also alludes to the band's earlier work, in particular to their big hit, "That's All." The video for that song artistically showed the band performing in a deserted warehouse in a story suggesting that they—especially Phil Collins, the vocalist—were down and out. Collins, also the drummer, did not touch his drums during that entire video. "Invisible Touch" is set in a similar warehouse, perhaps the same one, so most viewers of either video channel would recognize an allusion to the earlier work. This time, however, the story concerns not men laid low by love but musicians making a music video.

This is evident when Collins uses a Minicam to film both the other band members and the members of the video crew who, in alternating shots, are filming him. As a result, this video cannot be naively accepted as the transcription of a performance. In a similar vein, when Collins sings into his drum sticks as if they were a microphone, viewers cannot believe that these sticks are carrying the sound right to their own TV sets. Whatever the subject matter of the video, then, the viewers must accept these pictures on their TV screens as highly contrived and mediated constructions, not as neutral carriers of reality. This impression receives its final definition from the video's last scene, in which Mike Rutherford and Tony Banks, the other members of Genesis, imitate Collins's falsetto while joining him in a reprise of the chorus. More emphatically even than disclaimer notices or clapper-boards, this closing scene reminds the viewers that they are watching a video, not a band.

"Invisible Touch" demonstrates that videos are modular in the sense that they are composed, as films are, of discrete shots that can be edited, rearranged, and spliced into a multitude of final shapes. This fact opens the way for experiments such as Kevin Godley and Lol Creme's brilliant video for their song "Cry" (1985). To create the illusion that this song is being simultaneously sung by a crowd of people representing a broad range of age, race, and body structure, this video uses stunningly sophisticated dissolves among head shots of the actors. The viewer derives an impression of simultaneity. The viewer receives an even stronger impression of watching a film created by artists deeply immersed in their medium.

Many other videos exploit this technique with less polish. In a video broadcast on VH-1, the old Sly and the Family Stone hit "Everyday People," for example, uses fewer and less imaginative cuts to illustrate the many "everyday people" whose feelings might be conveyed through the song. Because lipsynching is inseparable from the video process, a viewer must be distracted through illusion or appeased through acknowledgement. When the latter route is adopted, as in this video—or in "You Can Call Me Al" (1987), where Chevy Chase lipsynchs Paul Simon's song with Simon at his side—a limitation of the medium can be converted into an asset through self-referentiality. In another familiar device, Sly is filmed in a sound studio before and after the principal part of the video. The narrative implication is that Sly has created the video we are now watching in order to adapt his old song to a new medium. We know, in any case, that someone has done so.

The creator's presence can also be signaled in various other ways. Stanley Jordan's video for "What's Goin' On," broadcast on BET, depends for some of its more striking effects on the sort of computer graphics made popular by Herbie Hancock's video "Rockit." To show that there is a personal force behind such artistic effects, the video for "What's Goin' On" presents shots of Jordan's hand, encased in a color-keyed glove, before a computer screen. Later shots of a disembodied hand interacting with computer graphics therefore have dual impacts, both as visual entertainments and as reminders that the screen has been filled with great deliberation. The same may be said about the device, illustrated by a Cheap Trick video on

MTV, in which comic-book-style balloons are superimposed on live action. In the "Can't Stop Fallin' in Love" video, some of these balloons contain lyrics. Others, like the one saying "Guitar Solo," serve the same self-referential function as the clapper-board shots used by REO Speedwagon in "Live It Up." Perhaps the predictable sentiments and arrangements of both songs demanded some sort of ironic insulation to make the filming seem acceptable. Perhaps this triteness also explains the use of balloons containing sound effects such as "Sigh" and "Ring, Ring" in the Cheap Trick video. For precedents, one might cite the TV show *Batman*, an earlier rhetorical wink at a hypermediated audience.

The video for Phil Collins's "Something Happened on the Way to Heaven," broadcast on MTV, also trades on the audience's video experience. As in a similar piece by the Beach Boys, the narrative introduces comic mishaps into the familiar story of filming a music video. In "Something Happened," the filming is established at the outset when Collins asks the band to play the number again because something is not quite right. This performance obviously must be for the cameras, because there is no audience present, despite the sophisticated onstage lighting. The trouble begins when a dog gets onto the soundstage. Although there is considerable burlesque foolishness, none of the subsequent action really distinguishes this video from those produced for Pirates of the Mississippi or Bon Jovi. The Collins video does develop a more interesting contrast between color and black-and-white film, however. To simulate the animal's colorblindness, all shots filmed from the dog's perspective appear in black and white. This is true also of the dog's dream fantasy of rescuing a silent-movie heroine from an oncoming train. Although this scene is somewhat less plausible zoologically, it clearly illustrates the video's sense of itself as part of the history of film.

The Beach Boys' venture into this territory, broadcast on VH-1, involves additional layers of mediation. The story here has the band recording the title song for the film *Problem Child*. This is established by the expected shots of a soundstage and control booth as well as by signs outside the studio containing all the pertinent information. Scenes from the film are also included in the video, both as full-screen shots and as projected on a screen behind the musicians. Finally, Michael Oliver, the "problem child" in the film, plays the starring role in the video, so that his antics become doubly self-referential. Whereas the dog in the Collins video does not do anything very disturbing, Oliver, in accordance with his film role, is much more troublesome. He knocks over a line of guitars so that they fall on Carl Wilson's foot. He pulls on a cable that yanks the microphone away from Brian Wilson. He pours soap suds into Mike Love's saxophone. Speakers blow out, people receive electric shocks, but—significantly—the sound track gives no indication of all these disruptions. The song sounds as perfect as it would in a movie theater, on a CD, or on VH-1. Mike Love is no more playing those saxophone notes through soap suds than all the judiciously chosen actors are singing "Everyday People." These events are, as the viewers well know, only scenes in music videos.

The highly derivative video for "I'm Into Something Good," sung by Peter Noone and broadcast on VH-1, brings together many of the self-referential devices we have seen in these other works. As in the case of the Beach Boys' "Problem Child," one purpose of this video is to advertise a film, here *The Naked Gun*, starring Leslie Nielsen and Priscilla Presley. Since the movie is itself a parody of the police-action film, it is unsurprising that the video parodies many conventions of its own medium. The more romantic passages in the lyric are often supported by parodic shots from the film, as when a starry-eyed Priscilla bumps into a doorjamb and when Nielsen, hand-in-hand with Priscilla, runs out of the surf wearing tennis shoes.

Video conventions are parodied as Nielsen, while performing the song as part of Noone's band, exudes sexual vibrations toward comically stereotypical women in the audience. Since Nielsen is obviously not playing the instrument he is holding in these scenes and since Noone is lipsynching amateurishly, no illusion of performance is intended. In an essay entitled "The Aesthetics of Rock," Richard Meltzer notes a similar segment in the Beatles' film *A Hard Day's Night* in which John Lennon can be heard playing harmonica behind his own vocal on "I Should Have Known Better" (246). The goal in both cases is surely to ridicule the falsity of other musical dramatizations. In the video under discussion, this goal might account also for the laughably inept dancing during the performance scenes.

A significant narrative thread in this video—as in many others, including Fleetwood Mac's "Skies the Limit"—is developed by superimposing the current performance on historical footage of the group, in this case of Herman's Hermits. The black-and-white film of screaming teenage girls effectively undercuts any hint of sexuality in the performance by Noone and Nielsen, and perhaps in the filmed scenes featuring Presley and Nielsen. What remains of both narratives is purely mediated visual experience, a fact signaled in the video's conclusion by shots of an audience watching the video on a huge screen in an arena/stadium.

Many videos self-referentially signal their invention in this way, by stressing that this form of musical experience is predominantly visual. MTV-award-winning videos by Peter Gabriel ("Sledge Hammer," 1986) and the Cars ("You Might Think," 1984) combined live action and animation to emphasize that they were artistically created for the screen, not discovered through a journalistic lens. Another video starring Phil Collins, "Don't Lose My Number" (1988), illustrates this principle with especial clarity. The narrative premise here is that a series of creative video-makers come to Collins with suggestions for his newest video. After the first genius proposes a western story mildly suggestive of *Shane,* ensuing shots develop the proposal up through Collins's death in a shoot-out with the blacksmith/sheriff. Understandably, this concept is rejected, and proposals from six other geniuses follow, some developed at length, others merely suggested. A futuristic *Road Warrior* idea is quickly succeeded by a "sensitive" black-and-white treatment that echoes the video for "Every Move You Make" (1983) by the Police. A Michael-Jackson-like aerobic concept follows, followed in turn by a playboy-on-the-beach scene that suggests videos by David Lee Roth and Elton John. Then comes a Japanese segment that possibly may allude to *The Karate Kid.* The next idea, based on the Cars' video for "You Might Think," shows Collins's head attached to a cartoon fly's body. Immediately following the fly sequence is a shot of Collins asking, "How does it end?" This is followed by the same shot of Collins asking again, "How does it end?" This continues until the fade-out.

Several reflections occur. This video for "Don't Lose My Number" is self-referential first of all because its narrative subject is how to make a video. It is self-referential also in showing that none of the visual treatments proposed by the video-makers is particularly relevant to the song's lyric—the video advertises that this medium is primarily visual. And thus, the video becomes self-referential finally in its references to, or parodies of, other music videos and Hollywood films. The videos for Cindy Lauper's "Time After Time" (1984) and Madonna's "Material Girl" (1985) stimulated a similar awareness through allusions to familiar motion pictures or film genres. Viewers of such videos are made constantly aware, thorough their own mediated experiences, that they are viewing something on a screen.

This community of reference transcends musical fields. The video for Cee Cee Chapman's "Everything," broadcast on TNN, exploits a structure closely resembling that of "Don't Lose My Number" without evincing any incompatibility with the country lyrics or instrumentation. The plot of the video is that Chapman is approached by a sleazy producer who wants her to make a film that will reach "the kids," a market he claims to understand fully. Chapman is then shown in a video setting that parodies one used by the Red Hot Chili Peppers, a distinctly noncountry act. As in the Collins video, sequences of unequal duration follow, each suggestive of a recognizable video or video genre. After the Chili Peppers segment, Chapman is shown playing guitar in front of a background of three male singer-automatons, an allusion to Michelle Shocked's "On The Greener Side" (1989). Since Shocked's video was itself a parody of Robert Palmer's "Addicted to Love" (1986), the depth of reference becomes particularly rich, a fact validated when Chapman's male backup singers are next presented wearing black cocktail dresses like those featured in the Palmer video.

Probably because cross-dressing is such an alien concept in a country music video, the next sequences are broadly comic—parodies of generic rock and rap videos. The final sequence then shows Chapman in a Madonna-like costume that would not ordinarily constitute part of a country music performance. As in the case of the Collins video, however, there is little illusion of performance here. In most scenes, Chapman does not even lipsynch, a sign probably intended to show the dramatized singer's discomfort with the unacceptable staging. The overall effect is to emphasize that this video is a visual experience, a piece of television, not a real or simulated concert. It is surely significant that this message can be conveyed to audiences with such varied musical tastes. Apparently, everyone may be assumed to watch television.

Such "media references abound in rock video" (18), according to "Music, Television, and Video: Historical and Aesthetic Considerations," an article by Gary Burns and Robert Thompson. Perhaps this explains the fondness for still photography manifested in so many music videos. Theatrical films such as Michelangelo Antonioni's *Blow-Up* and Alfred Hitchcock's *Rear Window* earlier demonstrated that a contrast between still photography and moving pictures could heighten the impact of the latter. The gain, as might be expected in a highly mediated culture, accrues largely as a result of increased self-referentiality. The film-maker signals that he makes pictures just as the photographer does. A similar effect is often achieved in videos, the most striking recent case being Billy Joel's "We Didn't Start the Fire," broadcast on VH-1. As earlier efforts such as "Keeping the Faith" revealed, Joel's videos often assume the viewer's familiarity with various forms of visual media. The earlier video testifies to this by exploiting newspaper headlines in the manner of old black-and-white films and stop-action shots in the manner of print journalism.

In "We Didn't Start the Fire," the lyric is supported throughout by references to news photos and to television, both as entertainment and as a source of news. The story of the video shows a family evolving from the 1950s to the present through entirely mediated images. Sometimes the events in this family's history recall television entertainment figures like Lucy and Davy Crockett; sometimes, big stories on the evening news like bra-burning and anti-war activism. All of these events are filtered through television, however, and thus accorded equivalent significance in the lives of the fictional family members. Intercut with the family's story are shots of Joel, simulating synthesized drum sounds on a table, lipsynching the lyrics against huge blown-up black-and-white photographs of major news events: Jack Ruby shooting Lee Harvey Oswald, the South Vietnamese police officer shooting the bound viet cong suspect in the head (the same photo blown up on Woody Allen's apartment wall in *Stardust Memories*), Ollie North. As Joel explained in many interviews, the song was intended to bring the importance of history home to young listeners. Even more clearly, the video brings home the viewer's relation to experience that is mediated through television and print journalism. Another significant form of such experience is, needless to say, the music video.

The video "Banned in the USA," performed by 2 Live Crew and broadcast on MTV, confirms all these assumptions. Even more than in Joel's video, the subject matter is derived from the media. As most viewers of MTV surely would know, police officials in several American cities opposed the lyrics of 2 Live Crew on grounds of obscenity. Newspapers and television stations across the country reported on the charges and on the band's claims of censorship motivated by racism. The song and video address these issues entirely through mediated imagery. The tune of the song, first of all, derives from Bruce Springsteen's "Born in the U.S.A.," another big video hit on MTV. The video contains actual television news film of the controversy, actual shots of Broward County, Florida, scene of a particularly acrimonious encounter, and actual newspaper headlines. The video also contains mock headlines intended to support the lyric and courtroom scenes that are obviously dramatizations, although in the latter case the distance from some "soft" TV news programs may not be so obvious.

The actual and dramatized materials work effectively together to ridicule the officials' actions and to support the band's view that they were "banned" because their success was unacceptable to the white power structure. Effective cutting between the video's contemporary story and historical television film of the civil rights movement lends thematic support to this narrative. At the same time, this device illustrates television's equalizing effect on experience, what Salman Rushdie calls, in *The Satanic Verses*, "a Procrustean bed for the twentieth century" (405). By giving equal visual authority to the actual struggle for justice in the 1960s and a band's desire for a bigger piece of the economic pie in 1990, the video vividly demonstrates how everything on television may be viewed only as "television."

One final, but well-documented, example must suffice. E. Ann Kaplan identifies the self-referential essence of Dire Straits' "Money for Nothing" (1985) when she says in *Rocking Around the Clock* that the video "comments baldly on MTV itself, and on the alternate blandness and sensationalism of [the] videos shown" (35–36). Sue Lorch discusses what she calls the "deeply self-reflexive" nature of the video more extensively in her essay "Metaphor, Metaphysics, and MTV" (152–54). Both critics correctly see this video as central to the genre. The reason is apparent in the first two lines of the lyric, spoken by a computer-animated blue-color TV viewer: "Look at them yo-yo's, that's the way to do it / Play the guitar on the M.T.V." The direct address in the verb form *look* anchors the video in self-referential immediacy, an effect reinforced by the later verbs *see* and *look at* and by the pronouns *them* and *that*. Since the objects of these references are elements of a fictional music video, viewers are asked to accept what is filling their screens as something like a metavideo. It is, in any case, not a window on reality.

The visual content of "Money for Nothing" further establishes this impression. As most viewers probably know already, the story of the video concerns two computer-animated workmen who envy the live-action members of Dire Straits, whom they view on a series of animated TV screens. As several previous examples have shown, mixing two visual media in this way cannot help but emphasize the artificiality of both, thus establishing a pronounced sense of self-referentiality. Lorch argues in this direction when she observes that even as "we watch the band's performance without the computer-graphics frame . . . we are aware of the computer-generated effects: Mark Knopfler's head band and guitar are outlined in a glow of neon color" (153). Thus, in some scenes, the viewer is watching an actual television screen that shows a picture of an animated, fictional television screen that shows a picture of Dire Straits lipsynching a song about watching videos on television.

More clearly than any other example of the genre, "Money for Nothing" recognizes the viewers' awareness of the conventions defining the purely mediated experience of the music video. This recognition, furthermore, enables the makers to turn the viewers' participation in a hypermediated rhetorical community to highly creative purposes. By now we all know that when we see a piece of film showing Janet Jackson, Mike Jagger, or Steve Earle grimacing in passion on MTV, VH-1, TNN, or BET, it is part of an overall performance called a music video. Someone may have sung a song somewhere—probably in a recording studio, and probably ten or twelve different times—but that singing certainly was not done on top of a mountain, by a cartoon figure, or by a group of statistically representative Americans. Just as *Spaceballs* and *It's Garry Shandling's Show* can communicate fully only with audiences steeped in the conventions of their media, so the self-referential music video challenges only to affirm conventions that have become almost second nature to today's generation of hypermediated television viewers.

WORKS CITED

Abt, Dean. "Music Video: Impact of the Visual Dimension." In *Popular Music and Communication,* edited by James Lull, 96–111. Newbury Park, Cal.: Sage, 1987.

Bennett, H. Stith, and Jeff Ferrell. "Music Videos and Epistemic Socialization." *Youth and Society* 18 (1987): 344–62.

Burns, Gary, and Robert Thompson. "Music, Television, and Video: Historical and Aesthetic Considerations." *Popular Music and Society* 11, no. 3 (1987): 11–25.

Denisoff, R. Serge. *Tarnished Gold: The Record Industry Revisited.* New Brunswick, N.J.: Transaction, 1986.

Kaplan, E. Ann. *Rocking Around the Clock: Music Television, Postmodernism, and Consumer Culture.* New York: Methuen, 1987.

Kinder, Marsha. "Music Video and the Spectator: Television, Ideology, and Dream." *Film Quarterly* 38 (1984): 2–15.

Lorch, Sue. "Metaphor, Metaphysics, and MTV." *Journal of Popular Culture* 22, no. 3 (1989): 143–55.

Lynch, Joan D. "Music Videos: From Performance to Dada-Surrealism." *Journal of Popular Culture* 18, no. 1 (1984): 53–57.

Meltzer, Richard. "The Aesthetics of Rock." In *The Age of Rock*, edited by Jonathan Eisen, 244–53. New York: Vintage, 1969.

Rushdie, Salman. *The Satanic Verses.* New York: Viking, 1989.

CHAPTER 9 **Comic Strips**

Fearless Fosdick Comes

to Doonesbury County

Comic strips have long operated as significant elements of American culture. In his book *Comics as Culture* (1990), M. Thomas Inge analyzes interactions between comic strips and such diverse cultural elements as American slang, motion picture comedy, and the fiction of William Faulkner. Today, comic strips are undeniably part of the enormous web of economics and publicity that constitutes the hypermediated world of American popular culture. Evidence can be found, for example, in "Comics as Inspiration: Are We Having Fun Yet?" Richard B. Woodward's insightful tracing of the comics' influence on television programs, Hollywood films, consumer goods, "serious" fiction, and hieratic art, in the 23 April 1989 edition of the *New York Times*. In addition to Broadway shows such as *Li'l Abner* (1956) and *Annie* (1977), Woodward discusses the enormous success of *Batman* (1989) as well as the bonanza then anticipated from *Dick Tracy*. As a further example, Maurice Horn's entry on "Peanuts" in *The World Encyclopedia of Comics* recounts not only Charles Schulz's artistic struggle to establish the strip but also the uncountable millions that success has brought him through syndication, TV specials, and merchandising. Woodward adds that in 1988 Schulz was ranked sixth in income among American entertainers, joining the ranks of Bill Cosby, Sylvester Stallone, and Bruce Springsteen.

Television, newspapers, and magazines all over America reported the fortieth birthday of Charlie Brown in 1989 and Superman's fiftieth in 1988. On the twentieth anniversary of original syndication of "Doonesbury," Garry Trudeau appeared on the cover of *Newsweek* (15 October 1990). In the accompanying profile, Trudeau demonstrated an acute sense of how the American system of mediation operates—and perhaps just a touch of disingenuousness—when he told Jonathan Alter that America is "the only country where failure to promote yourself is widely considered arrogant" (62). During the late 1950s, Al Capp apparently entertained no similar qualms during his long and very successful string of appearances on the Jack Parr show. Despite their differences, Trudeau, Capp, Schulz, and other cartoonists too numerous to mention are all in some sense part of the mediated world of American popular art. It is entirely predictable, therefore, that their work should reveal forms of self-referentiality comparable to those we have already seen working in television, film, and music. In fact, self-referentiality has become so widespread in comics that, in *Great American Comics: 100 Years of Cartoon Art* (1990), Inge has invented the critical term *metacomics* to encompass the whole phenomenon (33–34).

In their introduction to *The Smithsonian Collection of Newspaper Comics* (1977), Bill Blackbeard and Martin Williams offer the following definition: "A comic strip may functionally be defined as a serially published, episodic, open-ended dramatic or narrative series of linked anecdotes about recurrent, identified characters, told in successive drawings regularly enclosing ballooned dialogue or its equivalent and minimized narrative text" (13). While this definition is very useful in itself to anyone who wants to think seriously about the funnies, it is valuable also in demonstrating that, like any other artistic medium, the comics have identifiable conventional properties. These conventions provide easy access to more complex questions surrounding self-referentiality in the comic strips.

Consider, first of all, Blackbeard and Williams's insistence on ballooned dialogue. As early as the 1920s, Otto Mesmer's "Felix the Cat" strip made practical use of this convention by attributing the power of helium to the balloons so that Felix could use them to float out of threatening situations. More recently, a Sunday strip of Jerry Scott's "Nancy" (1990) shows the youthful heroine circumventing her teacher's prohibition against talking by cutting out a balloon that says, "I'm done." In Gary Larson's "The Far Side" (1990), a boss says to an employee who considers him a "big, dumb geek," "Lewis, you're fired! You apparently forgot this is a cartoon, and I can read every word you think!"

Strips using an "equivalent" for speech balloons can exploit this convention as well. A Sunday "Frank and Ernest" by Bob Thaves begins with Frank asking, "Hey, Ernie, how do you spell 'caption?'" Ernie points to Frank's speech and says, "Just look above you." The ensuing panels develop variations on this thin joke in order to set up Frank's exclamation, "Who's the dumb bozo we've been trusting to transcribe our dialogues?" The final panel shows Ernie telling a headless Frank that "an apology might be in order." These examples demonstrate that comic strip speech—within or without the balloons that Pierre Couperie technically identifies as "philacteries" (179)—may be treated not only as an organic part of a larger joke but as a visual joke in itself.

The physical appearance of comic strip dialogue provides many other opportunities for the artist's self-expression. In *Li'l Abner: A Study in American Satire,* Arthur Asa Berger recalls Al Capp's eccentric reliance on multiple exclamation points in dialogue and on a "large number of grunts and groans" (107). Reinhold Reitberger and Wolfgang Fuchs draw similar attention to Walt Kelly's typography in their *Comics: Anatomy of a Mass Medium.* The gothic lettering of Deacon Mushrat's speeches and the circus poster typography of P. T. Bridgeport's, they argue, constituted an equally distinct advertisement of Kelly's creative presence behind "Pogo" (49).

Walt Kelly would agree. In his collection *Ten Ever-Lovin' Blue-Eyed Years with Pogo,* he notes, "The emergence of P. T. Bridgeport marked the second time that the lettering in the balloons was so styled as to indicate the tone of voice of the character" (43). Kelly does not explain how the appearance of such lettering affects the readers' consciousness of the strip, although this effect is significant here, as it is when his character Sarcophagus MacAbre speaks in a typeface usually reserved for printing obituaries and death notices (85). Kelly does explain the comic intent behind the strips (282–83) in which unruly gnats spell out words that Beauregard the dog refuses to take responsibility for: "It may be of interest to archaeologists who chip away this far to know that the entire sequence of the gnats (I think it ran for a couple of weeks) evolved out of merely trying to find a fit vehicle for one gag." For our purposes here, it should suffice to observe that forty years ago Kelly saw the technical apparatus of his strip as potential material for comedy.

Another historical discovery lurking in Kelly's collection is the Sunday strip in which Barnstable Bear's writing is shown in reverse (220). The joke is that Barnstable can write but not read. The effect on the reader is a heightened consciousness of where Kelly stands behind his strip. We need not consult history for the Sunday strip by Berke Breathed, reprinted in *Bloom County Babylon*, in which the speeches of Opus, Milo, and Binkley are all printed backwards (190). The day's topic, according to Binkley, is that American priorities have become twisted; thus, the typographical device can be interpreted as part of an organic message. In fact, however, this message takes second place to the medium, whether the reader holds the strip up to a mirror or labors through it word by word. Ultimately, Breathed emerges more prominently in the reader's thoughts than does the alleged cultural malaise. In an earlier strip concerned with newspaper censorship, reprinted in *Bloom County: Loose Tails* (25), Breathed creates a similar effect by covering a supposed obscenity by Editor Thornback with a smudge of black ink. Like the more traditional device of suggesting obscene words through typographical marks such as asterisks and stars, this smudge communicates symbolic meaning visually. Because it is a departure from the traditional, it probably also forces the reader to recognize Breathed's originality.

As should be expected from one of today's younger cartoonists, Breathed deliberately reveals that he is working in a tradition bristling with conventions. A Sunday strip from 1987, entitled "The Official Handbook for Better Comix Comprehension," identifies and illustrates the typographical devices conventionally used in comic strips to represent sudden ideas, motion, anxiety, and intoxication. Breathed is, of course, not the first cartoonist to reveal these secrets of the trade. It is significant, however, that, while Mort Walker anatomizes the conventions in prose in his 1975 book *Backstage at the Strips* (26–31), Breathed does so in a Sunday strip.

Walker is not really a member of the conservative old guard, however. The strip "Boner's Ark," which he developed in cooperation with Bud Jones, revealed an advanced degree of self-referentiality from its early years. In a strip from 1971, reprinted in Walker's book (20), Boner is walking along the deck when he trips with a "FLOP!" over the signature *Addison* at the bottom of the middle panel. Readers may not know that "Addison" is the pen name adopted by the artistic partnership, but they must know that their attention is being directed to a convention of the medium.

This is even more apparent in a Pogo strip from the *Ten Ever-Lovin' Blue-Eyed Years with Pogo* collection (17) in which Walt Kelly directs his readers' attention to the subtleties of his craft. In the first panel Howland Owl explains to Porky that the numbers at the lower left, representing the day's date, constitute "the first bit of convulsive waggery" in any comic strip. Howland uses a stick in the second panel to point to the required copyright notice, a convention that Porky calls "a true guffaw . . . possibly a boffola." In the third panel, Howland, Porky, and a bug use the stick to poke at the balloons above their heads, which they claim to be "glutted . . . with attic wit." In the last panel, Howland points to a box at the lower right containing the Latin phrase *O Tempora, O Mores*, which he takes to be an Irish name. He explains to the others: "The last laugh is the first thing a artist *got* to *git*. So he *must* learn to sign his name . . . big and black with a box 'round her." Supposedly, the joke is that the ideas in a cartoon matter less than the conventions. Actually, the joke is Kelly's betrayal of these conventions for the sake of some shared fun.

Kelly does not mention, but very well might, the black lines surrounding each of these "Pogo" panels. Like the balloons, these defining lines have attracted the self-referential attention of many cartoonists. In a 1989 "Boner's Ark" strip, for example, Boner solves a navigational problem by sailing the ark from left to right through "an opening in the panel." At the far right, the ark crashes into the black line with a "BUMP!" In a 1990 "Adam" strip by Brian Basset, the title character runs from left to right in pursuit of a pop fly while playing baseball. In the third panel he collides with the right-hand border: "CRASH." The fourth panel shows Adam on the ground with a thought balloon containing the conventional signs for obscenity and the words "Comic Strip Borders." If some readers have never before noticed that black lines surround the spaces in which comic characters operate, strips like these cause them to become more aware. If—as seems more likely—the readers have already noticed this convention, a community of shared allusion is hereby reinforced.

Another visual convention apparent in many strips is the narrative summary. Perhaps since comics closely resemble early films, as Earle J. Coleman demonstrates in "The Funnies, the Movies, and Aesthetics," the practice may correspond to the use of narrative placards in silent films. Since the device has continued to appear in films even up through the marvelous introductory crawl in *Star Wars*, it may be essential to some kinds of visual narrative. In any case, such summaries have long been associated with adventure strips such as "Wash Tubbs" and "Captain Easy," both created by Roy Crane and both amply illustrated in Blackbeard and Williams's *Smithsonian Collection*. This book also contains examples of the narrative teasers that Harold Gray used at the beginnings of his "Little Orphan Annie" Sunday strips as well as Harold Foster's characteristic use of summary to preface "Prince Valiant," a device he always called "Synopsis." The parallels with continuing adventure series on film and radio seem obvious.

At least they must have seemed obvious to Berke Breathed, probably because readers were so willing to take them for granted. In an early strip reprinted in *Bloom County: Loose Tails* (120), Breathed devotes the first panel of a daily strip involving Steve Dallas, Cutter John, and Bobbi Harlow to the following summary: "In order to clarify things for new viewers, dim viewers and us, we interrupt this feature for a quick review of the key players on the torrid *Bloom County* romantic scene." The three following panels present these characters (and Opus) over mildly ironic descriptions of their plot functions. Very likely the comic strip *was* acquiring new readers in the mid-eighties—In *Penguin Dreams and Stranger Things* (28–30), a whole week of strips is devoted to welcoming readers of the *Tulsa Daily Herald* to the syndicate—but the romantic summary carries far more resonance as a self-advertisement than as an actual aid to the reader. Breathed is signaling his presence behind the strip, as Mel Brooks might do in a film.

Confirmation of this intention can be found in the series of strips, reprinted in *Bloom County Babylon* (197), dealing with Opus's rhinoplasty. As in the earlier example, the narrative text refers to the strip as a "feature." In both cases, the language presents this comic strip as a mediated experience, rather than as a comic drama done in pictures or as social commentary. In the earlier strip, Breathed addresses his summary to his "viewers." In one of the ones dealing with Opus's nose, he writes, "We now return to the hilarious comic already in progress," as if he were announcing a TV show. Perhaps if early adventure strips resembled silent serials, then contemporary strips such as "Bloom County" resembles television programs.

It is clear in any event that cartoonists such as Breathed see their relation to their audience in terms of a shared experience of mediation. Readers may be assumed to know a good deal about who draws a comic strip, how it is produced, and how it relates to the larger world of popular entertainment, just as they may be expected to know about Madonna and Sean Penn or the latest antics of Spuds MacKenzie. By reading Jonathan Alter's *Newsweek* article on Garry Trudeau, for example, readers learn that his Sunday "Doonesbury" strips must be completed five weeks before publication. Readers may then fully comprehend the significance of Trudeau's strip for the first Sunday following the 1988 presidential election. Now occupying the last page in *Read My Lips, Make My Day, Eat Quiche and Die!* the strip shows Marvelous Mark Slackmeyer and his assistant recapping the election in their radio studio. Each recounts when he first realized that George Bush would win. After reading *Newsweek*, the reader can only marvel while imagining Trudeau drawing these panels almost five weeks before the election. Even in November 1988, the effect of the strip would have been highly self-referential. If readers did not know how far in advance the strip was prepared, they at least must have suspected that it was not done in the immediately preceding days. Even if they did not realize this much, Trudeau signals the point by having Mark's assistant say that if Bush has not won the election, "We sure look like jerks right now." Obviously Trudeau was confident that they, and he, would not look like jerks. Obviously, too, readers were expected to recognize this.

In a strip reprinted in the same collection (51), Trudeau gives further evidence of what he assumes about his readers. The premise is that Sal Doonesbury, Mike's younger brother, is addressing a group of parents on the subject of Dr. Whoopee condoms. The realistically drawn parents ask realistic questions about health and sexuality for five panels. In the last, someone asks whether comic strips might be used for sex education. Sal replies, "No, no, it's too serious a subject." Rhetorically, this strip is an example of apophasis, the device through which orators pretend not to say what they are saying. Self-referentially, this strip exploits the readers' knowledge of what is usual in comic strips in order to do ostentatiously something else.

Breathed is also very fond of such self-advertisements. When, in a strip reprinted in *Penguin Dreams* (14), Mrs. Limekiller incredibly meets Opus in the middle of the South Atlantic, she says, "Small World!" Opus says, "Small strip." When, in a strip reprinted in *'Toons for Our Times* (37), Milo pummels Bill the Cat in a mock aerobics exercise, Milo says that the folks in Bloom County "aren't ever ashamed to indulge in a little physical fitness." Bill adds, "Or physical humor." On the last page of *Bloom County Babylon*, Opus and Oliver Wendell Jones engage in a debate about whether Opus's spilled ice cream is, from a statistical point of view, a tragedy. The strip concludes with the ice cream cone smeared on Oliver's face and Opus saying, "Statistically speaking, there was about a one in one chance that you'd be wearing that cone by this last frame." In all of these examples, Breathed freely uses the terminology of his medium as part of normal dialogue, confident that his readers will understand his meaning and respond to his humor even if—perhaps because—he is making some very old jokes.

In these examples, the enabling act for Breathed's humor is his open acknowledgement that he conceives and draws his work, rather than just jotting down impressions as he observes life passing by. Other artists sometimes follow this avenue to similarly productive ends. In a "Far Side" strip published in 1990, Larson draws two outsized, grinning faces in the foreground of a panel whose background shows a proportional farmer, wife, and bird in a living room. The caption reads: "Suddenly, two bystanders stuck their heads inside the frame and ruined one of the funniest cartoons ever." Visually, a joke results when Larson violates the depth of field that conventionally governs the drawing of cartoons, a matter thoroughly discussed in Lawrence L. Abbott's 1986 article "Comic Art: Characteristics and Potentialities of a Narrative Medium." In light of what we have seen elsewhere, a more sophisticated joke results when Larson violates convention by mentioning his "frame" and the fact that the work is in fact a "cartoon."

Two of Tom Wilson's "Ziggy" strips printed in 1989 show that even less adventurous cartoonists occasionally adopt this self-referential route. In one strip, a doctor says that he is going to refer Ziggy's case to Rex Morgan, M.D., "since you're a cartoon character." In another, Ziggy is telling his psychiatrist "and I'm in my panel for the whole world to see, and he forgot to draw my clothes!" Obviously, many cartoonists today work with a sense of their audience's hypermediation that is at least as clear as that held by the creators of self-referential music videos.

A closely related self-referential device is the introduction of visual forms other than black-lined panels into the strip. In recent years, Trudeau has frequently turned toward this practice. A Sunday strip reprinted in *You're Smokin' Now, Mr. Butts!* contains a form letter complimenting George Bush for doing a "great job" as president. Dotted lines give the reader an opportunity to fill in the specific information that will make the form letter more personal. George Bush and mass mailing are equally satirized in the strip, but the conventions governing how space is used in the Sunday comics also come under close scrutiny. The same collection also contains a Sunday strip (76) about flag burning, two-thirds of which consists of a drawing of an American flag. The problem posed by Marvelous Mark is how to dispose of the comic page without committing some symbolic desecration. Again, the primary object of the strip is satire, here of the conservative politicians who were agitating in favor of a constitutional amendment to prevent flag burning. Another effect is an increased awareness on the reader's part of how Trudeau operates within the space available to him in his chosen medium.

A last example, printed in 1989, comes from a series of strips in which America's political cartoonists supposedly grant incoming President Bush a week without editorial criticism. In this strip, the spokesman for the cartoonists tells Marvelous Mark for three panels what a warm, caring person Bush is. Then Mark receives a call from the Bushes, asking for a copy of the strip—not a transcript of the fictional radio program—"for their fridge." Mark and the cartoonist advise that the Bushes clip the strip out of their paper, using "the dotted lines." Readers either notice these lines for the first time at this point, or they finally learn why the strip looks different today. In either case, Bush's political persona is attacked, the popular American practice of hanging things on the refrigerator is humorously lampooned, and readers are reminded forcefully of Trudeau's presence behind the strip.

Breathed is even more attracted to this form of self-referentiality. An early Bill the Cat Sunday strip, reprinted in *Bloom County: Loose Tails* (137), has Milo interrupt a story about Steve Dallas in order to hawk Bill the Cat merchandise. One unconventional stroke shows Milo pulling back the first panel as if it were a stage curtain and screaming, "Hold it! Stop the comic!" In the last panel, he unrolls the panel so that we may "return to today's feature." Between the first and last frames is a direct appeal to the readers to buy nonexistent products. The most unconventional use of space is a coupon drawn with a dotted-line border so that the reader may cut it out and mail it to "Save Bill the Cat / P.O. Box 45 / Bloom County,

U.S.A." Probably there were readers who contemplated sending in the coupon until they saw the last line of the address. Surely there were readers who felt an increased sense of how clever Breathed is. Related devices appear in strips reprinted in *Bloom County Babylon* and also devoted to Bill the Cat. Probably because of Breathed's unceasing hostility toward the commercialism surrounding Garfield, one Sunday strip (206) contains an order blank for Bill the Cat Christmas gifts. Another (207) gives information about a contest with prizes for the best and worst drawings of Bill. (The winning drawings are reproduced on 222.)

There are precedents for some of these devices. The Blackbeard and Williams *Smithsonian Collection* (112) reprints a Sunday "Gasoline Alley" strip containing a framed drawing of "Mr. Whicker," the seventh stamp in a series that "Boys and Girls" were encouraged to clip and save. Also reprinted in the collection (200–216) are several Sunday strips of "Thimble Theatre" containing a "Funny Films" feature that could be cut out and assembled to create a simple kind of animation. Like the "Crimestoppers' Textbook" that Chester Gould later included in the Sunday "Dick Tracy," these features probably had as their goal closer involvement in the strip, especially on the part of younger readers. Because of today's heightened media-consciousness, even such benign manipulation must be viewed through a prism of suspicion. By ironically imitating the devices used with apparent sincerity by their predecessors, contemporary cartoonists call on their readers' mediated experience, perhaps developing thereby an even "closer involvement in the strip" than their predecessors sought.

The key ingredient may be the cartoonists' conviction that we all, cartoonists and readers alike, share the same hypermediated relation to contemporary American culture. Early in 1991, for example, Tom Wilson shows Ziggy sitting in front of his TV set—as Wilson or any of his readers might recently have been doing—saying with shock, "I never thought that rabbit would come in beating the bass drum during *The State of the Union Address.*" Readers probably need some familiarity with Ziggy's character to appreciate his nebbish-like chagrin, but they certainly need to know about the Eveready commercials featuring the mechanical bunny to get the point of the joke. In all likelihood, most readers share this knowledge with Ziggy and with Wilson.

Berke Breathed makes similar assumptions about our common

involvement with the media. Throughout the history of his strip, celebrated media figures such as Madonna, Diane Sawyer, and Michael Jackson have figured prominently, both as characters in the stories and as photographs inconspicuously hanging on walls. *Penguin Dreams* begins with a series of black-and-white drawings supposedly representing photographs of the characters living in Milo Bloom's boarding house. Although these drawings never appeared in the newspaper strip, Breathed apparently found them compatible with his overall design for the collection. The same might be said about Gary Larson's 1990 collection *Wiener Dog Art*, in which paintings of dachshunds drawn as parodies of artistic masterpieces are presented side by side with daily strips of "The Far Side." In these ways, cartoonists reveal that they see their medium as existing on a horizontal artistic plane with other mediated forms of contemporary expression.

Other illustrations abound in "Bloom County." One variation on the critique of materialism emanating from the Bill the Cat story is a Sunday strip, reprinted in *Bloom County: Loose Tails* (117), in which Bill is transformed into a "Billie," a feline clone of Little Orphan Annie. The satiric object is the commercialism surrounding the hit Broadway show, but this satire can function only if Breathed's readers know about *Annie* and how it exfoliated commercially. Clearly, this is what Breathed expects. Mediated commercialism is also the target in the recurrent strips in which Opus feels compelled to buy useless products he has seen advertised on television. In a particularly clever strip, reprinted in *Penguin Dreams* (62), the voice from Opus's TV set claims credit for the success of Jimmy Carter as well as "Cabbage Patch Dolls." TV is also the target of the strip from *'Toons* (49) in which Dan Rather grows irate at his own journalistic offensiveness while interviewing himself for CBS News. While the darts probably hit close to home here, it is important to realize that only an experienced watcher of Dan Rather could catch—or make—this joke.

By the same token, considerable familiarity with popular films is required to appreciate the joke behind the strip, reprinted in *Penguin Dreams* (65), in which Steve Dallas succeeds in selling the story of his client Alice, "The Bloom County Axe Murderess," to Disney films. To comprehend the humor fully, readers must know the type of movie the Disney studio formerly made, the different direction adopted by the new ownership, and who Don Knotts, Dean Jones, and Annette Funicello are. The vast number of contemporary Americans possessing this knowledge should be taken as evidence of how far hypermediation has progressed. After turning to his new strip, "Outland," Breathed continued to make the same sorts of assumptions, as in the 1989 strip in which Mickey and Mortimer Mouse, Snow White, Dopey, and Roger Rabbitt lament the changes that Michael Eisner has brought to the Disney corporation.

Because of his commitment to contemporary satire, Garry Trudeau might be expected to make similar assumptions about his audience, and he does. In the 1989 series about the political cartoonists' giving President Bush a week free of criticism, Trudeau includes a panel in which he duplicates the signatures of editorial cartoonists including Oliphant, Auth, and Conrad, apparently confident that readers will recognize the autographs. Needless to say, Trudeau must have been long familiar with their work to think of the joke in the first place. The same might be said of all the political figures who have played parts in his Vietnam, Watergate, Carter, and Reagan strips. Fairly advanced political sophistication would be required to catch the nuances of the strip, reprinted in *Read My Lips, Make My Day, Eat Quiche and Die!* (65), in which Lee Atwater dictates to a docile ABC News executive the content of their evening news reports on the electoral campaign. It is unsurprising, given his political engagement, that Trudeau would satirize television in terms of its political coverage. Like Breathed, and like most of us, Trudeau also participates in the general field of TV mediation. For example, in two strips from the same collection, B.D. is revolted by the sentimentality of a television program called "Forty-Something" (22) while Mike and Zonker see a *Donahue* show featuring Geraldo Rivera (54). Assuredly, the referents in these strips are not as remote as Atwater, but our common knowledge of all of them derives from the same media sources.

Naturally enough, the most significant sources of mediated references for cartoonists are other comic strips. Reitberger and Fuchs provide a helpful account (53) of how Al Capp parodied other comic strips, including "Mary Worth," "Peanuts," and "Dick Tracy." In the last case Li'l Abner was depicted as fanatically devoted to an absurd Dick-Tracy-like comic strip called "Fearless Fosdick," which was drawn by a Chester-Gould-like artist called Lester Gooch. In Gooch's strip, Fosdick was unrelentingly subjected to—and miraculously indifferent to—the fiercest physical abuse, including enormous gunshot wounds right through his torso. The naive Abner always worried as to whether his "ideel" would survive this current crisis and always laughed uproariously when he, unsurprisingly, did. In his book on Capp, Arthur Asa Berger says concerning this strip-within-the-strip, "Capp is able to laugh at us as we laugh at Abner who laughs at Fosdick, and a hierarchy of superiorities is established, with Capp at the top" (96).

Because Berger is so determined to place Capp in the historical tradition of corrective satire, he perhaps overemphasizes the artist's thematic intentions. It might be more useful for our purposes to consider "Fearless Fosdick" and a comparable strip-within-the-strip in "Pogo" stylistically as commentaries on the genre of the comic strip. In his introduction to the *Li'l Abner Dailies* collection for 1944, Max Allen Collins suggests this dimension of "Fosdick" by noting Capp's careful parodies of Gould's style of drawing, especially his exaggerated treatments of violence (10–11). Collins also discusses the highly self-referential "Fosdick" story from 1942 in which Gooch himself persuades Abner to perform a life-threatening stunt in order to see how Fosdick might escape from the same predicament (8).

This self-referential note is also explicitly sounded in the series discussed in Couperie's *A History of the Comic Strip* (150–51). In this story from 1964, the fabulously wealthy General Bullmoose kidnaps Gooch and forces him to draw "Fosdick" only for Bullmoose's pleasure. Every day Gooch draws a new installment, and every day Bullmoose destroys the strip after reading it, thereby depriving millions of their favorite pastime. Chaos naturally ensues. Naturally, also, everything works out all right in the end, to the satisfaction of both Li'l Abner and Capp's readers. The point to be grasped from the series is not so much the idiocy of those who depend on comic strips for aesthetic release as the recognition that comic strips contribute pleasurably to the lives of a large community of Americans, a large enough community to make Capp's system of cross- and self-references rhetorically effective in 1964.

Similar strips appeared from time to time in "Pogo," particularly "Li'l Arf An' Nonny," based, of course, on Harold Gray's "Little Orphan Annie." In a series reprinted in *Ten Ever-Lovin' Blue-Eyed Years With Pogo* (58–59), Pogo decided that, to escape the pressures of his presidential campaign, he is "gone be a runaway gal orphan for fifty years an' talk my head off to my faithful dog like in the *funny papers.*" Beauregard agrees to play the part of the dog and say "arf," but he explains that "to be a *orphan gal* like in this funny paper, you gotta have *blank eyeballs.*" Eventually, these blank eyeballs cause Pogo to fall into the creek. The equally blank-eyed Beauregard is saved from making the plunge by his "keen nose." No one is really hurt, not even Harold Gray. There is probably some satiric edge to Kelly's joke about the eyeballs and to his observation that not much changes in "Little Orphan Annie" despite the passage of decades. The principal effect, however, must be a heightening of the reader's sense of how comic strips—including "Pogo"—operate.

Another old comic strip given to cross-references to other strips is "Gasoline Alley." Significantly, however, the strips in question were drawn between 1988 and 1990, by Jim Scancarelli rather than by the originator, Frank King. In the 1988 strip the older characters reminisce about their favorite comic characters from the past, ranging from Harold Teen to the Yellow Kid. Each recollection is drawn in imitation of the original artist's style. In the last panel, Walt Wallet says that "the best strip was started by a fellow named Frank King in 1918," and, just in case the self-reference might escape some readers, Phyllis adds, "Somehow that always reminded me of us!" (In a comparable case published in 1989, Hank Ketcham has the hoary Dennis the Menace say to Joey, "My Dad says it's just a kwinsidence that this kid in the comics looks like me.")

The allusive "Gasoline Alley" strip for 1989 has Walt complaining to Phyllis that the Sunday funnies are "just not like they used to be." When he goes out for a walk in the next panel, he encounters Mutt and Jeff, Smokey Stover, Krazy Kat, and other famous cartoon characters, all drawn in their original styles. In the last panel, it turns out that he has been dreaming. In the 1990 strip, Walt tells his grandson about other old-time comics, including "Terry and the Pirates" and "Toonerville Folks," once again rendered with great artistic accuracy. Walt's grandson concludes that he is "gonna' go live in a comic strip!" The reader, of course, knows that the boy already does, but this joke can hardly be the purpose of the strip. As in films like *Blazing Saddles*, highly polished allusion and parody can be used ironically to direct the audience's attention back to the parodist rather than to the original sources.

For example, in an "Arlo and Janis" strip by Jimmy Johnson published in 1990, Arlo is wrestling with the idea of turning forty as he sits down at a lunch counter next to Charlie Brown. Arlo says, in reference to Charlie Brown's more famous fortieth birthday, "At least I've still got my hair!" The joke is not very funny, but the drawing is good enough to win the reader's admiration. The allusion to Schulz's work serves to elevate Johnson's. Schulz also gives a boost to a "Frank and Ernest" strip from 1989 when Frank says to an Oriental waiter, "I'm sure I said 'Snow Peas,'" after the latter has brought him a tray of Snoopy-shaped beagles. While Thaves's drawing is less accurate than Johnson's, his joke is probably funnier. Neither strip would work on any level, however, if the readers did not recognize the allusions to "Peanuts." A 1990 "Marvin" by Tom Armstrong relies equally on such recognition when the title character finds himself sharing a nursery school with babies borrowed from "Popeye," "The Family Circus," "Snuffy Smith," and "Hi and Lois." Here, the accuracy of Armstrong's stylistic parody is crucial since the punchline—"There's something funny about this day-care center"—is senseless without the drawing. The accuracy of the readers' visual memory is, of course, equally crucial.

Once again, Berke Breathed provides many clear examples of the self-referential device. Sometimes his references to other strips are only passing mentions, as when he uses his nemesis Garfield as a foil for Bill the Cat's first appearance in the strip (*Bloom County:Loose Tails* 79). Breathed seems equally unimpressed in his brief mentions of "Nancy." Opus considers dropping "Nancy" from the Bloom County *Beacon* when he becomes features editor (*'Toons* 55). In a strip reprinted in *Bloom County Babylon*, an editor's note proposes *Nancy* as the negative pole of contrast while discussing "impressive literary devices" (204). More positive, but equally passing, is the mention of Garry Trudeau's sabbatical during the series, reprinted in *'Toons*, in which Milo dreams of becoming a syndicated cartoonist (58–59). One effect of this sort of allusion, beyond praise or blame of other artists' work, is to situate "Bloom County" in the context of other American comic strips as well as of American culture more generally.

More elaborate references often have the same effect. In two strips reprinted in *Bloom County Babylon* (182, 185), Opus seeks therapy at the five-cent psychiatric booth operated in "Peanuts" by Lucy Van Pelt. Breathed feels no need to explain who Lucy is or why it would be funny for Opus to cross cartoon boundaries in search of her assistance. (Bill Holbrook apparently assumed the same in his "On the Fastrack" strip, printed in 1988, in which Bill Watterson's Calvin receives Lucy's advice about his stuffed animal Hobbes: "Look, Kid . . . the Tiger ain't real!") When Breathed satirizes Bob Woodward's sensationalized biography of John Belushi in a strip republished in *Bloom County Babylon* (99), he provides no identification for Dagwood, Mickey Mouse, and Charlie Brown, who come to testify at the "Comics Guild hearings" about Bill the Cat's scandalous life-style. In fact, Breathed draws Dagwood only from behind and draws black patches instead of the faces of Mickey and Charlie. The device conveys additional satire of sensationalistic newspapers, of course, but this satire is possible only because readers can recognize the other cartoon characters even when they are only partially drawn.

Breathed's sense of the surrounding comic world is perhaps most pronounced in the strips he used to close out "Bloom County" in 1989. Steve Dallas moved to "Cathy," Oliver Wendell Jones went to integrate "The Family Circus," Milo became a creature of some sort in "The Far Side," Binkley became "a wild boar skinner" in "Prince Valiant," and Portnoy and Hodge became janitors in "Marmaduke." The range of reference is so broad in these strips that we must assume Breathed's deep immersion in the whole American comic strip milieu, but Breathed makes the same assumptions about his readers.

By treating the end of "Bloom County" as material for the strip, Breathed illustrates another form of self-referentiality, one popular with the creators of many other comic strips. Even the venerable "Bringing Up Father" by George McManus made self-references of this sort. In a strip reproduced on the back cover of the collection *Jiggs is Back*, Jiggs wakes up early on Sunday morning and spends ten panels wordlessly looking for something to do. In the eleventh panel Jiggs says to the readers, "Well, folks, I just 'phoned McManus. He's not up yet, an' I don't know what to do. So-o-o-o—" In the last panel, Jiggs goes back to bed. While this is McManus's only appearance in the collection, Al Capp was a more familiar presence in "Li'l Abner." One good example, appearing in Arthur Asa Berger's book on Capp (161), shows the artist at his drawing table in conversation with his character Daisy Mae. Another (137) shows him discussing the appearance of a new character, Roger the Lodger, with Mammy Yokum. The readers are, naturally, included in this Dogpatch community when they overhear the conversations between the creator and his creations.

Will Eisner also advertised his presence frequently in "The Spirit." In one example, reprinted in his *Comics & Sequential Art*, Eisner draws a crew of laborers hacking their way through a tunnel. In the first two panels, they dig, and their balloons set forth their criminal boss's plan to subvert the city's construction plans. In the third, they encounter the Spirit, casually leaning against the wall of the tunnel. The first villain cries, "Hey Look!" The second answers, "THE SPIR-IT" in caps and oversized letters. The third adds, "And by Will Eisner too!" in lettering that reproduces the artist's characteristic signature (50). Another example from the same collection (60) presents a rear view of a lonely, trench-coated figure heading for an office building on New Year's Eve. In the third panel, he is greeted by an elevator operator, who says, "Evenin', Mr. Eisner! I didn't expect t' see you workin' on New Year's Eve!" The last three panels show this cartoon Eisner entering his office, sitting down, and desperately trying to come up with "a good New Year story idea." Readers would have to be very dense indeed not to realize that Eisner did come up with a good idea, not in some imaginary seventh panel, but several weeks ago when he drew this whole strip.

Contemporary cartoonists are just as outrageous, probably more so. A "Shoe" strip by Jeff MacNelly, published in 1989, shows two avian journalists discussing Garry Trudeau's sabbatical and the end of "Bloom County," clearly suggesting that MacNelly sees his own career as a legitimate subject for his strip. This is confirmed in the last panel when the Perfesser says, "I've always wanted to start a comic strip." Even more direct is the "Fusco Brothers" strip by J. C. Duffy, also printed in 1989, in which the brothers discuss the shameful behavior of "a lot of successful syndicated cartoonists [who] don't draw their own strips after they get big." If readers are unaware of this practice, they can be instructed as well as pleased by the strip. If readers already know about this exploitation of "other struggling artists," they can admire Duffy for speaking out. In either case, they are probably flattered by the invitation into an inner circle of professional cartooning.

These practices are admittedly contrary to the aesthetic stance adopted by some other cartoonists. In a column by James O. Clifford concerning the fortieth anniversary of "Peanuts," for example, Charles Schulz says decisively, "A comic strip should not make self-conscious statements" (1E). Thus, according to Schulz, his strip will take no notice of the anniversary or of any other actual event surrounding the author's life and work. Increasingly, however, Schulz's position appears to represent a minority view.

It is surely unsurprising to discover that Breathed often refers directly to himself and his strip in "Bloom County." In one strip, reprinted in *Penguin Dreams* (107), Binkley's anxiety closet produces a watch symbolic of mortality to remind Binkley that his life is flying by. One of the more disturbing disclosures is that Binkley wastes his time reading "Bloom County." In the same collection appears the Sunday strip in which the Dean of the Harvard Law School replies editorially to Breathed's satiric slaps at lawyers. In addition to reminding the readers of a past "Bloom County" series, this strip focuses attention on Breathed by mentioning "the young fool who draws this daily outrage" (46). This young fool's actual name is included in the strip, reprinted in *'Toons* (47), in which Yaz Pistachio challenges Opus to think of a more ridiculous name than hers. She is slightly cheered when he suggests, "Berkeley Breathed." It is interesting that the fictional Opus knows the name of an actual cartoonist, but, given the fields of reference in contemporary comic strips, it is not incredible.

Garry Trudeau also indulges in this form of self-referencing. In March 1990, a Sunday "Doonesbury" purported to offer the "Scheduled Spring Releases" for the strip. The twenty-one story ideas touch on most of the hot political issues of that time and feature most of the strip's better-known characters. In the two introductory panels carried only in some papers, Mike and Zonker discuss the suggested lineup, and Zonker complains that he is "underused, as usual." Obviously, Trudeau is attempting to involve his readers in a highly specific form of self-reference. This is even clearer in the concluding panel when Mike says to the readers, "Circled your favs? No? You say they were too small to read? Contact your local editor! 'Bye for now!" The rhetorical effect is very powerful since most readers have probably squinted carefully through the twenty-one tiny strips, engaged by all the fanciful plot suggestions and fearful of missing some subtle joke. The final level of self-reference becomes clear when readers realize that comic strips *have* been shrinking in size, a crisis also treated in a Sunday "Bloom County" strip, reprinted in *Penguin Dreams* (86), in which Binkley has a *Star Trek* dream about all the strips except "Doonesbury" being shrunk to make more room for the "Dear Abby" column.

Another self-referential joke about the contents of "Doonesbury" appeared in September 1990 when the possible implications of the Saudi Arabian crisis started to engage public attention. Four panels show Roland Hedley being dispatched to the front, Mike being asked to do public relations for big oil, Duke being solicited to run guns, and B.D. telling Boopsie that he has been called up for duty. A box poses Trudeau's question about these tempting story lines: "Where to begin." The last panel silently answers the question by repeating the panel showing B.D. and Boopsie. Readers thus know that the strip will focus on these two characters, but they also know that this focus was determined not by fate but by Garry Trudeau, who could have developed one of the other three stories if he had so chosen. In light of the *Newsweek* profile, readers might know further that this decision was made more than a week earlier.

Trudeau also draws readers into his professional circle in a series of strips published in 1989 and focused on the immense popularity of the *Sports Illustrated* swimsuit issue. Throughout the series, Boopsie and another model, Cynthia, don skimpy bathing suits and discuss the propriety of using sex to sell products. In the Saturday strip, Cynthia wraps up the discussion by saying, "Sex sells! It doesn't matter what it is—magazines, books, movies, T.V. shows! It's all about hyping sales and ratings!" Trudeau announces his own presence by having Boopsie look out at the readers while asking, "You don't suppose they have a sweeps week on the comics page!" The very sexy Cynthia, who is drawn provocatively in the foreground of the last panel, responds, "That was certainly my understanding!" With this drawing staring them right in the face, readers can only acknowledge their own complicity in Trudeau's joke, but they must also acknowledge the author's presence.

Probably the ultimate degree of self-referentiality is the comic strip about producing comic strips. Whether they are amused or not, readers of such strips cannot avoid thinking about their artists. This was surely part of Al Capp's intention when he would draw himself into "Li'l Abner" strips. It is just as surely the effect of the "Ernie" strips by Bud Grace, in which a cartoonist called Mr. Grace becomes the butt of professional misadventures. In a strip published in 1989, Mr. Grace is dragged from his desk by a medical attendant when the absurdities associated with T. Boone Pickens and Michael Jackson lose their comic appeal and unhinge his sanity. In a 1990 strip, Mrs. Grace is outraged rather than entertained by a strip in which her husband depicts sexual discrimination on the job. As in the

"Doonesbury" strips on "sweeps week" in the comics, satire can point within and without simultaneously, and the final gesture is toward the satirist himself.

Less pointed but equally self-referential was "Sam's Strip," produced between 1961 and 1963 by Mort Walker and Jerry Dumas. The premise was that a cartoon character named Sam lived in a comic strip and sometimes interacted with historical comic strip characters more elaborately even than the annual "Gasoline Alley" trips down memory lane. According to Richard Marschall's entry in *The World Encyclopedia of Comics*, the strip was "surreal and high camp" (2: 597). According to Mort Walker in *Backstage at the Strips*, "the satire [in the strip] just didn't sink in" with the mass public (223). One consequence of the strip's relative unpopularity in the 1960s is its relative unavailability today. The strip fits so smoothly into the patterns we have been discussing, however, that a few illustrations, gathered from various places, seem irresistible.

In two examples reprinted by Walker (221–22), Sam approaches Jiggs about taking part in the strip and passes a telephone message from Blondie along to Dagwood. In a strip reprinted to illustrate Paul Power's 1990 interview with Dumas, in David Kraft's *Comics Interview*, Sam berates Ignatz for two panels because he has thrown still another brick at Krazy Kat. Sam tells Ignatz that he has to leave the area and orders him to "take your shading with you!" (30). Here the strip is doubly self-referential in alluding to another comic strip and in focusing the reader's attention on a convention of cartooning: the shading used by George Herriman and many successors to indicate depth of field. In a series of strips reprinted to conclude Blackbeard and Williams's *Smithsonian* collection (323), a convention of cartoon characters takes place. The strip soon overflows with Mutt and Jeff, Betty Boop, the Yellow Kid, and other famous characters from the comics. The joke is hardly sidesplitting, but Dumas's drawing is uncannily accurate. Walker recalls, "It was a lot of work for Jerry to research all the old cartoon characters and to copy styles" (220).

Coupled with the lack of popular amusement, this demanding regimen would surely account for the strip's demise, but the conviction of both Dumas and Walker that comic strips may furnish material for comic strips has lived on and flourished. The problem with "Sam's Strip" was perhaps as much historical as rhetorical. With today's heightened sense of self-referentiality in all of the popular arts, something like "Sam's Strip" might very well delight audiences attuned to *It's Garry Shandling Show* and *Pee Wee's Playhouse.* Most probably there are even more extreme experiments to come.

WORKS CITED

Abbott, Lawrence L. "Comic Art: Characteristics and Potentialities of a Narrative Medium." *Journal of Popular Culture* 19, no. 4 (1986): 155–76.
Alter, Jonathan. "Real Life with Garry Trudeau." *Newsweek,* 15 Oct. 1990: 60–66.
Berger, Arthur Asa. *Li'l Abner: A Study in American Satire.* New York: Twayne, 1970.
Blackbeard, Bill, and Martin Williams, eds. *The Smithsonian Collection of Newspaper Comics.* Washington, D.C.: Smithsonian, 1977.
Breathed, Berke. *Bloom County: Loose Tails.* Boston: Little, Brown, 1983.
———. *Bloom County Babylon.* Boston: Little, Brown, 1986.
———. *Penguin Dreams and Stranger Things.* Boston: Little, Brown, 1985.
———. *'Toons for Our Times.* Boston: Little, Brown, 1984.
Clifford, James O. "Charlie Brown Turns 40." *The (Nashville) Tennessean,* 5 Oct. 1989, 1E+.
Coleman, Earle J. "The Funnies, the Movies, and Aesthetics." *Journal of Popular Culture* 18, no. 4 (1985): 89–100.
Collins, Max Allan. "The Strip Within a Strip." Introduction. *Li'l Abner Dailies, Volume Ten: 1944.* Princeton, Wis.: Kitchen Sink, 1990.
Couperie, Pierre, et al. *A History of the Comic Strip.* Translated by Eileen B. Hennessy. New York: Crown, 1968.
Eisner, Will. *Comics & Sequential Art.* Tamarac, Fla.: Poorhouse, 1985.
Harvey, Robert C. "The Aesthetics of the Comic Strip." *Journal of Popular Culture* 12 (1979): 640–52.
Horn, Maurice. "Peanuts." In *The World Encyclopedia of Comics,* edited by Maurice Horn, 2: 542–43. New York: Chelsea House, 1981.
Inge, M. Thomas. "Comic Books." In *Handbook of American Popular Literature,* edited by M. Thomas Inge, 75–99. Westport, Conn.: Greenwood, 1988.
———. *Comics as Culture.* Jackson: University Press of Mississippi, 1990.
———. *Great American Comics: 100 Years of Cartoon Art.* Washington, D.C.: Smithsonian, 1990.
Kelly, Walt. *Ten Ever-Lovin' Blue-Eyed Years with Pogo.* New York: Simon and Schuster, 1959.
Larson, Gary. *Wiener Dog Art: A Far Side Collection.* Kansas City, Mo.: Andrews and McMeel, 1990.
Marschall, Richard. "Sam's Strip." In *The World Encyclopedia of Comics,* edited by Maurice Horn, 2: 597. New York: Chelsea House, 1981.
McManus, George. *Jiggs is Back.* Edited by Bill Blackbeard. Berkeley, Cal.: Celtic, 1986.

Power, Paul. Interview with Jerry Dumas. *David Anthony Kraft's Comics Interview,* #88, 18–30. New York: Fictioneer, 1990.

Reitberger, Reinhold, and Wolfgang Fuchs. *Comics: Anatomy of a Mass Medium.* Translated by Nadia Fowler. Boston: Little, Brown, 1972.

Trudeau, Garry. *Read My Lips, Make My Day, Eat Quiche and Die!.* Kansas City, Mo.: Andrews and McMeel, 1989.

———. *You're Smokin' Now, Mr. Butts!.* Kansas City, Mo.: Andrews and McMeel, 1990.

Walker, Mort. *Backstage at the Strips.* New York: Mason/Charter, 1975.

Woodward, Richard B. "Comics as Inspirations: Are We Having Fun Yet?" *New York Times,* 23 Apr. 1989, sec. 2, 1+.

CHAPTER 10 **I'm OK / You're OK /**
**Most of Us Are OK**

The self-referential art forms examined in the previous chapters demonstrate the presence of a contemporary rhetorical community based on a mutual recognition of mediated experience on the parts of senders and receivers of cultural messages. It is evident that film-makers such as Mel Brooks and Jim Henson presupposed that their viewers were nearly as familiar with the subjects and techniques of popular American films as they were themselves. Thus they, and their colleagues Woody Allen and Rob Reiner, felt free to engage in elaborate self-references in their work. The TV producers responsible for *SCTV* and *Moonlighting* made similar assumptions about their viewers' familiarity with many forms of popular culture, including films and network television. Moreover, in films and TV shows of this class, audiences were often expected to recognize subtle references to various dimensions of popular music: Frank Sinatra and Duke Ellington, for example, or—in the case of Rob Reiner—British rock groups. Such references show that pop music may be assumed to constitute a universal element of popular cultural experience. As a consequence, such music is empowered to engage in the types of self-references that foster a sense of mediated experience, not of pure representation. It is unsurprising, therefore, that the producers and performers of this music—especially in its contemporary manifestations in rock and country music and in music videos—presume their listeners' previous familiarity with the music and its conventions.

As we have seen, such assumptions are reinforced by the continual interventions of the publicity media between the senders and receivers of these cultural forms. Television shows, magazines, newspapers, and tabloids continually inform the public about the real and alleged doings of TV and film stars. Music performers are equally well covered in all dimensions of their careers, whether the topic be a torrid romance, a megabucks record deal, or some artistic soul-searching. Since this same publicity industry also focuses on the producers of comic strips, the absorption of comics' readers into this hypermediated community of reference is equally to be expected. To return to a question I asked earlier, who can not know about these people and what they do and how they do it? Who, under such circumstances, can be naive about the means of producing popular culture? Why, then, should producers pretend that people do not know what they clearly do know? Such questions are the basis of the community of culture we have been examining in this study.

Although they seem to be universally syndicated, the self-referential cultural forms described in the foregoing chapters have attracted negative commentary from a number of sources. Both cultural conservatives, interested in "restoring" a privileged hieratic culture that never attracted a substantial segment of the American public in the first place, and left-wing intellectuals, committed to subverting the existing culture in order to erect a hypothetical culture of liberation, have excoriated the only culture actually including substantial portions of the American population today.

From the old cultural right, Allan Bloom has lamented the influence of popular culture on the young in his *Closing of the American Mind* (1987). The almost universal popularity of rock music, in particular, seems to Bloom symptomatic of America's decline into narcissistic barbarism. The correct cultural procedure, according to Bloom, would be to adopt the attitude of Plato and Nietzsche, who saw music as an attempt "to give form and beauty to the dark, chaotic, premonitory forces in the soul—to make them serve a higher purpose, an ideal," an attitude of which "Bach's religious intentions and Beethoven's revolutionary and humane ones are clear enough examples" (72). The incorrect attitude—adopted by nearly every young person in America and most of their parents—has been to accept a music based on "three great lyrical themes: sex, hate and a smarmy, hypocritical version of brotherly love." Bloom sadly observes, "Such polluted sources issue in a muddy stream where only monsters can swim" and concludes: "A glance at the videos that project images on the walls of Plato's cave since MTV took it over suffices to prove this" (74).

If *The Closing of the American Mind* had been spun off into a TV series, Gale Gordon would have been wonderful in the role of Bloom. Older movie goers might be reminded by Bloom's jeremiad of Margaret Dumont's efforts to bring Groucho Marx around to the beauties of high culture in *A Night at the Opera* (1935). Another generation might recall the plots of the many rock exploitation films of the 1950s and 1960s in which a stuffy high school principal or the wife of the town's leading banker viewed with alarm the young people's attraction toward all that "animal music." In those films, Elvis Presley or Chubby Checker could usually convert the old fussbudget to demotic values in a way that Margaret Dumont failed to do on the hieratic plane.

Despite its success as the second best-selling hard-cover nonfiction book of 1987, many readers apparently cast themselves in the roles of Elvis and Chubby and responded negatively to Bloom's book. One of the more useful reactions appeared in Lawrence E. Levine's *Highbrow/Lowbrow: The Emergence of Cultural Hierarchy in America* (1988). Levine carefully documents historical parallels between Bloom's charges and hieratic lamentations over the state of American culture voiced at the end of the nineteenth century by Henry Adams and Henry James, among others. Levine recognizes in Bloom and his predecessors in the 1890s "the same sense that culture is less something that *is* than something that *was* . . . something created by the few for the few, threatened by the many, and imperiled by democracy . . . the belief that culture is finite and fixed, defined and measured, complex and difficult of access, recognizable only by those trained to recognize it, comprehensible only to those qualified to comprehend it" (251–52). The hierarchical advantages of this cultural view to college professors such as Allan Bloom should be readily apparent. The unlikelihood that such a view might actually lead to practical changes in the ways American culture is brokered by the media should be equally clear. The odds are approximately the same as those that Wagner's *Ring* cycle will become more popular than Coppola's *Godfather* cycle.

It is interesting, however, that Bloom sees MTV as the clinching evidence for his argument, since E. Ann Kaplan denounces music videos with equal vigor from the other political direction. She writes, in *Rocking Around the Clock: Music Television, Postmodernism, and Consumer Culture* (1987), "MTV, more than other television, may be said to be *about* consumption. It evokes a kind of hypnotic trance in which the spectator is suspended in a state of unsatisfied desire but forever under the illusion of *imminent* satisfaction through some kind of purchase" (12). Apparently the American rock music industry is as morally culpable in Kaplan's eyes as in Bloom's, though on different grounds, even if she does not echo Bloom's scurrilous charge that rock has "all the moral dignity of drug trafficking" (76). For Kaplan the sin consists in MTV's manipulation of fools into the mistaken belief that material things can bring transcendence, a belief that she naturally considers herself too intelligent to accept.

Even Wayne C. Booth, a rhetorical critic who usually stays out of political debates, worries about the public's vulnerability to the "pornography" of TV advertising. In his essay "The Company We Keep: Self-Making in Imaginative Art, Old and New" (1982), Booth writes: "It could be said, of course, that not just TV ads, but the whole of modern culture leads to the 'I want, I want . . . ' that Saul Bellow attributed to Henderson. But TV culture makes previous 'want-makers' seem puny" (409). Although Bloom, Kaplan, and Booth might be understood to share few other attributes or attitudes, they all see themselves as immune to some sort of cultural virus to which the general public is vulnerable.

Another presumed defect of contemporary culture recognized by Kaplan is a widespread public mistaking of "simulations" for reality. In this respect, Kaplan joins forces with the many contemporary critics of American popular culture who draw their ideas and their vocabulary from Jean Baudrillard, particularly from his essay "Simulacra and Simulations" (1981). In a typical passage in this essay, Baudrillard writes, "Disneyland is presented as imaginary in order to make us believe that the rest is real, when in fact all of Los Angeles and the America surrounding it are no longer real, but of the order of the hyperreal and of simulation. It is no longer a question of a false representation of reality (ideology), but of concealing the fact that the real is no longer real, and thus of saving the reality principle" (172). Taking her cue from Baudrillard, Kaplan explains that television, "with its celebration of the look–the surfaces, textures, the self-as-commodity—threatens to reduce everything to the image/representation/simulacrum" (44). As a consequence, the unawakened consumers of popular culture live an inauthentic existence in which they constantly encounter, but naively misapprehend, "hyperreality," a universal, interlocking grid of simulacra created by powerful media forces. Unsurprisingly, MTV seems to Kaplan to be the wellspring of simulacra.

A more lively version of this indictment appears in the title essay of Umberto Eco's arresting collection *Travels in Hyperreality* (1986). The structure of this essay is a quest conducted by Eco through the major theme parks, wax museums, ghost towns, and historical reconstructions in America. The topic is, of course, simulation, as in his characterization of the quintessential American wax museum, which "shows Brigitte Bardot with a skimpy kerchief around her loins, it rejoices in the life of Christ with Mahler and Tchaikovsky, it reconstructs the chariot race from *Ben Hur* in a curved space to suggest panoramic Vista Vision, for everything must equal reality even if, as in these cases, reality was fantasy" (15). By implication, Eco is proposing hierarchies of "reality" according to which a wax museum is less "real" than, say, an Italian church.

The explanation for this reality gap seems to lie in the fact that wax museums and other American tourist attractions sell souvenirs, presumably unlike Italian churches. At Knotts Berry farm in Los Angeles, Eco notes that "the dry-goods store is fake nineteenth-century and the shopgirl is dressed like a John Ford heroine." However, "the candies, the peanuts, the pseudo-Indian handicrafts are real and are sold for real dollars, just as the soft drinks, advertised with antique posters, are real, and the customer finds himself participating in the fantasy because of his own authenticity as a consumer" (41). Eco does not say whether he purchased a ten-gallon hat to wear on the plane back to Rome or whether he stuck his head through a wooden mock-up of a western gunslinger to have his photograph taken. Perhaps, like Kaplan and Baudrillard, he was strong enough to resist the seductions of materialism.

In his conclusion, however, Eco clearly casts some doubt on the existence of such strength in others: "[O]n entering his cathedrals of iconic reassurance, the visitor will remain uncertain whether his final destiny is heaven or hell, and so will consume new promises" (58). Again, an intellectual "untainted" by American popular culture—except, of course, for knowing about Disneyland, Ripley's "Believe It or Not!" Museum, and *Ben Hur*—claims to see through the simulacra of contemporary American to the festering late capitalism beneath.

Not all observers of American culture accept the conclusions derived from the concept of hyperreality. In a highly critical review of Baudrillard's book *America,* published in *The New York Review of Books* (1 June 1989), Robert Hughes says that he is willing to accept Baudrillard's proposition that "Americans are immensely influenced by television," but Hughes insists that "it is by no means clear just how this influence works, whether it acts on everyone to the same degree or in the same way, whether the Box 'substitutes' for reality when it is on" (30). Finally, Hughes rejects Baudrillard's characterization of contemporary culture as merely "hyperrealization" and not reality itself.

Hughes does not—although he probably should—adopt the strategy invented long ago by Samuel Johnson to address the issue of Berkelean idealism. According to James Boswell's *Life of Johnson,* the great lexicographer was asked how he would respond to Bishop Berkeley's "ingenious sophistry to prove the non-existence of matter, and that every thing in the universe is merely ideal." "Striking his foot with mighty force against a large stone, till he rebounded from it," Johnson said, "I refute it *thus*" (333). Perhaps continental cultural nihilism might be refuted in the same fashion, by questioning why some purely putative alternative culture more in keeping with Baudrillard's politics would possess any greater degree of authenticity than the culture in which we live. Reifications are reifications, no matter whence they arise.

Hughes does level an un-Johnsonian, but very telling, charge against the entire concept of simulacra when he writes, "Baudrillard's American fans revel in this, perhaps because his apocalyptic view of mass media excites a deep vein of snobbery in them" (30). As in the examples cited earlier of cultural critics who feared advertisers' seduction of the indiscriminate masses, the assumption that consumers of popular culture cannot distinguish the true from the false turns out to be an elitist act of self-aggrandizement. Zoltan Tar makes this point in connection with another European critique of contemporary American culture, that arising from premises established by Max Horkheimer, Theodor W. Adorno, and the Frankfurt School. Because of their accurate perception that large groups of people were manipulated through Fascist propaganda, these Critical Theorists postulated an unthinking mass public easily manipulated by capitalist forces. Tar observes, "A somewhat ambivalent elitism was an omnipresent ingredient . . . because concern for the masses has always accompanied fear and/or ignorance of the masses for the Frankfurt theorists" (179).

George Lipsitz extends this critical history to include later epigones such as Walter Benjamin and Herbert Marcuse and concludes, "Although their theoretical perspectives remain important, the Frankfurt School never offered a convincing explanation as to how forms of communication which they 'saw through' should be so effective in fooling their audiences" (56). The problem is that such critiques are perpetually launched from premises hostile to popular culture. The alleged desire to liberate inferiors from bondage to the media is perhaps best described in a wonderful German phrase that Tar quotes from Walter Benjamin: *"linke Melancholie* (left melancholy)" (10). Leftist melancholics simply do not like Bugs Bunny and Jerry Lee Lewis, and they do not think other people should like them either. Thus, they hypothesize dangers of control through popular cultural artifacts, which they can then warn against. Such Marxist critiques of American popular culture may be understood pragmatically as naive idealizations. Even a simple deconstruction would expose the nostalgia of these critics for some putative cultural "presence" as an invalid and sentimental form of "logocentrism."

A more plausible method of analyzing contemporary American culture has been developing over several years in the work of John Fiske. Fiske's basic premise is enunciated in his *Television Culture* (1987): "I do not believe that 'the people' are 'cultural dopes': they are not a passive, helpless mass incapable of discrimination and thus at the economic, cultural, and political mercy of the barons of the industry" (309). In fact, the whole concept of "the people" or of "the masses" is probably best understood as another reification by those whose thinking requires an undifferentiated and powerless mass as an alternative to their own elite incisiveness. Fiske conjectures that the mass public "is neither a unified nor a stable concept, but one whose terms are constantly under reformulation. . . . In the cultural domain, then, popular art is an ephemeral, multifarious concept based upon multiple and developing relationships with the practices of the dominant ideology" (310). Fiske offers in evidence, "Twelve out of thirteen records fail to make a profit, TV series are axed by the dozen, expensive films sink rapidly into red figures" (313). One might add the failures of the Edsel and of New Coke. If contemporary American culture is supposedly controlled by some irresistible elitist hegemony, the people in charge are not doing a very effective job of dominating.

It would seem from the evidence that American popular culture is actually governed by some sort of transactional rhetoric rather than by domination. Further, it seems likely that this transactional culture vests considerable power in the consumer. Again, evidence from different sources may be used to suggest the same conclusion. In his essay "*A World of Confusion*," George Lipsitz claims that because music videos "manifest a concern with images, a reflexive sense of self, a propensity for pastiche, and a sense of the present as a 'post' period . . . their self-reflexivity can critique as well as describe reality." In an attack of Marxist nostalgia that would please Baudrillard, Lipsitz sadly observes that "there is not enough oppositional content for us to read [videos] as directly subversive to contemporary myths." He adds more cheerfully, however, "There are too many internal references and humorous bits of self-reflection in these videos to see them as uncritical conduits for dominant ideology" (58–59). In other words, self-referential music videos credit their viewers with some understanding of the mediational processes at work, probably because the creators of these videos were acutely conscious of their own perceptions of mediation. Unlike the saviors slouching from the cultural left and the right, then, creators in the heart of the culture often credit their audience with as much sense as they have themselves.

Despite great reservations concerning the capitalist message of music videos, E. Ann Kaplan also recognizes the potentially liberating qualities of their self-referential style when she writes, "The sanctity of the image of illusionist texts is completely questioned by these devices"(38). Perhaps we might rephrase Kaplan's remark to propose that viewers of music videos cannot help but know that they are looking *at* television not *through* a window on reality or "hyperreality." Margaret A. Rose postulates an empowering rhetorical relation of this sort in a chapter with the very tony title, "The Parodistic Episteme," in her *Parody/Meta-Fiction* (1979). While discussing self-referential fiction, such as the works by John Barth, Robert Coover, and William Goldman discussed in my introductory chapter, Rose argues that, by "reflecting the author through other texts, as well as self-critically through his own," the creator of self-referential fiction may subvert "the unreflective work . . . [and] present an attack on the naive obsession with style as a mirror to either the external or the internal world of the author" (177). In developing Rose's argument, we might say that postmodern fiction presumes that its readers are experienced, that they have a strong sense of convention, and that they can distinguish between art and life.

In fact, distinguishing the "real" from the simulated probably proves difficult for most members of any audience only when artists strive to create works that are mimetic, realistic, or representational. Keith Cohen explains the sources of possible confusion skillfully in *Film and Fiction/The Dynamics of Exchange* (1979): "The dominant informing characteristic of representational art is the transparency of the mode in which the fictional world is created. It is as though we were to become oblivious, in a realistic novel or a figurative painting, to the materials that produced the world of figures" (8). Such "oblivion"—or willing suspension of disbelief— might in the most extreme case lead to a temporary misbelief that the fictional character Tom Joad, whether created by John Steinbeck or John Ford, was a real, suffering human being. Even in this hypothetical case, the misapprehension would have to be temporary because something—a noise from the next room, the need to turn pages, dust floating in the projection beam, a noisy cruncher of popcorn—would surely break the spell created by the fiction. In the case of self-referential fictions, even temporary confusions seem unlikely. Who could confuse Woody Allen's Zelig with a "real" person? What sort of TV watcher might believe that Bruce Willis's David Addison really solved crimes?

As Silvio Gaggi points out in his *Modern/Postmodern* (1989) viewers of realistic painting might also be temporarily confused about the relations of art to life. According to Gaggi, "A painting is a two-dimensional rectangle covered by colored pigments; but the two-dimensional surface 'pretends' to be, creates an 'illusion' of being, an opening into a three-dimensional world" (5). A viewer's eye might momentarily be tricked into some sort of misapprehension. Perhaps one might even find a bowl of painted fruit sensuously appealing. As soon as the viewer remarks on how life-like the painting is, however, the illusion dissipates and—as Samuel Johnson might assure us—sanity returns. Again, the contrast to self-referential contemporary art forms seems obvious. When "Doonesbury" encourages readers to cut out a strip "along the dotted lines," there is no opportunity to escape into a cartoon world of realistic illusion. The same should be said about most music videos. When David Lee Roth hardly pretends to sing on the screen, viewers can hardly believe that a camera just happened to catch him in the act of joyous self-expression. Such self-referential art forms have little intention of "deceiving" anyone into mistaking them for reality.

As I have been arguing, viewers know full well that these presentations are highly mediated because they have seen so many like them before. Cohen throws some light on this issue in *Film and Fiction* when explaining how viewers can apprehend film in the first place. He plausibly conjectures that "psychologically and historically, a certain apprenticeship of the eye precondition[s]" our experience of film, that we learn how to watch movies just as we learn to understand human speech (73). Cohen's interests do not lead him into speculations on how we learn to watch TV, listen to music, or read comic strips, but his conception of "apprenticeship" may surely be extended to these cases, perhaps as a more connotatively attractive term than *mediation*. The point is, in any case, that prolonged exposure to any form of communication inevitably leads to an internalization of its conventions, no matter how unconscious this process may be. Self-referentiality simply raises this awareness to a higher level of consciousness.

The effectiveness of this cultural apprenticeship is undeniable and, perhaps, unavoidable. Whatever their dissatisfactions with the place, Eco and Baudrillard knew about Disneyland, just as Mel Brooks and Berkeley Breathed probably do. When Bloom needed a figure to epitomize all that is wrong with rock culture, he may not have had the expertise of Rob Reiner or Phil Collins, but he was familiar enough with the culture to refer, very plausibly, to Mick Jagger. To make her case against the politics of rock videos, E. Ann Kaplan had to watch plenty of them, fewer perhaps than the producers of other videos, but enough for her to establish a clear hierarchy of preference. Though he probably could not have written a parody for *SCTV* or *SNL*, Roger Ailes watched *Jake and the Fatman* enough to write a gag for George Bush. Bush criticized Garry Trudeau often enough to supply jacket copy for *Read My Lips, Make My Day, Eat Quiche and Die!*. In this sense, these celebrities can be seen as parts of a very large contemporary cultural community, a community embracing most—if not all—Americans.

This community's shared body of popular cultural experience gives evidence that, even if those motivated by right-wing elitism or "left melancholy" do not appreciate Woody Allen, the Muppets, and TV shows like *Moonlighting*, a great many contemporary Americans do. America today does not consist of a homogeneous population rendered uniformly quiescent either by Beethoven and the Great Books or by folksongs about economic oppression, played on homemade musical instruments. While it is possible for media critics to imagine a theoretical form of American culture resembling either of these alternatives, neither is practically attainable. By the same token, it is possible to imagine flying without machinery, but it is not possible to fly. Instead of entertaining utopian or dystopian fantasies about American culture, the goal of contemporary criticism should be an accurate description of the conditions actually constituting the cultural state that I earlier defined as "what we are all in together."

While writing this book, therefore, I have assumed that there actually exists in America today a population of great demographic complexity, which interacts transactionally with mediational agencies steeped in conventions long grown familiar to both producers and consumers. I have assumed more specifically that, through a prolonged apprenticeship in popular culture, contemporary Americans have become accustomed to the knowledge that the media mediate experience, that representations are not reality. In recognition of this awareness, the individual artists and agencies responsible for the television programs, films, songs, music videos, and comic strips that I have examined in the book have produced Metapop. By openly encouraging the audience to recognize the mediated status of the forms themselves, their contents, their producers, and, significantly, their consumers, such self-referential popular art forms are simply somewhat ahead of the game in facing these undeniable facts.

WORKS CITED

Baudrillard, Jean. *America*. Translated by Chris Turner. New York: Verso, 1989.
———. "Simulacra and Simulations." 1981. Translated by Paul Foss, Paul

Patton, and Philip Beitchman. In *Selected Writings*, edited by Mark Poster, 166–84. Stanford, Cal.: Stanford University Press, 1988.

Bawden, Liz-Anne. *The Oxford Companion to Film*. New York: Oxford University Press, 1976.

Bloom, Allan. *The Closing of the American Mind*. 1987. Reprint. New York: Touchstone, 1988.

Booth, Wayne C. "The Company We Keep: Self-Making in Imaginative Art, Old and New." 1982. Reprint in *Television: The Critical View*, edited by Horace Newcomb, 382–418, 4th ed. New York: Oxford University Press, 1987.

Boswell, James. *Boswell's Life of Johnson*. 1791. Reprint. New York: Oxford University Press, 1953.

Cohen, Keith. *Film and Fiction/The Dynamics of Exchange*. New Haven: Yale University Press, 1979.

Eco, Umberto. "Travels in Hyperreality." In *Travels in Hyperreality: Essays*, translated by William Weaver, 1–58. New York: Harcourt, 1986.

Fiske, John. *Television Culture*. 1987. Reprint. London: Routledge, 1989.

Gaggi, Silvio. *Modern/Postmodern: A Study of Twentieth-Century Arts and Ideas*. Philadelphia: University of Pennsylvania Press, 1989.

Hughes, Robert. "The Patron Saint of Neo-Pop." Review of *America*, by Jean Baudrillard. *The New York Review of Books*, 1 June 1989, 29–32.

Kaplan, E. Ann. *Rocking Around the Clock: Music Television, Postmodernism, and Consumer Culture*. New York: Methuen, 1987.

Levine, Lawrence E. *Highbrow/Lowbrow: The Emergence of Cultural Hierarchy in America*. Cambridge, Mass.: Harvard University Press, 1988.

Lipsitz, George. "*A World of Confusion*: Music Videos as Modern Myth." *ONE TWO THREE FOUR: A Rock 'N' Roll Quarterly* 5 (Spring 1987): 50–60.

Rose, Margaret A. *Parody/Meta-Fiction: An Analysis of Parody as a Critical Mirror to the Writing and Reception of Fiction*. London: Croom Held, 1979.

Tar, Zoltan. *The Frankfurt School: The Critical Theories of Max Horkheimer and Theodor W. Adorno*. New York: Wiley, 1977.

Trudeau, Garry. *Read My Lips, Make My Day, Eat Quiche and Die!*. Kansas City, Mo.: Andrews and McMeel, 1989.

# INDEX

"Prince Valiant" (Harold Foster), 165, 175

*Princess Bride, The*, original novel, 101, 103; relations to TV, 101–02; allusions to film, 102–03; metadiegetic film, 103–05; mentioned, 96

*Producers, The*, 60

*Purple Rose of Cairo, The*, metadiegetic Purple Rose, 82–83; Tom Baxter and Cecilia, 83; Gil Shepherd and Cecilia, 84; ambiguous conclusion, 85; mentioned, 11, 60, 80, 199

Pryor, Richard, 61, 88, 121

*Radio Days*, 73, 81

Radner, Gilda, 27, 29, 55, 56

Rampling, Charlotte, 74

Rawls, Lou, 12

Reagan, Ronald, 14, 16, 171

*Reds*, 79

Reiner, Carl, 42, 51, 56, 59, 72, 96

Reiner, Rob, TV origins, 96; *This Is Spinal Tap*, 96–101; *The Princess Bride*, 101–05; mentioned, 27, 28, 72, 182, 191

REO Speedwagon, "Live It Up," 148, 152

Reynolds, Burt, 102

Rigg, Diana, 91, 93

Rivers, Joan, 68, 91

Rivers, Johnny, "Tunesmith," 113

Road, life on the, Spinal Tap, 97; Grand Funk, 112, 119; Johnny Rivers, 113; Waylon Jennings, 113–14, 127; Lynyrd Skynyrd, 119–20; Jackson Browne, 120–21; Bob Seger, 121–23; Willie Nelson, 139–40; mentioned, 13, 142

Roberts, Tony, 74

Rock music, romantic elements, 107–08; signs of the artist's presence, 108–09; dramatic monologues, 109–10, 118–19; autobiographical references, 109–14; insider references, 114–18; life on the road, 119–23

Rogers, Ginger, 41, 83

Rogers, Kenny, "She Believes in Me," 127

*Rolling Stone*, 14, 30, 116, 117, 118, 128, 135

Rooney, Mickey, 92, 94

Rosato, Tony, 29, 30, 31, 34

Rose, Jack, 92

Rose, Pete, 15

Rose, Margaret, 189, 190

Rota, Nino, 75

Roth, David Lee, "Just a Gigolo," 149; "California Girls," 149, 154

*Rowan & Martin's Laugh-In*, 24, 25, 30

Rushdie, Salman, 22, 157

Safire, William, 6, 19

Salinger, J. D., 21

*Sam and His Friends*, 87

"Sam's Strip" (Mort Walker and Jerry Dumas), 179–80

*Saturday Night Live (SNL)*, origins, 26–27; "Killer Bee" sketches, 27–28; "The Last Voyage of the Starship *Enterprise*," 28–29; mentioned, 11, 24, 30, 40, 46, 48, 49, 52, 56, 59, 71, 88, 96, 97, 98, 99, 191

Savage, Fred, 101, 103, 105

Scholes, Robert, 76

Scorsese, Martin, 96

Scott, Randolph, 61

*SCTV (Second City Television)*, origins, 29–30; cast, 29–30; McKenzie brothers, 30; Guy Caballero, 30–31; characters, 31–32; *The Adventures of Shake 'n' Bake*, 32; *Night of the Network Stars*, 32–33; *Maudlin's Eleven*, 33; *The Lone Ranger Show*, 33–35; mentioned, 11, 24, 37, 40, 44, 47, 52, 59, 62, 71, 97, 182, 191

Second City comedy troupe, 29

Seger, Bob, "Turn the Page," 121–23, 126; "Old Time Rock & Roll," 142; mentioned, 14, 140

Self-referentiality in, advertising, 4–6; politics, 6, 16; literature, 7–10, 107–08; art, 10; radio, 10; film, 11, 60–61, 66–67, 71, 72–73, 105; television, 11–13, 20–24, 37–38; music videos, 13, 147–53, 158; rock music, 13–14, 116, 123; country music, 13–14, 124–27; comic strips, 14–15, 165–69, 179–80

*Sesame Street*, 87, 94, 95

Shaffer, Paul, 96, 100

Shakespeare, William, 7, 20, 32, 43, 108

www.ingramcontent.com/pod-product-compliance
Lightning Source LLC
Chambersburg PA
CBHW020610270326
41927CB00005B/271